preface

This book is intended to fulfill a wide range of needs in the college composition course.

First, in each of its ten chapters there is a headnote containing a lesson in rhetoric. In these, we have let a spirit of moderation be our guide, and the student is given counsel rather than prescription. We have never hesitated to say that on this matter or that, no absolute rule is possible. Thus, we have sought to enlist not the student's compliance but his thought.

What we have to say about writing has been required to pass tests of neither commonplace nor novelty. It has passed tests of usefulness, of usefulness to us and to our students. For our purpose is admittedly didactic; it is to produce a textbook that will assist its users to be better students and, especially, better writers than they were before using it.

Second, in the headnotes and in a set of Suggestions for Discussion in each chapter we have tried to present unobtrusively something of the logic of clear expression. This has been done without the use of a special technical language or formidable apparatus. It is our supposition that the course in writing is likely to be taught by the instructor of English, not of logic.

Third, we have built each chapter around two or more worthwhile and interesting selections for reading and study. These selections are varied in style, time of composition, and length. They are, however, of a kind in subject matter, for each presents some body of facts or opinion about the English language. In this manner, we have offered a subject matter for the college composition course. It is perhaps not the only acceptable subject matter, but it is a thoroughly useful one. Indeed, we agree with Professor Albert R. Kitzhaber in *Themes, Theories, and Therapy: The Teaching of Writing in College* (The Carnegie Series in American Education; McGraw-Hill, 1963), that "a freshman English program ought to contain a serious introduction to the study of language, with special attention to English" (p. 140). We hope, of course, that this book will give reading pleasure to the student as well as have a useful content for the student who merely reads the material on the language he speaks. It is not designed to be an anthology only, but it does contain worthwhile and enjoyable readings on English.

Fourth, in the Suggestions for Discussion and Writing, at the end of each chapter, we have endeavored to lead the student to a comprehension of the lesson in rhetoric and of the main points of the selections for reading and to a state of consciousness about them that will enable him, with true effort on his part, to write about the subjects treated in the readings. At times the exercises will lead him to a critical examination of points raised by others; at times they will lead him to original and, we hope, creative thinking and writing of his own.

There is no busy work in this book. As a rule, the Suggestions for Discussion add up to no more than four or five matters, and the Suggestions for Writing are of a similarly small number. Even so, we expect that we have provided more ideas for student writing than most teachers will choose to assign. So be it. Each suggested assignment in the Suggestions for Writing grows logically out of the readings for the chapter at hand, but we have tried to give four or five suggestions in order that the student or his teacher may have the chance to select according to his own taste or interest. Nowhere have we tried to do the student's work for him or to usurp the teacher's place.

J. R. G.
J. S.

4.50

a language reader

NOTES *for writers*

Jacques Barzun : pp. 189 — "English as she is not taught."

PRENTICE-HALL INTERNATIONAL, INC., *London*
PRENTICE-HALL OF AUSTRALIA, PTY., LTD., *Sydney*
PRENTICE-HALL OF CANADA, LTD., *Toronto*
PRENTICE-HALL OF INDIA (PRIVATE) LTD., *New Delhi*
PRENTICE-HALL OF JAPAN, INC., *Tokyo*

a language reader
~ for writers ~

JAMES R. GASKIN

University of North Carolina
at Chapel Hill

JACK SUBERMAN

North Carolina State University
at Raleigh

Prentice-Hall, Inc., Englewood Cliffs, New Jersey

Current printing (last digit):

11   10   9   8   7   6   5   4   3

Library of Congress Catalog Card Number: 66-10237

Printed in the United States of America   [52277-C]

contents

*Ten Rhetorical Patterns
for Exposition* **xiii**

Chapter One

unity **1**

the nature of grammar **2**

> SHAKESPEARE
> AND THE GRAMMAR SCHOOL
> **2** Marchette Chute
> SCHOOLS OF GRAMMAR
> **8** James R. Gaskin

suggestions for discussion **30**

suggestions for writing **31**

additional readings **32**

Chapter Two

coherence **33**

the english dictionary **34**

> THE HISTORY
> OF THE ENGLISH DICTIONARY
> **34** Margaret M. Bryant
> HOW TO READ A DICTIONARY
> **37** Mortimer Adler
> PREFACE TO THE DICTIONARY
> Samuel Johnson
> **39** A REVIEW OF WEBSTER'S
> THIRD NEW INTERNATIONAL
> DICTIONARY
> **44** Sumner Ives

suggestions for discussion **55**
suggestions for writing **56**
additional readings **58**

Chapter Three
the effective paragraph **59**
dialect **61**

EXPLANATORY
61 Mark Twain
INTRODUCTION TO THE ADVEN-
TURES OF HUCKLEBERRY FINN
61 Lionel Trilling
FROM THE DEVELOPMENT
OF MODERN ENGLISH
Stuart Robertson and
63 Frederic Cassidy
REGIONAL AND SOCIAL
VARIATIONS
65 Albert Marckwardt
83 THE TOWER OF BABEL

suggestions for discussion **83**
suggestions for writing **84**
additional readings **85**

Chapter Four
variety in the paragraph **86**
the history
of the english language **87**

THE PERIODS
OF THE ENGLISH LANGUAGE
87 Albert Marckwardt
THE YEAR 1066
88 Albert C. Baugh
FROM IVANHOE
91 Sir Walter Scott
WHY THE LANGUAGE
HAS CHANGED
J. N. Hook and
93 E. G. Mathews

suggestions for discussion   **99**
suggestions for writing   **100**
additional readings   **102**

Chapter Five
emphasis in the sentence   **103**
social problems
in the language   **104**

SOCIAL ASPECTS:
CLASS, TABOO, AND POLITICS
104   Margaret Schlauch
PROVOCATIVE PRONOUNS
FOR PRECISE PEOPLE
107   Lodwick Hartley
ON LANGUAGE
110   James Fenimore Cooper
suggestions for discussion   **114**
suggestions for writing   **116**
additional readings   **117**

Chapter Six
diction   **118**
the meaning of words   **119**

WHAT DOES A WORD
STAND FOR?
119   L. M. Myers
CHANGING MEANINGS
AND VALUES OF WORDS
Stuart Robertson and
128   Frederic Cassidy
CATS AND BABIES
132   Stuart Chase
suggestions for discussion   **137**
suggestions for writing   **140**
additional readings   **141**

Chapter Seven
coherence in the theme
or transitions
between paragraphs   **142**
slang   **143**

143   NOW EVERYONE IS HIP
ABOUT SLANG
Bergen Evans

150   THE NATURE OF SLANG
H. L. Mencken

161   GOOD AND BAD LANGUAGE
Stephen Leacock

suggestions for discussion   **170**
suggestions for writing   **171**
additional readings   **173**

Chapter Eight
the effective beginning   **174**
the english language
in school   **175**

175   IGNORANCE BUILDS
A LANGUAGE
John S. Kenyon

184   THE SOCIAL SIGNIFICANCE
OF DIFFERENCES IN LANGUAGE
PRACTICE AND THE
OBLIGATION OF SCHOOLS
Charles C. Fries

189   ENGLISH AS SHE'S NOT
TAUGHT
Jacques Barzun

191   THE BEST REASON
FOR STUDYING GRAMMAR
AND THE SECOND-BEST REASON
FOR STUDYING GRAMMAR
Paul Roberts

suggestions for discussion **194**

suggestions for writing **196**

additional readings **196**

Chapter Nine

the effective ending **197**

the future of english **198**

198 LANGUAGE AND SOCIETY
Simeon Potter

201 THE FUTURE OF ENGLISH
Albert Marckwardt

WORLD ENGLISH?
Stuart Robertson and

214 Frederic Cassidy

suggestions for discussion **222**

suggestions for writing **223**

additional readings **224**

Chapter Ten

*organizing the whole
composition* **225**

the language of literature **227**

227 AN INSTRUMENT
OF COMMUNICATION
John Wain

232 HOW SHOULD ONE READ
A BOOK
Virginia Woolf

LITERATURE OF KNOWLEDGE
AND LITERATURE OF POWER

242 Thomas DeQuincey

suggestions for discussion **248**

suggestions for writing **249**

additional readings **251**

ten rhetorical patterns for exposition

Analogy

social aspects:
class, taboo, and politics **104** Margaret Schlauch

cats and babies **132** Stuart Chase

Analysis

the history
of the english dictionary **34** Margaret M. Bryant

the periods
of the english language **87** Albert Marckwardt

english as she's not taught **189** Jacques Barzun

Cause and Effect

from ivanhoe **91** Sir Walter Scott

why the language J. N. Hook and
has changed **93** E. G. Mathews

changing meanings Stuart Robinson and
and values of words **128** Frederic Cassidy

cats and babies **132** Stuart Chase

ignorance builds a language **175** John S. Kenyon

language and society **198** Simeon Potter

the future of english **201** Albert Marckwardt

* We must caution those who will expect these essays to be pure exhibits of a rhetorical pattern. The truth is that no author who has something to write about deliberately designs his piece around one or even two rhetorical patterns. In fact, an author will use as many patterns as necessary to develop effective order in his writing, and in most cases these patterns are so combined as to defy any attempt of analysis to derive the rhetorical pattern in use. For this reason some of the essays are listed twice as exemplifying two different rhetorical patterns.

Classification

explanatory **61** Mark Twain

regional and
social variations **65** Albert Marckwardt

periods
of the english language **87** Albert Marckwardt

what does a word stand for? **119** L. M. Myers

Comparison and Contrast

introduction to the
adventures of
huckleberry finn **61** Lionel Trilling

good and bad language **161** Stephen Leacock

the social significance
of differences
in language practices
and the obligation of schools **184** Charles C. Fries

world english? Stuart Robertson and
214 Frederic Cassidy

literature of knowledge
and literature of power **242** Thomas DeQuincey

Deduction

provocative pronouns
for precise people **107** Lodwick Hartley

now everyone
is hip about slang **143** Bergen Evans

the best reason
for studying grammar
and the second-best reason
for studying grammar **191** Paul Roberts

Definition

schools of grammar **8** James R. Gaskin

what does a word stand for? **119** L. M. Myers

the nature of slang **150** H. L. Mencken

literature of knowledge
and literature of power **242** Thomas DeQuincey

Induction

a review of webster's
third new international
dictionary · **44** · Sumner Ives

*an instrument
of communication* · **227** · John Wain

Narration

shakespeare and the grammar
school · **2** · Marchette Chute

the tower of babel · **83**

the year 1066 · **88** · Albert C. Baugh

Process

how to read a dictionary · **37** · Mortimer Adler

preface to the dictionary · **39** · Samuel Johnson

from the development
of modern english · **63** · Stuart Robertson and
Frederic Cassidy

how should one read a book · **232** · Virginia Woolf

a language reader
for writers

Chapter One

~ A ~

unity

In this chapter, your attention will be directed to the quality of unity in the paragraph. The word *unity* means singleness, and the paragraph that has unity or that may be considered *unified* is a paragraph that presents but a single idea or aspect of an idea. If it presents facts, they are facts of a kind, facts that point to a single conclusion, or that pertain to a single process.

Unity, to be sure, is not the only quality that is essential to a good paragraph, but it is of great value. A paragraph, or any other unit of writing, that lacks unity will have the weakening effect of scattering the reader's attention over several unrelated bits of information or opinion. It will prevent his seeing clearly what the writer's purpose is; consequently, it will offset or counteract all the hard work the writer has done in gathering material, collecting his thoughts, and putting them into written form.

For generations, textbooks and teachers have urged the student-writer to adopt a very simple device for achieving unity in the paragraphs that he writes. That device consists of a single sentence within the paragraph that presents, in a nutshell, the main point of the paragraph; this is the *topic sentence*. A topic sentence may be, and usually should be, directly expressed; in each of the first two paragraphs above, it is the opening sentence. It may occasionally be implied, as in the paragraph you are now reading.

Topic sentences may be developed along many lines, as may their paragraphs. For example, the topic sentence may express a general truth, the rest of the paragraph providing illustrations; it may state a fact, with the rest of the paragraph showing how the matter being discussed is of a similar—or different—kind of fact. And so it goes. There is no hard and fast rule; you must be attentive to the practices of good writers, and, above all, deliberate in your own practices.

Keep each paragraph limited to one idea, or to one important aspect of your subject.

~ B ~

the nature of grammar

SHAKESPEARE AND THE GRAMMAR SCHOOL

Marchette Chute *

As a Stratford boy grew older he found less time for roaming, for school was a serious business in his community. There had always been a free school in Stratford, financed before the Reformation by the Guild of the Holy Cross and since then by borough revenues. The Stratford charter stipulated that the town was to have a "free grammar school for the training and education of children" to be "continued forever," and the boys in Stratford were expected to enter it for a free education as soon as they knew how to read and write.

By the end of the century there was a man in Stratford who taught the children reading and writing while his wife taught needlework,

---

* From the book *Shakespeare of London* by Marchette Chute. Copyright, 1949, by E. P. Dutton & Co., Inc. Reprinted by permission of the publishers.

and unless there was a similar arrangement when William Shakespeare was a small boy he probably learned his letters from the
parish clerk. The Stratford grammar school was not supposed to
handle elementary work of this kind, although it was apparently
sometimes forced to assume what it called the "tedious trouble" of
teaching the young to read. It was a trouble to the young also, and
one weak-minded English uncle of the previous decade spent twenty
times as much on sugar plums as on hornbooks before his nephew
succeeded in learning his letters.

The hornbook was a slab of wood on which a page full of letters
had been fastened and which was covered over with a thin, trans-
parent sheet of horn to protect it from grubby small fingers. Count-
less generations of children had learned to read clutching the handle
of a hornbook and William Shakespeare could hardly have been an
exception. From that he probably graduated to *The ABC and Little
Catechism,* which gave the youth of England their letters and their
religious instruction simultaneously and sold in England at the
rate of ten thousand copies in eight months.

Shakespeare learned to form his letters in the way all the little
boys in rural districts formed them. The new Italian hand, which
corresponds roughly to the modern way of writing, had made great
headway in court and city circles, but the medieval way of writing,
the one called the secretary hand, was still being used in the country. Some of Shakespeare's fellow-dramatists, like George Peele, used
the new Italian way of writing; some of them, like Thomas Kyd and
George Chapman, used both fashions interchangeably, and at least
one of them, Ben Jonson, worked out an efficient compromise between the two. The few signatures which are all that remain of
Shakespeare's writing are done in the old-fashioned secretary hand
he was taught in Stratford, and it is probable that he did not
bother to change it after he came to London.

As soon as he could read and write and knew his Catechism,
young William Shakespeare was ready to enter Stratford grammar
school. He was the son of one of the most prominent men in Stratford, but he received the same education that was democratically
open to every boy in town and there was no charge for the instruction.

The curriculum of Stratford grammar school, like that of every
other grammar school in England, was serious, thorough and dull.
There was no attempt whatever to fit the boys for the ordinary life

they were going to find when they graduated, for all school theory in England was based on the medieval system. The purpose of schools in the Middle Ages was to turn out learned clerks for church positions, and therefore what the little boys of Renaissance England learned was Latin, more Latin and still more Latin. About a decade after Shakespeare entered the classroom a London teacher urged that English should also be taught in the schools, but no one paid any attention to so radical a suggestion.

The chief difference between the education given Shakespeare and that given Geoffrey Chaucer two centuries earlier was that Chaucer's comparatively simple instruction book, called the Donat, had been replaced by an authorized Latin grammar written by William Lily. Lily was the first headmaster of the school at St. Paul's Cathedral, and his book must have made him more cordially hated by harassed seven-year-olds than any man before or since. The whole of the English educational system united to pound Lily's Latin grammar into the heads of the young, and if a schoolboy was wise he resigned himself to having to memorize the whole book.

Not one boy in a hundred had any real use for Latin in his subsequent career, and it is sad to think how the young Quineys and Walkers and Shakespeares worked over their construing in the schoolroom, in what one London teacher compassionately called "an unnatural stillness," while the whole of the sunlit world waited for them outside. One of their number was eventually to become an actor and no doubt the strict training in memory-work did him a certain amount of good, but it is hard to see how their work in the schoolroom really benefited most of them.

In the average grammar school the boys worked at their grammar about four years, although an earlier educationalist had urged a little more consideration of the boy's own point of view. "By the time he cometh to the sweet and pleasant reading of old authors, the sparks of fervent desire for learning is extinct with its burden of grammar." Another reformer agreed that it was "cold and uncomfortable" for both teacher and pupil when grammar was taught without an allied course of reading, but he added gloomily that it was "the common way." It was much easier to teach rules than to give boys a real love of Latin literature, and the average teacher took the easier way.

Here and there an imaginative teacher who loved his work triumphed over Lily and kindled a love of Latin writers in the hearts of the young. William Camden, the great London teacher, lit such a fire in the heart of one of his students that Ben Jonson worshipped both Camden and the classics all his life. Somewhere at Cambridge Christopher Marlowe evidently found a teacher who did the same, but there is no indication that any schoolmaster set off a similar spark in young William Shakespeare. Like Geoffrey Chaucer before him, Shakespeare preferred to approach his Latin authors through a translation whenever he could.

Like Chaucer, Shakespeare's one real love among the schoolroom worthies was Ovid, but it was never difficult to arouse a schoolboy's interest in Ovid. The chief difficulty, rather, was to distract his mind from that amorous and delightful story-teller. Nearly all the mythology that Shakespeare knew came from Ovid's *Metamorphoses,* as did that of most of his fellow writers, but it is evident that Shakespeare was much more familiar with the first book or two than he was with the rest of it and even in the case of Ovid he was not above working with a translation.

Apart from learning to read Latin and write Latin, an English schoolboy was also expected to recite Latin, and here again was an aspect of the curriculum that might conceivably be of some use to a future actor. There was considerable emphasis on good public speaking and a controlled, intelligent use of the voice, and many schoolmasters let their boys act out Latin plays by Plautus and Terence to give them experience in handling the spoken word.

Richard Mulcaster, who was head for many years of the excellent school conducted by the Merchant Tailors in London, always kept the spoken word in the forefront of his mind when he taught Latin. When he expounded the mysteries of punctuation to his classes he did it as a singing teacher might, with the emphasis on "tunable uttering." A parenthesis meant the use of a lower and quicker voice, a comma was a place to catch the breath a little, and a period was a place where the breath could be caught completely. This sort of training would have been of great use to William Shakespeare when he started work as a professional actor and had to learn to translate the words written on a cue sheet into the sound of a living voice, and if he did not learn it from some imaginative teacher in the schoolroom it was one of the many things he had to pick up for himself after he reached London.

Apart from teaching him Latin, Stratford grammar school taught Shakespeare nothing at all. It did not teach him mathematics or any of the natural sciences. It did not teach him history, unless a few pieces of information about ancient events strayed in through Latin quotations. It did not teach him geography, for the first (and most inadequate) textbook on geography did not appear until the end of the century, and maps and atlases were rare even in university circles. It did not teach him modern languages, for when a second language was taught at a grammar school it was invariably Greek.

What Shakespeare learned about any of these subjects he learned for himself later, in London. London was the one great storehouse in England of living, contemporary knowledge and in that great city an alert and intelligent man could find out almost anything he wanted to know. It was in London, for instance, that Shakespeare learned French; and French was taught by Frenchmen who worked in competition with each other and used oral, conversational methods that were designed to get colloquial French into the student's head as quickly as possible.

When French was finally accepted into the grammar school curriculum it was subjected to the heavy emphasis on rules and grammar with which the Latin tongue was already burdened, and Shakespeare was probably very fortunate that no one tried to teach him English by the same system. All the rules, the ritual and the reverent embalming were focussed on Latin, and as a result the writers of the late sixteenth century had a lighthearted sense of freedom where their native tongue was concerned because it had never been laid out in the schoolroom and expounded. Much respect was given to the Latin language, but all the affection, the excited experimentation and the warm sense of personal ownership went into the English. If a writer needed an effective word he could not go to a dictionary for it. There were no English dictionaries, although Richard Mulcaster remarked it would be a praiseworthy deed to compile one. The writer could either reach back into his memory, a practice that forced every writer to be also an alert listener, or else he could invent a new word entirely.

There was still some doubt among thoughtful men whether it was quite respectful to the language to use it in so light-hearted a fashion. George Puttenham apologized for using such "strange and unaccustomed" new words as *idiom, method, impression, numerous, penetrate, savage* and *obscure.* Gabriel Harvey was scolded for using such abnormalities as *theory* and *jovial* and *negotiation;* and Ben Jonson, who could never forget his classical education, was horrified by a fellow playwright who used such outlandish words as *damp, clumsy, strenuous* and *puffy.*

This use of new words could degenerate into complete confusion in the hands of incompetent writers but it gave Shakespeare exactly the freedom he needed. He felt at complete liberty to pick up effective new words and combinations of words wherever he could find them, and a play like *Hamlet* is so full of them that it would have made a schoolmaster turn pale if he had had any responsibility for teaching his charges the English language. Fortunately he had no such responsibility, and young William Shakespeare was free to discover the great reaches of the English language as a free-born and independent citizen.

Every weekday, summer and winter, from the time when he was about seven years old, young Shakespeare went to school. He walked down Henley Street, turned at the Market Cross and went the two long blocks to the guild buildings. During most of Shakespeare's boyhood the schoolroom was upstairs over the Council room, except for a short period when it had to be repaired, and the same bell that called William to school every morning called his father about once a month to the Council meeting in one of the rooms downstairs.

No single schoolmaster can be assigned the honor of having given William Shakespeare his schooling, since there happened to be a succession of teachers in Stratford during Shakespeare's boyhood. When he entered school the master was Walter Roche, who left because he was given a rectory. Roche's successor was Simon Hunt, who left in 1575 to become a Jesuit. The teacher for the next four years was Thomas Jenkins, and when Jenkins left his post Shakespeare was fifteen and certainly no longer in school. All these men were university graduates, each of them holding a degree from Oxford, for the pay in Stratford was excellent and the twenty pounds a year that went to the schoolmaster was almost twice what he would have received in a large town like Warwick. All three men were presumably competent and well-trained, since there must have been many candidates for the post. It is to be hoped that at least one of them had a spark of Mulcaster's imagination, but they may have been merely the routine pedagogues that the educational system of the time encouraged.

When a boy had completed the curriculum of the grammar school in Stratford, he would have his head well stocked with the principles of Latin grammar and also with a miscellaneous collection of quotations from Latin authors, designed to illustrate the different parts of speech and supply him with a little moral education besides. He had probably been taught to keep a commonplace book, in which he was encouraged to write down any quotations that pleased him in his reading from ancient authors. He had learned how to make a pen neatly, cutting off the goose feathers with his penknife and softening the nib with his tongue. He had learned to sit upright when he was writing so that the humors of the brain would not fall down into his forehead and affect his eyesight, and he had learned how to endure the discipline of long hours of labor.

The school hours for the average English boy were long, usually extending from seven in the morning to five at night, with two hours off in the middle of the day to go home for dinner. The only difference made by the coming of summer was that the school hours were generally longer because there were more hours of daylight. Since curfew was at eight in the summertime, a well-brought-up little Stratfordian had comparatively few hours to play. For the rest, each small scholar was supposed to supply his own books and satchel and pens and ink, with candles extra in the winter; and, as William Lily opened his grammar by pointing out sternly, he was also supposed to come to school with his face washed and his hair combed, and on no account was he to loiter by the way.

Schools of Grammar *

James R. Gaskin

The student may regret that the word "grammar" has conflicting meanings and that all of them are in common use. To some of us, the word refers to a kind of social conduct or manners applied to speech and writing; thus, as we would call eating peas with a spoon bad table manners, we would call saying "He ain't here" bad grammar. To others, grammar summarizes the patterns by which native users of a language combine forms (such as "boy" and "ish") into

---

* This rather long essay has four parts: The first is introductory and is intended to define the subject; the second, third, and fourth are, respectively, sketches of traditional, structural, and generative grammar. While it should be read in its entirety, the essay does not have to be covered in one sitting.

larger forms ("boyish") and then include these in still larger forms ("his boyish conduct"); these persons, who include in their number many professional linguists, frequently say such things as that the child has a reliable command of the grammar of his language before he begins his formal education. They do not mean that he has conceptions or verbalized ideas that would enable him to talk about this grammar that he commands; they mean only that the difference between, say, an organization of words into a statement ("Daddy is working") and into a question ("Is Daddy working?") is a difference that the child can be counted on to *observe* even if he is unable to state rules that would account for the difference. A statement of such rules is a third meaning of grammar. The statement may simply *describe* a set of speech forms that make up a language or a part of it, or it may indicate how one forms the phrases and sentences possible in the language.

When we try to sort out this diversity, we see that the first meaning of grammar—good manners in language—is fundamentally different from the others but that the second and third are at bottom little more than different points of view from which the language habits—not the manners—of a group of people may be studied. Sometimes, to make sure that we will be understood, we specify the first kind of grammar by calling it *normative* or *prescriptive* grammar. These words imply that the grammarian has a grammatical standard by which a given bit of speech or writing may be reckoned correct or not, good or bad. Grammar of the second and third kinds is not so clearly described. But since both are clearly based on the supposition that the grammarian will first observe very carefully the language patterns actually employed by a group of speakers before he states any rules at all, let us agree, for want of a better term, to call them scientific grammars.

Of the kinds of grammar that we have identified, the one most consistently represented in the school books has been the prescriptive. That this is so should not surprise anyone, for the social processes that have operated over the past two or three centuries to make opportunities for book learning available to nearly all citizens of the English-speaking countries have been grounded in a political philosophy that encourages personal ambition. Everyone may hope to be a foreman where his father was a sweeper, or he may hope to be a teacher although his father may have been barely able to sign his name; and ambitious people require a safe way to write and speak. The schools have assumed the social burden of trying to teach the children a way of expressing themselves that may not be eloquent or poetic or forceful, but that is designed to render them free of the kind of discrimination that they might suffer if they used verb forms that the boss' daughter would not use (like "He clumb" or "He seen" instead of "He climbed" or "He saw").

Some of the people who by "grammar" would mean one of the kinds of scientific grammar would say that the effect of prescriptive grammar has been all bad. Others are more tolerant of it. All of them, however, would like to see it replaced by one or another scientific approach. They may—and do—claim that the conventional emphasis on errors and their correction has not led our students to a thoughtful, adult concept of language, that, indeed, this emphasis has not succeeded in its own purpose because the number and seriousness of "errors" have not declined. The prescriptivists of every generation find as much to do as did their predecessors. The advocates of the scientific grammars, or of any one of them, commonly hold that the student should be presented facts about the structure or organization of his utterances in their entirety and not only to those parts of his speech or writing that offend someone's sense of linguistic propriety.

Because in our time the effort of language scholars is all but exclusively scientific in its methods, one can but suppose that in the future the books of prescriptive grammar will be put aside by the teachers in our schools. If so, we have really no cause to worry, for despite their near monopoly on the materials of instruction in the schools, the prescriptivists have not had much success anyhow. The forces of usage—the sum of our habits of speaking and writing—are too powerful to be turned back or, even, restricted to a consistency with the usage of the recent past.

The spokesmen for the various kinds of scientific grammar not uncommonly talk as if only the laziness or general backwardness of those who teach, or only some other simple dishonor having nothing to do with themselves, were all that delays the triumph of their cause. Thus good men and women delude themselves. For such is the diversity of points of view among serious grammarians that it is most unlikely that there will soon be anything approaching a consensus on *which* grammar ought to be put into the schools. It would be reckless, then, for us now to try guessing what the grammar textbooks of twenty years hence will be like. But we can take a look at some of the different schools of grammar that now claim the attention and efforts of sizeable numbers of scholars.

Before setting about that chore, let's be sure that we have our terms defined. At the beginning of this article, it was said that to some persons, the word "grammar" summarizes the patterns by which native users of a language combine small forms into larger ones and these into still larger. According to this concept, which is a valid one, the speech of every normal user of language has its grammar; it has, that is, a set of devices that organizes it into meaningful utterances and that keeps it from being nothing more than random noises. We gain control over these devices by imitating the speech of persons among whom we grow up. At school when we study them, we do so from a formal statement—the third kind of grammar mentioned above—and it is over the kind of statement that would best fill our needs that we have differences of opinion among grammarians. Eventually, from these differences we shall gain, for where one point of view offers us insights of one kind, another may afford us a better approach to a different grammatical device. No one should, then, regret that differences exist, but neither should anyone ignore the differences.

Of the kinds of grammar that may be described as scientific, two have *description* as their main objective; that is to say, they are intended to be statements that show how utterances are constituted. And since both of them have supporters who differ among themselves, at least over details, we shall have to speak of them in rather broad terms. The two kinds of descriptive grammar that we shall look at are reasonably called *traditional* and *structural* grammar.

TRADITIONAL GRAMMARS   The older of these is traditional grammar, which is often erroneously identified with the prescriptive or normative grammar of the school books. The error of this identification rests in the fact that, while the prescriptive textbooks have customarily borrowed their technical terminology and something of their organization from traditional grammar, there is nothing inherent in traditional grammar that would cause it to be normative. In truth, the large traditional grammars of the Englishman Henry Sweet, the Dane Otto Jespersen, the American George O. Curme, and the Dutch grammarians Kreusinga and Poutsma are about as liberal on the subject of correctness as are the writings of the structural grammarians. Therefore, it is not a preoccupation with correctness that marks them as traditional; it is instead their following a long and honorable literary-scholarly tradition of basing their work on the written language, of referring to the grammars of the classical tongues, especially of Latin, for a guide or index to the language features that should be described, and of being, in the main, inexplicit about the methodology of their work.

It is consistent with—and perhaps owing to—their lack of explicitness on method that the traditional grammars have had a tendency to shift from one to another basis of definition with no apparent hesitation. For example, most of them define *nouns* and *verbs* according to the kinds of meanings that these groups of words have. (A *noun,* we are told, is the name of something: a *verb* is a word expressing an action, a state of being, or an occurrence.) On the other hand *adjectives* and *adverbs* have been defined according to the kinds of relationships that may exist between them and members of other groups of words. (An *adjective* is a word that modifies a noun or a pronoun. An *adverb* is a word that modifies a verb, an adjective, an adverb, or sometimes a whole sentence.) These definitions of nouns and verbs are said to be *notional;* those of adjectives and adverbs are *syntactic* or *functional.*

To the extent that traditional grammars fail to employ a single basis for defining comparable entities, they must be held unscientific. But here we are counting as scientific the kinds of grammar that grow out of the grammarian's observation of real specimens of the language. What we have done, therefore, amounts to isolating a serious, procedural weakness of traditional grammar; we have not necessarily justified its complete dismissal.

Had most of the traditional grammars been confined to a single basis of definition, it would be the notional. Thus, the sentence is usually defined as the expression of a complete thought. Of the verb, the *indicative* mood is the mood of fact ("He *ran*"); the *imperative* is the mood of command or request *("Run"* or "Please *run*"); and the subjunctive mood is the mood of wish, supposition, and, among others, condition contrary to fact ("If he *run*"). If the adjectives are customarily defined on the syntactic basis, they are just as regularly subclassified on the notional basis: The *descriptive* adjective denotes a quality, or it describes ("The *pretty* girl"); the *limiting* adjective denotes quantity or number (*"Some girls"*);

demonstrative adjectives specify or point out (*"That* girl, not *this* one"). And so it goes, with many classifications and subclassifications that are, more often than not, notional.

In practice, another noticeable—apparently unavoidable—quality of a traditional grammar is the fact that it is given to repetition. In a section likely to be called "Parts of Speech," a given word class, say, the adjective, will be defined; its subclasses will be described, with illustrative sentences to show how each is used; and any peculiarities of inflection, such as that for comparison of the adjective ("tall, taller, tallest"), will be sketched. Later in another section likely to be called "Syntax" or "Sentence Structure," many of the same points will appear, along with demonstrations of how other words and whole phrases and clauses that are *not* adjectives yet perform the modification function that, by definition, is supposed to be typical of adjectives. All in all, the performance is at best uneconomical.

This lack of economy and the amount of attention given to many notional categories and their subheads tend to cause the traditional grammar to take on great length. The student or young teacher who feels oppressed by the strangeness of some of the new approaches to the language might well look into Jespersen's seven-volume *A Modern English Grammar,* into Curme's two-volume work, or into the large grammars of Poutsma and of Kruisinga. Complexity and length are not of recent invention.

Earlier in this article, the absence of explicitly identified method was referred to. Nobody would claim, of course, that all traditionalists have been equally inexplicit as to how they discover grammatical truth; nor would anybody claim that even the least explicit of them *resolved* to be so. But it is still a fact that in the main these books do not reveal how things get decided in grammar.

For example, in his well-known and widely used *Principles and Practice of English Grammar,* which, as a volume in the Barnes and Noble College Outline Series, may be the serious work of a traditional grammarian that is best known to the general run of students and teachers in this country, Curme calls *other,* with its plural *others* and genitives (or possessives) *other's* and *others',* an indefinite pronoun (p. 50). Yet, he correctly associates "an S-sound" added to the singular with the "regular" plural of English *nouns* (p. 36) and forms in _____'s and _____s' with the genitive case of nouns (p. 43). It will appear to most of us that a consistent regard for method would have led Curme to consider as nouns words with regular noun endings; it is owing to his lack of a consistent regard for method that he did not do so. (His calling *other* a pronoun reflects, too, his reliance on notional considerations; *other* is not recognizably the name of anything.) Indeed, his entire list of indefinite pronouns is a hodgepodge that could hardly be accepted by anyone with a strong sense of procedure.

But our purpose is not a detailed criticism of a single grammarian; it is, rather, to try to gain some understanding of the most fundamental attributes of traditional grammar. Only a complete review of the books themselves can show these attributes in full clarity, and only such a review can show how the traditional grammarians differ among themselves.

These differences aside, we may say that the goal of traditional grammar is to resolve the sentence into its components and to place one or more labels, which constitute the technical terminology of the grammar, on each component. Thus in the sentence "The man is reading the book," the *phrase* (a group of words behaving as one) "The man" will be called the *subject* and "is reading the book" will be called the *predicate*. Within the subject, "The" is identified as the *definite article* and "man" as a *noun* acting as the *simple subject;* "man" will also bear additional labels: its *gender* is *masculine,* its *number* is *singular,* and its *case* is *nominative* (or *subjective*). Within the predicate, *is reading* constitutes a *verb phrase,* with *is* (*the 3rd person singular indicative present tense* form of "be") an *auxiliary verb* and "reading" (the *present participial* form of "read") the *principal verb;* "reading" will bear additional labels as follows: it is *transitive* (because it has a *complement* of the type called the *direct object*), it is in the *present tense, indicative mood,* and *active voice* (because the action it denotes is performed by the *subject* "man"). The phrase "the book" is the *complement* of the verb, and, as we have seen, in this instance the complement is a *direct object* (defined usually as the receiver of the action denoted by the verb). And, as was true of "man," the word "book" will bear other labels: it is *singular, neuter* in its *gender* (and customarily regarded as *objective* or *accusative* in *case*). All this—which is a fairly thorough but doubtless not exhaustive or complete analysis of the sentence is called *parsing*. And parsing is a descriptive process. Its object is to describe a sentence with whatever degree of thoroughness may suit the grammarian's purposes at the moment.

For better or worse, the terminology of traditional grammar is that which is known to most of us who know anything of grammar as an intellectual discipline. Often the adequacy and the accuracy of this terminology have been questioned. Sometimes questions have been asked and changes proposed by traditionalists themselves. Here we lack space to take these attacks and alterations under consideration, but it will be worth our while to observe that those classes of words called *parts of speech* have been a focus of dissatisfaction.

The reasons for this dissatisfaction are numerous. For one, we have already noticed that historically the definitions employed by traditional grammar have had bases that are sometimes syntactic and sometimes notional. Thus we have frequently been left with the thorny problems that have come about when a word that, notionally considered, might be a noun, for instance, but that, syntactically regarded, is something else. Too, the inclusion of nouns and verbs, both of which terms cover thousands and thousands of words, and prepositions and conjunctions, which are terms that apply to only a few dozens of words, in the same list, as apparently coordinate word classes, has caused the logicality of the traditional view of parts of speech to be questioned. (Again, it should be said, some traditional grammarians have been among the critics.)

STRUCTURAL GRAMMARS Of the scholars who have felt and expressed dissatisfaction with the traditional grammars, none have been more persistent than the structural grammarians. These grammarians, who differ among themselves even more than do the traditionalists, are identifiable by their holding to a set of scholarly attitudes and employing several basic procedures. These are:

1. They base their investigation of a language firmly—one might say dedicatedly—on the *spoken* forms or structures that constitute the language.
2. They proceed on the assumption that while the act of speech is a continuum of sound (as if it might be represented graphically by a wavy line of indefinite length), it may be studied as a sequence of small entities or segments. The first stage in their description of a language is to recognize and classify these segments (which may be likened to the single waves in a wavy line of indefinite length).

3. They regard features of speech such as *pitch* or *tone* (highness or low-ness of speech or transitions from one level of tone to another) and *stress* (relative loudness of a syllable or word among other syllables or words) to be of importance equal to that of the sound segments them-selves and, therefore, to require close study.
4. Their description proceeds from observations of the smallest identifi-able speech feature to the next larger, and so on, to the sentence. This fact is one of the more important ways in which the structural and traditional approaches differ, for, as we have observed already, the tra-ditional grammar has as its aim the parsing of the sentence.
5. They base definitions and grammatical distinctions on functional or structural patterns, not on the meanings of words as words. Thus, for example, no grammatical difference exists between "boy" and "man" although one might speak of "the man's grandchildren" and not of "the boy's grandchildren." The difference lies in the fact that "man" and "boy" have different meanings as words; they are, however, equally suited to such grammatical groups as "the man's (or boy's) house, mit-tens, hat, or mother."
6. One of the prominent descriptive procedures that represents a deep-seated scholarly conviction of the structuralists is their resolution to produce a grammar of a language without recourse to the history of the language, to the kinship of the language and other languages, and to the grammars of other languages. This means, for example, that the fact that English once had some nouns with plural forms ending—*u* is irrelevant, as is the fact that the word "ear" once had plural forms like the plural of "ox," for structural methods are based on the assump-tion that one may arrive at a valid description of a language as it is spoken at the time and without reference to its history.

Finally, as far as our purposes are concerned, the structural gram-marians consider language to be a social function of man. Accord-ingly, they expect persons in one community to speak at least a little differently from speakers of another community; moreover, within a community, they expect that members of two social groups will differ somewhat in their speech patterns. "He isn't here" and "He ain't here," then, are likely to be regarded by these scholars as being fully and equally grammatical; the difference is that one of them is less likely to be typical of the speech of the college-educated part of the community than it is of the less well-schooled citizens. But all native speakers of the language speak grammati-cally; that is, they use patterns of speech sounds and arrangements of words that are accepted by other native speakers with whom they live, play, and work. It is not surprising that the structural gram-marians have been disinclined to produce manuals of usage and otherwise to tell us how we should speak. And it is not surprising that they have been often harshly criticized by persons who consider the mission of the teacher and other professional users of language to be to maintain "standards." But, as we have seen, the serious, scholarly traditional grammarians have also taken a liberal view of usage; in short, with respect to usage some of the blame (or, if one wish, praise) heaped on the structuralists is hardly justified.

In their kind of language analysis, as we have indicated, the structuralists pay attention first to the smallest recognizable speech feature—the segment of sound that the layman might call, for instance, "the *h*-sound" or "the *a*-sound" or "the *p*-sound." Now, chiefly by illustration, let us see what we can learn about the way these scholars arrive at some helpful conclusions about this level of language.

Let us assume that we ourselves are structural linguists for the moment and that our professional task is to examine the segments of sound used in someone's English. Let us, more particularly, examine the segments that would pass in the mind of most speakers as "the *p*-sound." In our record of the sample of English (produced by one whom we would call our "informant"), we have caught the words "play, prune, topmost, reptile, spoon, and spill." Most of us can easily demonstrate to our satisfaction that really we are not dealing with a single "*p*-sound" but with at least three special varieties of "*p*-sound." One of these varieties occurs in "play" and "prune"; it is *articulated* (the phonetician's way of saying "made" or "spoken") to the accompaniment of a strong puff of air; it is, then, called an *aspirated* sound. We can demonstrate that the puff of air or aspiration is present by simply holding a slip of paper two inches or so from the lips as we say "play." As we utter the initial sound, the paper will be visibly blown over. On the other hand, when we say "spoon" or "spill," the articulation of the consonant we are concerned with is not accompanied by aspiration. We might notice, however, that in "play" and "spill," although we have different varieties of "*p*-sounds" as far as aspiration is concerned, both are alike in that we articulate them by first closing the lips rather tightly and then by opening them suddenly. But when we say "topmost" and "reptile," we close the lips and hold them closed until we make the following sound; this type of *p*-sound is said to be *unreleased* or *imploded*.

Aside from trying to be sure that we are aware of these differences and of the significance of them, we shall not go further into this analysis. The point is that when we say the three words "play," "spill," and "reptile," we make not "the *p*-sound" but we make a special and different variety of *p* in each of them. What counts, of course, is not the special kinds of *p* but the fact that all the special varieties belong to a group of similar sound-types to which, as native speakers, we assign the same values. Such a group of related sounds or sound-types is called a *phoneme* by structuralists; each member or special variety of such a group is called an *allophone* of the phoneme. The differences among allophones of a phoneme are habitually ignored by native speakers of our language; differences among phonemes are significant or contrastive and are, therefore, interpreted by users of the language. Thus, the presence of aspiration in the initial consonant of "play" is not noticed by most of us till it is called to our attention, but replacing the initial consonant *p*- by *f*- to produce the word "flay" would be noticed at once by all of us. "Flay" begins with a special member or allophone of a phoneme that is different from the *p*-phoneme.

We have a few phonemes that occur in only one form or allophone, but most consist of a group of allophones which, in general, occur in different environments. For example, after *s*-, our *p*- phoneme occurs in its unaspirated form.

In a structural description of a language, the principle of small groups or systems that consist of one or more subtypes (as each phoneme consists of one or more allophones) is an important one, and it carries over into grammar. Here again, we shall depend chiefly on an example or two to make the idea clear.

Let us recall that whenever we say things like "He plays/he sings/he writes/he blushes," the verbs end with the spelling "-s." Now, by pronouncing the forms "plays" and "sings" slowly, most of us can actually hear that the "-s" spelling represents a *z*- sound; in "writes," it represents an *s*-sound; and in "blushes," it represents something like -*iz*. Each of these three different values of the "-s" as a grammatical form (or as the third-person singular present tense ending) occurs according to very precise rules:

1. If the verb to which the ending is affixed, is pronounced with a final sibilant or hissing sound (as do such verbs as "kiss, bruise, cherish, gauge, pitch, and cringe"), the ending will take the -*iz* form.
2. If the verb is pronounced with a final *f*, *p*, *t*, or *k*-sound, the ending will take the -*s* form.
3. Otherwise, the ending will be -*z* when the word is spoken.

In summary, this so-called ending is really the sum of three different subtypes, each of which occurs under set conditions.

Grammatical elements like the ending that we have just examined are not the only ones that have more than one form. For example "wife" and "knife" end in the consonant -*f* when spoken alone or when used as the base to which the genitive or possessive case ending is added (as in "my wife's hat"). But in such a phrase as "King Solomon's wives," the base to which the plural ending is affixed terminates in -*v*. In short, the word "wife" has two forms, each of which occurs under conditions that can be fully described. (Incidentally, spelling is unreliable as a guide to the separate grammatical forms of a word or other element. Thus, "child" denotes one form when it occurs alone or before the ending -'*s*, as in "This child lost that child's coat." But the same spelling denotes a separate form when the ending -*ren* follows, as "The children had a good time.")

From all this, what we want to learn is that, as is true of sounds, grammatical elements represent small groups or systems that consist of one or more forms or subtypes. The structural grammarian calls the group or system a *morpheme* and the different forms that make up the morpheme, *allomorphs*. Thus he speaks of the *s* morpheme for the third-person singular present tense verb and of its three allomorphs -*s*, -*z*, and -*iz*. And he may speak of the "wife" morpheme and its allomorphs *wife* and *wiv-*, the latter being the allomorph to which the noun plural morpheme (which in turn has several allomoprhs) would be affixed.

In classifying words, the structural grammars regularly differentiate one set of word classes, which they call the *parts of speech*, from another set, which are often called *function words*. There are actually many ways in which these kinds of word classes differ. We shall consider enough of them to make the basic contrast clear.

But first, let us try to make sure that we know what we are talking about. The parts of speech include essentially what we would call nouns, verbs (less the auxiliaries), adjective (less words that are commonly called limiting adjectives—"each, some" and the like), and adverbs (less words that, like "very," modify adjectives, as "*very* good," and adverbs, as "*very* quickly"). The excepted groups plus prepositions, conjunctions, and a few other small groups are the function words.

Some of the reasons that the parts of speech and function words are kept separated are the following:

1. In number, the parts of speech constitute all but about 300 of the words in our vocabulary.
2. As distributed in our speech, the function words include a relatively small number of words that recur over and over. (It would be enlightening for us to count the number of times "the, and, of, in, for" and a few other words are repeated in the space of ten pages of this or any other book.)
3. The parts of speech contain words that supply most of the lexical meaning in our utterances; the function words, on the other hand, have little lexical meaning but are indispensable as carriers of grammatical signals. Put another way, most of our one-word utterances would make use of a member of a part of speech, as "Stop" or "Run" or, in response to a question as to our destination, "Home."

To this time, the structural grammarians have based definitions of the parts of speech on the basis of word form, on the basis of the substitutability of words in given positions in a sentence, or on a combination of these two bases.

Those who use word form as the basis for definition, might proceed in this manner: From any sizeable sampling of the speech of a user of English, it will be observable that:

1. Some words have forms that in the manner of "hats, boys, churches, men, oxen, and children" contrast with the base forms of the words ("hat, boy, church, man, ox, and child") and many of these same words will occur in such forms as "boy's and man's"; these words are *nouns;* pronouns typically show contrasts like those of "I, my/mine, me" and "who, whose, whom."
2. Other words show forms that in the manner of "liked, loved, chided, ran, thought, and spent" contrast with the base forms of the words ("like, love, chide, run, think, and spend"); further, these same words occur in the forms "likes, loves, chides, runs, thinks, and spends"; they constitute the verbs of the language.
3. Some words occur in forms ending with the affixes *-er* and *-est*, as do "softer: softest, plainer: plainest," in contrast with the base forms "soft" and "plain"; these are adjectives.
4. Still another group are derived words with the affix *-ly* applied to what in their base forms would be adjectives: "softly, plainly"; these are adverbs. It is not uncommon for the first three groups—nouns, verbs, and adjectives—to be also at least partially defined by reference to derivation; thus, for example, "-(a)tion, -er, and -ism" are familiar noun-deriving elements (as in "creation, restriction, reader, and paganism").

Those who classify parts of speech by virtue of the fact that each word class has at least some special positions that it alone can occupy proceed along these lines: 1) Words that occur in the positions indicated by blanks in "The tall _____ went to the (or, a/an) _____" are nouns; 2) those that occur in the blank positions of "The very _____ boy is very _____" are adjectives; 3) those that occur in the blank positions of "_____ he wrecked his car _____" are adverbs; and 4) words that occur in the blank position of "He is/does_____the roof" are verbs.

Grammarians who employ both word form and position as joint bases for defining the parts of speech may work in any of several ways, but one clearly effective use of the two is to permit substitution in a given set of sentence positions to yield a long list of grammatically interchangeable words; then, considering that the list represents words that are members of the same word class or part of speech, one studies the forms that occur in the list and inductively draws up a statement of the formal characteristics of whatever part of speech is represented. This procedure has been used in several published grammars that are widely used in college and university courses, and it is likely that many persons regard it as the orthodox structural method with respect to parts of speech. One of its advantages is that it permits us to accommodate our definitions to a wide range of facts—formal and positional. It does not permit, or at least, encourage, the statement of brief, economical definitions; but at the expense of brevity, we gain in exactness and comprehensiveness.

The function words, which comprise several small word classes, are identified by substitution. For example, words that occur in the positions of "at" and "of" in "*at* the end *of* the row" are *prepositions;* and words that occur in the positions of "the" and "a/an" in "*the* man in *a* red coat" are a class of function words usually called *noun determiners.* As a group the function words represent classes of words that the native speaker of the language has, for all practical purposes, memorized; they lack formal features that would render them identifiable out of context.

In all kinds of grammars, sooner or later we are called on to resolve utterances or parts of utterances into their components. We have said that the traditional grammars had the parsing of sentences as their chief goal. The structural grammars seek to identify what are called the *immediate constituents* of constructions that are made up of more than a single part. Analysis of a grammatical entity into immediate constituents is applicable at the levels of word and sentence structure. Thus, the word "manly" has the forms "man" and "-ly" as its immediate constituents, and the sentence "He slept" has "He" and "slept" as its IC's (to use a common abbreviation).

In the practice of the grammars, there are rules that govern this kind of analysis. Of these, the fundamental one is that, save for structures of coordination, which often consist of several grammatically equal parts (such as "apples, peaches, pears, and plums"), at each stage, one establishes a single division, which, of course, will have the effect of resolving the structure being examined into *two* parts; these two parts constitute the IC's of the structure. For example, the word "mindful" has "mind" and "-ful" as its IC's; "unmindful" has "un-" and "mindful." It is not till the analysis is carried one stage further that "mindful" as an IC of "unmindful" would be further divided.

In their descriptions of words, structuralists frequently speak of *free* and *bound* forms. The nature of these may be illustrated with words that we have used for other purposes. We have just observed that "mindful" may be resolved into the constituents "mind" and "-ful." Of these the first occurs with no affix, as in "He changed his mind." It is, then, a *free* form. The other constituent, the weakly stressed (i.e. relatively unloud) "-ful" occurs only as a constituent of a larger word, such as "mindful, merciful, and helpful." (Once again we should remind ourselves that the spelling of these forms is not the basis of our observations; their pronounced or spoken forms alone are the grounds for what we have said of them. Thus, while "-ful" and the free form spelled "full" are semantically similar—i.e. similar in meaning—they are different in that the weak stress on "-ful" characterizes the bound form; it is incidental that the spellings of the two are different.) All words are, by definition, free. Some consist of a single free form. They are words that cannot be divided into smaller components which would not be mere segments of sound. A few of them are the words "boy, girl, book, school." Some words, on the other hand, are described as being made up entirely of bound forms (although, as always, the entire word is itself free). A few of these are "impress, digestion, and procedural," which, respectively, contain two, three, and four bound forms.

In concluding our survey of structural grammars, let us recall that one of the attitudes underlying this kind of grammar is that the speech features denoted by such terms as *stress* and *tone* or *pitch* are of great importance.

Stress, once again, is a technical term that refers to the relative loudness of a syllable or of a word among other syllables or words. Stress may be of genuinely grammatical value. Thus, the word "object," with the first syllable stressed—or louder than the second —is a noun, a word that might appear in the sentence "A small object was left on the sofa." In contrast, the word "object," with the second syllable stressed is a verb and might appear in the sentence "He can hardly object to our new policy." We do not have many such pairs, but a few others are "cónduct (noun): condúct (verb), présent (noun): presént (verb), and pérmit (noun): permít (verb)."

In the grammar of the sentence, stress has value also. For example, structural grammarians often point out that the heaviest (i.e. the relatively loudest) grade of stress marks the end of a phrase in our speech. In the sentence "Mayor Jackson went home" the words "Jackson" (on its first syllable) and "home" bear the heaviest stresses; the first of these marks the end of the subject and the second the end of the predicate of the sentence. Longer sentences, of course, have more phrases and, therefore, more heavy stresses.

With no pretense that we have treated stress with anything approaching fullness, let us examine briefly the speech phenomenon of *tone* or *pitch. Tone,* to settle down on one term, refers to the highness or lowness of speech sounds. In English, tone is used for grammatical purposes, of which we may illustrate one or two of those that are most easily recognized. Let us suppose that one of us forms a sentence consisting of the words "He will be here soon" but with no rise or fall in tone at the end. The words will then, in a way, be no real sentence at all. But let us suppose that the sequence of words is repeated, this time with a slight rise and then a fall in tone as the word "soon" is spoken; this time, the words do constitute a sentence—a *statement* sentence. Again, let us suppose that the sequence of words is repeated, this time with a final rise in tone; again, it is a sentence, but it is now a question to which a yes-or-no—or a repetition—response would be expected. Thus it is that a given series of words is helped to become a true grammatical structure by the addition of tone; indeed it is helped to be one kind of sentence as clearly opposed to another kind according to the tone that is added.

From even so cursory a sketch as this, it should be apparent that the structural grammars differ considerably from the traditional ones. In their attentiveness to spoken forms they are highly detailed with respect to some features of language on which the traditional grammars had little to say. And, while it is not evident in this essay, the structural grammarians have developed a whole new terminology. In fact, they have developed sets of terminology that reflect disagreement not only with the traditionalists but also among themselves. The degree to which we are successful in producing an accurately descriptive grammar in terms that will be at least acceptable to other grammarians will have an effect on the future of this general approach to the grammar of a language like English, which, of course, already has a scholarly literature about it. That the structuralists have made us more acutely aware of the patterning—the orderly formation of structures—in our speech than we were, is already a fact.

There has not yet appeared a structural grammar of English that is claimed to be exhaustive.

GENERATIVE GRAMMARS   Since the publication in 1957 of a work of little more than a hundred pages, *Syntactic Structures* by Noam Chomsky, a great deal of attention has been paid to what is called *transformational* or *generative grammar*. This is a kind of grammar, rigidly disciplined in nature, that has the professed aim of developing a set of rules by which one may form or generate all the grammatical sentences possible in a language and *only* the grammatical sentences. This implies, among other things, that one can accurately define grammaticality and that the statement of rules that will not permit the generation of ungrammatical sentences is possible.

Here, before proceeding with our survey of generative grammar, we ought to make certain that the term *grammatical* is understood. It does not mean that some rule of usage has been observed; therefore we are not saying that a *grammatical* sentence is one in which "ain't" is avoided or in which the speaker does not split an infinitive. It means that a sentence is one that would be accepted by native speakers as conforming to the patterns by which they actually do group smaller elements into sentences. One would say then that "The brave boy saved his cousin's life" and "Purple toes caused the fountain pen to fly" are grammatical. To be sure, the second one is nonsensical, but it in no way violates *grammatical* principles; we form sentences beginning with a noun phrase that consists of an adjective before a noun (as "Purple toes"), followed by a verb ("caused"), with a following noun phrase ("the fountain pen") and infinitive ("to fly"), as such sentences as "Gallant soldiers permitted the refugees to eat" will show. So, grammaticality and good sense, accuracy, or the use of words in familiar senses are different matters; and, of them, only grammaticality is the concern of grammar.

We can regret that to date no more or less thorough English grammar of the generative type has been produced. The large amount of publication on the subject has been on parts of the grammar, or it has been intended to demonstrate advances in method. What we shall do, therefore, is to rely chiefly on a small number of illustrations to demonstrate something of the methods employed in generative grammar.

Parenthetically, we might well observe that in part the technical terminology of this approach to grammar is a return to that of traditional grammar. And, especially in some of its procedures, to which we shall return, it puts to use the traditional device of assuming that some sentences may be represented as derived through modifications or changes in simpler sentences. On the other hand, through its practice of using formulaic representations and through its use of the technical terms of disciplines that are not known to most teachers of English—and to many professional linguists, as far as that is concerned—this new grammar has an awesome effect on many persons who are accustomed to the relatively discursive styles of traditional, and even structural, grammar. Too, its proceeding from step to step in the manner of a machine processing language data gives a generative statement an appearance that more than once has been described as cumbersome.

Now, as we have said, chiefly through the use of illustrations, we shall examine some of the procedures that are basic to the methods of generative grammar.

At or near its beginning, this type of grammar would state a small number of sets of rules by which a small number of basic or *kernel* sentences could be formed or generated. These sentences are of the type of "The man hit the ball" and "The man seemed ill." (These are recognizable as the simple declarative or statement sentences that are a part of the subject matter of other grammars.) These rules are stated as a series of *rewrite rules,* in each of which the symbol ———➤ is to be read as instructions to rewrite whatever is to the left of the symbol by giving it the value denoted to the right. Thus, in the following, the first rule "Sentence ———➤NP + VP" means "rewrite 'sentence' as 'a noun phrase plus a verb phrase.' " The example below is from page 26 of Chomsky's *Syntactic Structures* (The Hague: Mouton & Co., 1957):

$$\text{(i) Sentence} \longrightarrow \text{NP} + \text{VP}$$
$$\text{(ii) NP} \longrightarrow \text{T} + \text{N}$$
$$\text{(iii) VP} \longrightarrow \text{Verb} + \text{NP}$$
$$\text{(iv) T} \longrightarrow \text{the}$$
$$\text{(v) N} \longrightarrow \text{man, ball, etc.}$$
$$\text{(vi) Verb} \longrightarrow \text{hit, took, etc.}$$

What has just been stated is a grammar, i.e., a set of rewrite rules by which a kind of very common sentence may be written. Before actually deriving the sentence from the grammar, let us look back at the rules for a moment. Let us notice especially that they proceed from a highly abstract beginning: "Sentence ———➤NP + VP" is a statement that would fit what might well be an infinite number of actual sentences; it is doubtful that a less specific statement about these sentences could be made. Each successive rule, however, limits the applicability of this particular grammar. In rule (iv) we learn, for example, that "T," which appears first in rule (ii) is to be rewritten as the single word "The." "N" is to be rewritten as such words as "man" and "ball"; these are but specimen words, we should observe. "Verb," in rule (vi) means such words as "hit, took, etc."

We shall see now the application of this grammar to the production or derivation of the sentence "The man hit the ball"; what follows is from Chomsky, page 27: (The numbers at the right of each line refer to the rules in the grammar above by which the line is developed from the preceding line.)

Sentence

NP + VP

    (i) Meaning that by rule (i) above we have rewritten sentence, our starting point, as noun phrase + verb phrase.

T + N + VP

    (ii) Meaning that, according to rule (ii) we have rewritten NP as T + N, which, as we proved will also be rewritten according to the grammar.

T + N + Verb + NP   (iii)

The + N + Verb + NP   (iv)

The + man + Verb + NP   (v) By now we are far enough along to notice that in any single line we rewrite but *one* component of the preceding line.

The + man + hit + NP   (vi)

The + man + hit + T + N   (ii) Here we double back and rewrite NP—the *second* NP that we have to deal with—exactly as we did the first.

The + man + hit + the + N   (iv)

The + man + hit + the + ball   (v)

In trying to grasp an essential fact about generative grammar, we must observe that the procedures that we have just followed are the reverse of those employed by both traditional and structural grammar; in both of them we would have been led from "The man hit the ball" to recognition of the parts of the sentence. In traditional grammar, we would have *parsed* the sentence; in structural grammar we would have resolved it into its *immediate constituents*. Here we followed a set of rules that, step by step, account for the *derivation* of the sentence itself. The several lines in the grammar beginning "Sentence ———➤ NP + VP" show, according to generative theory, the order of grammatical events by which we proceed from an abstract statement to the actual statement of a sentence. These procedures, with refinement and with others that would yield sentences, like "The man seemed ill," make up the part of generative grammar that is called *phrase structure*.

The second part of generative grammar is called the *transformational* stage. The terms *transformation* and *transformational* refer to changes that are effected in simple sentences like "The man hit the ball" in order to derive more complex structures. There are transformational rules by which we can begin with "The man hit the ball" and derive the so-called *passive transformation:* "The ball was hit by the man," and the *interrogative transformation:* "Did the man hit the ball?"

It is this part of generative grammar that has been regarded by some persons as being the most likely to have a helpful effect on grammars for use in college and school courses. Actually, for many years teachers whose knowledge of grammar was taken from the traditional books (and from simplified rehashes of them) have employed an informal, unsystematic sort of transformational method. They have taught, for example, that many of our interrogative or question sentences are but statement sentences with the subject and verb in inverted order; thus:

> Statement: They are lost
> Question: Are they lost

Actually, the transformational rules employed by Chomsky (as in Chapter 7 of *Syntactic Structures*) and others are not simple and easy for the beginner to follow, and the order in which the rules must be employed lest the derived sentence lose grammaticality is a strict discipline. Perhaps another example will help us to see into the need for very precise rules and for applying these in a precise order. Let us suppose that we wish to proceed from "He plays tennis" to the derived sentence "Does he play tennis?" (We must be aware here that regularly the question transformation of sentences like "He plays tennis" requires the use of the auxiliary "do"; Shakespeare, in *Macbeth* could write "Dismay'd not this our captains, Macbeth and Banquo?" but we would say *"Did* this not dismay our captains?") Now, in the one-step-at-a-time method of generative grammar, *after* we have selected the inflectional ending *-s* that we use with the third person singular verb (as "he takes/ plays/ cherishes/") and *before* it is affixed to the verb "play," we must render the verb into the phrase "do play" so that the *-s* may be in due time affixed to "do" and thus eventually produce "does." If we were to reverse the order of these lines we might derive something ungrammatical, as "Do he plays tennis," which, being ungrammatical, would be rejected by native speakers of English.

With respect to its transformational rules especially, generative grammar is held by its partisans to have a decided superiority over structural grammar. And, once more, we shall use an illustration to demonstrate the nature of the claim, although we need feel no obligation to judge it. Let us, then, illustrate as follows: It is often asserted that structural grammar is perhaps at its weakest when it is called upon to draw a truly grammatical distinction between such a sentence as "We had hotdogs for lunch" and "We had guests for lunch." It is not mute on the question; a structural grammar might say that the blank position in "We had ＿＿＿＿ for dinner" is necessarily ambiguous—susceptible to more than one interpretation—because it may be filled with a word ("hotdogs" or "steak") that shows what we ate, or it may be filled with a word ("guests" or "friends") that shows who shared our lunch with us. The transformational approach, oversimplified considerably, would say that "We had hotdogs for lunch" and "We had guests for lunch" are each derived from two kernel sentences. The first comes from "We had guests" and "They were here (or, with us) for lunch." Therefore, the transformational rules accounting for "We had hotdogs for lunch" and "We had guests for lunch" are different rules. They provide a way of resolving the ambiguity or even of rendering the sentences grammatically unambiguous.

After generative grammar has stated phrase structure rules to account for the structure of a small number of basic sentence patterns and after it has presented what will very likely be a rather large number of transformational rules to account for our relatively complex sentences, it proceeds to state a set of rules that are designed to account for changes in the grammatical forms of words as they are used with other words in sentences. These last rules are no more complicated or difficult than others, but they require the use of phonological terms (i.e., terms pertinent to the study of the sounds occurring in a language) that have not been introduced in this article and that cannot be taken for granted. Let us depend upon one final illustration for some little insight into this last stage of generative grammar. One *could* with no great inconvenience present the phrase structure rules for deriving "The wives will meet today" by referring to "wives" as "wife + plural affix"; one could also apply the transformational rules to derive "Will the wives meet today" with no further refinement in the way "wives" as a word is identified. But before the kernel sentence and the question can be truly called English sentences, "wife + plural affix" will have to become "wives," and in grammar we shall have to have rules to yield the proper form.

We began our sketch of grammar by observing that there is more than one meaning to the word "grammar" and that, among systematic studies there are rival presentations of the grammar. Indeed the traditionalists are not all of a single mind. Nor are the structuralists, although among themselves they have more in common than they have with the traditional grammarians. The point is almost too subtle to be even mentioned in a general article like this one, but time and use have had a strange effect on the way we regard structural grammars produced in the early 1950's; some of them have already come to belong to a sort of new tradition and to seem conservative when, at the time they appeared, they were called radical and for their novelty accorded much praise by some reviewers and condemnation by others.

The generative grammarians have not yet had time to come into the degree of general consciousness as have the other schools of grammarians. But they appear already to be getting themselves differentiated, and it is likely that they will come to present a many-sided front also. The degree to which they will affect the grammars designed for class use in the schools cannot be predicted, for their methods and terminology are still being developed; still, efforts at simplification for the beginning student are already being made, particularly with respect to the transformational part of grammar.

The diversity is an amazement for the beginner, but it is, all in all, a healthy sign. From discussion, dispute, competition we gain knowledge and strength. And we gain appreciation of the marvelous instrument of language that we use daily for affairs great and small.

~ C ~

suggestions for discussion

1. Examine several paragraphs in Marchette Chute's account of the grammar-school days of William Shakespeare. Can you identify the topic sentence—the sentence that reveals the chief business of the paragraph—in them?

2. The fifth paragraph (beginning "As soon as he could read and write and knew his Catechism . . .") in the same selection contains two sentences that express distinct but related ideas. Propose a topic sentence that might have been written for the paragraph.

3. Marchette Chute's *Shakespeare of London* is a biography of the dramatist written for a general or popular audience. Does this suggest any reason for the generally short length of the paragraphs in it? Notice that the paragraph length in "Schools of Grammar," the second essay in this chapter, tends to be greater than in the first. The second was written expressly for this book, for, that is, a presumably thoughtful reading by students. Consider whether a difference in length introduces problems of unity in the paragraph.

4. Do you find that any groups of two or three of Miss Chute's paragraphs could be joined without loss of unity? If so, do you suppose that its being written for the type of audience referred to above led the author to make some paragraph divisions on an arbitrary basis?

5. In the second essay, do you think that some of the fairly long paragraphs could be divided without harm to the subject matter? Do you suppose that sometimes a writer may allow a given paragraph to take on considerable length as a means of holding the reader's attention longer on the chief ideas in the paragraph?

~ D ~

suggestions for writing

1. In the second essay in this chapter you were told that the traditional grammars of English had Latin models. From your reading of Marchette Chute's account of Shakepeare's schooling, can you propose reasons that Latin grammar affected the representation given English grammar when the latter became a school subject? State your response in two or three paragraphs.

2. Recall what you had thought grammar to be before you studied this chapter. Did your conceptions fit those of normative (prescriptive) grammar or of one of the scientific grammars? Which of the latter was the strangest or most foreign to what you regarded grammar to be? Write a paper of four to six paragraphs to express

the relation of your own ideas about grammar to what is said in the two essays reprinted above.

3. Write a paper of four to six paragraphs on the topic, "Everybody's Speech is Grammatical"; consider grammaticality to be as it is represented in "Schools of Grammar."

4. Do you feel a need for a prescribed standard of correctness in language? Write a one-paragraph response to the question. Be sure to consider the question carefully.

5. In Marchette Chute's essay appears the following statement: "All the rules, the ritual and the reverent embalming were focussed on Latin, and as a result the writers of the late sixteenth century had a lighthearted sense of freedom where their native tongue was concerned because it had never been laid out in the schoolroom and expounded." In a three or four paragraph theme write on your experiences with the learning of English in terms of freedom or the lack of it.

~ E ~

additional readings

Myers, L. M., *Guide to American English,* 3rd ed. (Englewood Cliffs, N.J.: Prentice-Hall, Inc., 1962), Ch. 3, "Patterns of Grammar."

Roberts, Paul, *English Sentences* (New York: Harcourt, Brace & World, Inc., 1962), Ch. 1, "What Is Grammar?" and Ch. 3, "Word Classes."

Bryant, Margaret M., *Modern English and Its Heritage,* 2nd ed. (New York: The Macmillan Company, 1962), Ch. 37, "The Nature of English Grammar"; and Ch. 38, "Form and Function."

Chapter Two

~ A ~

coherence

Coherence, the sticking together of ideas, is another principle of effective communication. It is the principle concerned with *how* the materials of your writing are unified. When coherence is missing in a unified collection of ideas, the writing may be criticized as being awkward, rough, obscure, disorganized, and even confused. To avoid such criticism of your writing and to communicate simply and easily, you must learn to think and write coherently.

Coherence may be developed in a unit of writing, like the paragraph, by placing the sentences in a reasonable order, i.e., an order understandable to the reader. For example, if the sentences describing actions have been placed one after the other because each causes the next action to develop, the writing is said to have a logical relationship based on a sequential pattern. Another way in which to order sentences would be to show the reader how each sentence must follow the next because of its chronological relationship. A third possible method could be called a natural ordering of sentences. In this method the writer presents his materials as he would be expected to by most people who have had similar experiences. Thus, in the process of listing and describing objects, a reason for putting one object before another might be one of recognition: the object with the brighter surface naturally would be seen first.

In addition to the ordering of sentences, coherence may be developed by the use of certain words and phrases called "transitional" because they make the reader cross from one paragraph to another, from one idea to another, and from one sentence to another. The first two words in this paragraph "in addition" illustrate the function of the transitional phrase. In this same way the pronoun also serves to develop coherence by making the reader look back to the antecedent of the pronoun. And finally, the repetition of words and phrases develop coherence because they too suggest a looking back to the original word or phrase.

~ B ~

the english dictionary

THE HISTORY OF THE ENGLISH DICTIONARY *

Margaret M. Bryant

Modern English dictionaries started with glossaries of Latin or some other foreign language and English. The first English dictionaries were those expounding hard words. The earliest was Robert Cawdrey's *The Table Alphabeticall of Hard Words,* a little book published in 1604 explaining some 3000 terms, importations from Hebrew, Greek, Latin, and French as well as archaic native words. Following it in 1616 are John Bullokar's *English Expositor* and in 1623 Henry Cockeram's *English Dictionarie,* both of which went through numerous editions. *The Glossographia* of Blount in 1656, the *New World of Words,* or a *General English Dictionary* (1658) by Edward Phillips, nephew of John Milton, and subsequent collections dealt only with the more difficult words. In 1721 appeared Nathaniel Bailey's *Universal Etymological English Dictionary,* the

---

* Reprinted with permission of The Macmillan Company from *Modern English and Its Heritage* by Margaret M. Bryant. Copyright © The Macmillan Company, 1948, 1962.

dictionary which was first and foremost until Dr. Samuel Johnson's epoch-making lexicon was published in 1755. The Renaissance period paved the way for the great lexicographical strides made in the eighteenth century and the centuries following. . . .

One of the great language needs was filled in 1755 when Dr. Samuel Johnson published his *Dictionary* in two folio volumes. He confessed in the Preface that he once had some idea of fixing the language, but by the time he had finished his great work he realized that it could not keep the language from changing and that he objected to establishing an Academy. He wrote, "With this hope, however, academies have been instituted, to guard the avenues of their languages, to retain fugitives, and repulse intruders; but their vigilance and activity have hitherto been vain; sounds are too volatile and subtle for legal restraints; to enchain syllables, and to lash the wind, are equally the undertaking of pride, unwilling to measure its desires by its strength. The French language has visibly changed under the inspection of the academy . . . and no Italian will maintain, that the diction of any modern writer is not perceptibly different from that of Boccace, Machiavel, or Caro." Even though Dr. Johnson opposed an Academy, his dictionary served practically the same purpose, setting for the eighteenth century a standard, an authority to which the public could turn. Johnson himself considered that his dictionary did for the English language what the dictionary of the French Academy did for French. In matters of spelling, accent, and meaning he assumed the responsibility of legislating. Boswell spoke of Johnson as "the man who had conferred stability on the language of his country." He undoubtedly was voicing the opinion of his day. Despite the defects of ridiculous etymologies, prejudiced definitions, and the inclusion of words which should scarcely be considered as belonging to the language, his work of seven years was a great step forward in lexicography in setting a standard for spelling, in supplying quotations illustrating the use of words, and in giving a better idea of the English vocabulary than had been done previously. It was a great achievement. Johnson said in his *Dictionary,* "When I took the first survey of my undertaking, I found our speech copious without order, and energetick without rules: wherever I turned my view, there was perplexity to be disentangled, and confusion to be regulated." Out of the disorder he established order. . . .

The aim of Dr. Johnson was to give the correct spelling, accent, and meaning of all words in good usage at that time. The matter of giving the exact pronunciation was left for later lexicographers, the first of whom was William Kenrick, who indicated the vowel sounds for the first time in a general dictionary in his *New Dictionary* of 1773. Previously two Scotsmen, James Buchanan and William Johnston, had published pronouncing dictionaries in 1757 and 1764 respectively. The precedent of indicating pronunciation has been followed ever since by lexicographers, both British and American. The most important American lexicographers of the early nineteenth century were Noah Webster and J. E. Worcester. Webster's *Compendious Dictionary of the English Language* first appeared in 1806. It was revised from time to time and was the chief authority for the greater part of the nineteenth century. Professor George Philip Krapp described the 1828 edition, *An American Dictionary of the English Language,* as "the most significant contribution to English lexicography between Dr. Johnson and the appearance of the first volume of the New English Dictionary." The first edition of this dictionary to be termed *Unabridged* appeared in 1864. The second edition, *Webster's New International Dictionary,* appeared in 1934 and the third in 1961. Two competitors of Webster's in the latter part of the nineteenth century were the *Century* and the *Standard.* The most eminent work in the field of lexicography, however, was the *New English Dictionary* (NED) or *Oxford* (OED), a dictionary built on historical principles, begun under Sir James Murray and finished under Sir William A. Craigie, both Scotsmen. The first volumes appeared in 1884 and the last in 1928. A supplementary volume appeared in 1933 containing the accumulated additions and corrections of the forty-four years during which the original work was being published. The original work treated within its volumes 450,000 words, 240,165 main words with their derivatives. The publication has had a far-reaching effect upon the study of language by showing the history of words and idioms, giving their various forms and spellings, and indicating changes in meaning through the centuries. This dictionary enables one to realize the rise and fall of words and the importance of usage. . . .

How to Read a Dictionary

Mortimer Adler *

. . . This brief history of dictionaries is relevant to the rules for reading and using them well. One of the first rules as to how to read a book is to know what sort of book it is. That means knowing what the author's intention was and what sort of thing you can expect to find in his work. If you look upon a dictionary merely as a spelling book or a guide to pronunciation, you will use it accordingly. If you realize that it contains a wealth of historical information, crystallized in the growth of language, you will pay attention, not merely to the variety of meanings which are listed under each word, but to their order.

And above all if you are interested in advancing your own education, you will use a dictionary according to its primary intention— as a help in reading books that might otherwise be too difficult because their vocabulary includes technical words, archaic words, literary allusions, or even familiar words used in now obsolete senses. The number of words in a man's vocabulary is as definite as the number of dollars he has in the bank; equally definite is the number of senses in which a man is able to use any given word. But there is this difference: a man cannot draw upon the public treasury when his bank balance is overdrawn, but we can all draw upon the dictionary to get the coin we need to carry on the transaction of reading anything we want to read.

Let me be sure that I am not misunderstood. I am not saying that a dictionary is all you need in order to move anywhere in the realms of literature. There are many problems to be solved, in reading a book well, other than those arising from the author's vocabulary. And even with respect to vocabulary, the dictionary's primary service is on those occasions when you are confronted with a technical word or with a word that is wholly new to you—such as "costard" (an apple), or "hoatzin" (a South American bird), or

* *The Saturday Review of Literature,* Dec. 13, 1941, pp. 4, 18, 19.

"rabato" (a kind of flaring collar). More frequently the problem of interpretation arises because a relatively familiar word seems to be used in a strange sense. Here the dictionary will help, but it will not solve the problem. The dictionary may suggest the variety of senses in which the troublesome word can be used, but it can never determine how the author you are reading used it. That you must decide by wrestling with the context. More often than not, especially with distinguished writers, the word may be given a special, an almost unique, shade of meaning. The growth of your own vocabulary, in the important dimension of multiple meanings as well as in mere quantity of words, will depend, first of all, upon the character of the books you read, and secondly, upon the use you make of the dictionary as a guide. You will misuse it—you will stultify rather than enlighten yourself—if you substitute the dictionary for the exercise of your own interpretative judgment in reading.

This suggests several other rules as to how *not* to read a dictionary. There is no more irritating fellow than the man who tries to settle an argument about communism, or justice, or liberty, by quoting from Webster. Webster and all his fellow lexicographers may be respected as authorities on word-usage, but they are not the ultimate founts of wisdom. They are no Supreme Court to which we can appeal for a decision of those fundamental controversies which, despite the warnings of semanticists, get us involved with abstract words. It is well to remember that the dictionary's authority can, for obvious reasons, be surer in the field of concrete words, and even in the field of the abstract technical words of science, than it ever can be with respect to philosophical words. Yet these words are indispensable if we are going to talk, read, or write about the things that matter most.

Another negative rule is: Don't swallow the dictionary. Don't try to get word-rich quick, by memorizing a lot of fancy words whose meanings are unconnected with any actual experience. Merely verbal knowledge is almost worse than no knowledge at all. If learning consisted in nothing but knowing the meanings of words, we could abolish all our courses of study and substitute the dictionary for every other sort of book. But no one except a pedant or a fool would regard it as profitable or wise to read the dictionary from cover to cover.

In short, don't forget that the dictionary is a book about words, not about things. It can tell you how men have used words, but it does not define the nature of the things the words name. A Scandinavian university undertook a "linguistic experiment" to prove that human arguments always reduce to verbal differences. Seven lawyers were given seven dictionary definitions of truth and asked to defend them. They soon forgot to stick to the "verbal meanings" they had been assigned and became vehemently involved in defending or opposing certain fundamental views about the nature of truth. The experiment showed that discussions may start about the meanings of words, but that, when interest in the problem is aroused, they seldom end there. Men pass from words to things, from names to natures. The dictionary can start an argument, but only thought or research can end it.

PREFACE TO THE DICTIONARY *

Samuel Johnson

The rigour of interpretative lexicography requires that *the explanation, and the word explained, should be always reciprocal;* this I have always endeavoured, but could not always attain. Words are seldom exactly synonimous; a new term was not introduced, but because the former was thought inadequate: names, therefore, have often many ideas, but few ideas have many names. It was then necessary to use the proximate word, for the deficiency of single terms can very seldom be supplied by circumlocution; nor is the inconvenience great of such mutilated interpretations, because the sense may easily be collected entire from the examples.

In every word of extensive use, it was requisite to mark the progress of its meaning, and show by what gradations of intermediate sense it has passed from its primitive to its remote and accidental signification; so that every foregoing explanation should tend to that which follows, and the series be regularly concatenated from the first notion to the last.

This is specious, but not always practicable; kindred senses may

---

* E. L. McAdams, Jr. and George Milne, eds., *Johnson's Dictionary* (New York: Pantheon Books, Inc., 1963), pp. 15-20.

be so interwoven, that the perplexity cannot be disentangled, nor any reason be assigned why one should be ranged before the other. When the radical idea branches out into parallel ramifications, how can a consecutive series be formed of senses in their nature collateral? The shades of meaning sometimes pass imperceptibly into each other; so that though on one side they apparently differ, yet it is impossible to mark the point of contact. Ideas of the same race, though not exactly alike, are sometimes so little different, that no words can express the dissimilitude, though the mind easily perceives it, when they are exhibited together; and sometimes there is such a confusion of acceptations, that discernment is wearied, and distinction puzzled, and perseverance herself hurries to an end, by crouding together what she cannot separate.

These complaints of difficulty will, by those that have never considered words beyond their popular use, be thought only the jargon of a man willing to magnify his labours, and procure veneration to his studies by involution and obscurity. But every art is obscure to those that have not learned it: this uncertainty of terms, and commixture of ideas, is well known to those who have joined philosophy with grammar; and if I have not expressed them very clearly, it must be remembered that I am speaking of that which words are insufficient to explain.

The original sense of words is often driven out of use by their metaphorical acceptations, yet must be inserted for the sake of a regular origination. Thus I know not whether *ardour* is used for *material heat,* or whether *flagrant,* in English, ever signifies the same with *burning;* yet such are the primitive ideas of these words, which are therefore set first, though without examples, that the figurative senses may be commodiously deduced.

Such is the exuberance of signification which many words have obtained, that it was scarcely possible to collect all their senses; sometimes the meaning of derivatives must be sought in the mother term, and sometimes deficient explanations of the primitive may be supplied in the train of derivation. In any case of doubt or difficulty, it will be always proper to examine all the words of the same race; for some words are slightly passed over to avoid repetition, some admitted easier and clearer explanation than others, and all will be better understood, as they are considered in greater variety of structures and relations.

All the interpretations of words are not written with the same skill, or the same happiness: things equally easy in themselves, are not all equally easy to any single mind. Every writer of a long work commits errours, where there appears neither ambiguity to mislead, nor obscurity to confound him; and in a search like this, many felicities of expression will be casually overlooked, many convenient parallels will be forgotten, and many particulars will admit improvement from a mind utterly unequal to the whole performance.

But many seeming faults are to be imputed rather to the nature of the undertaking, than the negligence of the performer. Thus some explanations are unavoidably reciprocal or circular, as *hind, the female of the stag; stag, the male of the hind:* sometimes easier words are changed into harder, as *burial* into *sepulture* or *interment, drier* into *desicative, dryness* into *siccity* or *aridity, fit* into *paroxysm;* for the easiest word, whatever it be, can never be translated into one more easy. But easiness and difficulty are merely relative, and if the present prevalence of our language should invite foreigners to this dictionary, many will be assisted by those words which now seem only to increase or produce obscurity. For this reason I have endeavoured frequently to join a Teutonick and Roman interpretation, as to *cheer to gladden,* or *exhilarate,* that every learner of English may be assisted by his own tongue.

The solution of all difficulties, and the supply of all defects, must be sought in the examples, subjoined to the various senses of each word, and ranged according to the time of their authours.

When first I collected these authorities, I was desirous that every quotation should be useful to some other end than the illustration of a word; I therefore extracted from philosophers principles of science; from historians remarkable facts; from chymists complete processes; from divines striking exhortations; and from poets beautiful descriptions. Such is design, while it is yet at a distance from execution. When the time called upon me to range this accumulation of elegance and wisdom into an alphabetical series, I soon discovered that the bulk of my volumes would fright away the student, and was forced to depart from my scheme of including all that was pleasing or useful in English literature, and reduce my transcripts very often to clusters of words, in which scarcely any meaning is retained; thus to the weariness of copying, I was condemned to add the vexation of expunging. Some passages I have yet spared, which may relieve the labour of verbal searches, and intersperse with verdure and flowers the dusty desarts of barren philology.

The examples, thus mutilated, are no longer to be considered as conveying the sentiments or doctrine of their authours; the word for the sake of which they are inserted, with all its appendant clauses, has been carefully preserved; but it may sometimes happen, by hasty detruncation, that the general tendency of the sentence may be changed: the divine may desert his tenets, or the philosopher his system.

Some of the examples have been taken from writers who were never mentioned as masters of elegance or models of stile; but words must be sought where they are used; and in what pages, eminent for purity, can terms of manufacture or agriculture be found? Many quotations serve no other purpose, than that of proving the bare existence of words, and are therefore selected with less scrupulousness than those which are to teach their structures and relations.

My purpose was to admit no testimony of living authours, that I might not be misled by partiality, and that none of my cotemporaries might have reason to complain; nor have I departed from this resolution, but when some performances of uncommon excellence excited my veneration, when my memory supplied me, from late books, with an example that was wanting, or when my heart, in the tenderness of friendship, solicited admission for a favourite name.

So far have I been from any care to grace my pages with modern decorations, that I have studiously endeavoured to collect examples and authorities from the writers before the restoration, whose works I regard as *the wells of English undefiled,* as the pure sources of genuine diction. Our language, for almost a century, has, by the concurrence of many causes, been gradually departing from its original Teutonick character, and deviating towards a Gallick structure and phraseology, from which it ought to be our endeavour to recal it, by making our ancient volumes the ground-work of stile, admitting among the additions of later times, only such as may supply real deficiencies, such as are readily adopted by the genius of our tongue, and incorporate easily with our native idioms.

But as every language has a time of rudeness antecedent to perfection, as well as of false refinement and declension, I have been cautious lest my zeal for antiquity might drive me into times too remote, and croud my book with words now no longer understood. I have fixed Sidney's work for the boundary, beyond which I make few excursions. From the authours which rose in the time of Elizabeth, a speech might be formed adequate to all the purposes of use and elegance. If the language of theology were extracted from Hooker and the translation of the Bible; the terms of natural knowledge from Bacon; the phrases of policy, war, and navigation from Raleigh; the dialect of poetry and fiction from Spenser and Sidney; and the diction of common life from Shakespear, few ideas would be lost to mankind, for want of English words, in which they might be expressed.

It is not sufficient that a word is found, unless it be so combined as that its meaning is apparently determined by the tract and tenour of the sentence; such passages I have therefore chosen, and when it happened that any authour gave a definition of a term, or such an explanation as is equivalent to a definition, I have placed his authority as a supplement to my own, without regard to the chronological order, that is otherwise observed.

Some words, indeed, stand unsupported by an authority, but they are commonly derivative nouns or adverbs, formed from their primitives by regular and constant analogy, or names of things seldom occurring in books, or words of which I have reason to doubt the existence.

There is more danger of censure from the multiplicity than paucity of examples; authorities will sometimes seem to have been accumulated without necessity or use, and perhaps some will be found, which might, without loss, have been omitted. But a work of this kind is not hastily to be charged with superfluities: those quotations which to careless or unskilful perusers appear only to repeat the same sense, will often exhibit, to a more accurate examiner, diversities of signification, or, at least, afford different shades of the same meaning: one will shew the word applied to persons, another to things; one will express an ill, another a good, and a third a neutral sense; one will prove the expression genuine from an ancient authour; another will shew it elegant from a modern: a doubtful authority is corroborated by another of more credit; an ambiguous sentence is ascertained by a passage clear and determinate; the word, how often soever repeated, appears with new associates and in different combinations, and every quotation contributes something to the stability or enlargement of the language. . . .

A Review of Webster's Third
New International Dictionary

Sumner Ives *

A language is, first of all, a medium of communication. Each living language reflects the total life of some present-day community, and it is the medium through which the social, technical, and intellectual life of this community is carried on. This intimate and necessary connection between a language and a community has several consequences, among them the fact that the language changes as the community changes. It follows, too, that an individual's command of his language is one measure of his ability to participate in community activities, including its business, and that deficiencies in his command of language impose restrictions on this ability. This mutual relationship between language and activity exists whether the subject is baseball, cooking, philosophy, or anything else.

The full social, technical, and intellectual life of the community which includes the speakers of English has become so varied and complex that no one person has a total command of the entire language. Thus everyone whose horizons are expanding—whose contacts occasionally touch unfamiliar territory, whose reading occasionally includes unfamiliar concepts—needs a dictionary, if, in these broader associations, he is to communicate efficiently with others or fully understand their attempts to communicate with him. The constant change resulting from cultural and linguistic interaction makes dictionaries constantly go out of date. The best dictionaries add new words from time to time, but eventually the time comes when a complete revision is in order. G. & C. Merriam Company's *Webster's Third New International Dictionary*, a Merriam-Webster, is such a complete revision.

This sixth in the series of Merriam-Webster unabridged dic-

---

* By permission. From December 1961 issue of *Word Study,* copyright 1961 by G. & C. Merriam Co., publishers of the Merriam-Webster Dictionaries.

tionaries is more than just a product of subtracting from and adding to the material in the fifth. It is, in fact, so thorough a revision as to constitute a new dictionary. The details of revision are too many for enumeration, but, in general, this newness results from three major developments. The first, of course, is the evolution of the language itself since the appearance of the 1934 edition. The second is the progress which has been made in linguistics—the systematic study of language as a kind of human behavior. This progress has given us a better understanding of the nature of language, a greater accumulation of details about English pronunciation, grammar, and usage, and a clearer notion of dictionary responsibility in these areas. The third is a very detailed review of lexicography, of the craft of dictionary making, which was made by the editorial staff that produced *Webster's Third New International* and used by it in evolving new dictionary procedures—new refinements in discriminating senses, new precision and grace in wording definitions, and new devices for making entries clearer and more informative.

It is obvious that, for good or ill, we have had a kind of cultural explosion within the twentieth century, not only in technology but also in the arts and in the studies of human behavior. Words such as *carbon 14, impressionism,* and *libido* are encountered by nearly everyone who reads as much as a daily paper. It is less obvious that other influences—the tremendous expansion in mass media, and the greater need for written communication in nearly all undertaking—have had profound effects on the nature of the standard language itself, especially as used in writing. When metropolitan newspapers have circulations running into hundreds of thousands, when a single weekly magazine will be read by millions, when a television program will be seen and heard by even more millions, and when the very existence of large enterprise depends on effective written communication, the language of public use is in the hands of the public; its utilitarian aspect has been expanded.

For these reasons it is likely that English has changed more during the past fifty years than during any similar period in the past, with the possible exceptions of the times just before Shakespeare and just before Chaucer, when profound social and intellectual movements were likewise taking place. Aside from the mere accumulation of new words this change has been evident in two major manifestations: the great increase in open compounds like *traffic island* and *hatchet job;* and a kind of popularization of the language which, apart from some changes in formal writing, has influenced the development of any informative informal style in writing for general readers and the development of special trade styles in writing for special audiences. In both instances the style of writing more closely approximates the style of speech. As a consequence the scope of standard written English has been broadened by the inclusion of words and constructions heretofore associated primarily with conversation and by greater employment of combining facilities already in the language, as in the making of new verbs with *-ize* and the making of new adverbs with *-wise.*

Thus, although we still have an aristocracy of letters, this aristocracy does not arbitrate written English to the extent it formerly did. Parallel to this aristocracy there is something like a middle class of letters. In other words, the use of written English by more people and for a greater variety of purposes has extended its utilitarian character. And the effects of this extension appear in all, or nearly all, uses of the language, spoken or written.

The responsibility of a dictionary regarding these developments is indicated by some present-day conclusions about the nature of linguistic standards. Although these conclusions are becoming better known, they have not yet become part of the general intellectual equipment of educated persons. Underlying this progress, there are a few deceptively simple premises which seem to be self-evident, although logically and experimentally verified conclusions from these premises deny some popular notions about linguistic standards. The premises which are here most relevant follow. First, each language is a system of human conventions rather than a system of natural laws. Therefore all languages are dynamic rather than static, and a valid rule in an individual language can be nothing other than an accurate statement of contemporary practice. Second, each language is unique in pronunciation, grammar, and vocabulary. Consequently, precedents in one language have no force or relevance in ascertaining rules in another or in describing the grammatical characteristics of another, and any attempt to prescribe usage in grammar or vocabulary by reference to "logical" grammar or "real" meaning is simply based on a false premise. These two premises imply the further conclusions that there is no such thing as grammar apart from the individual grammars of individual languages, that the real meaning of a word is nothing more or less than its communicative value in a customary context, and hence there is no such thing as pure English, if *pure* is to be given its common meaning. The third of these basic premises is that an individual's use of his native tongue is a primary index to his position within his community—socially, geographically, and often vocationally. From these premises it follows that a dictionary is reliable only insofar as it is a comprehensive, accurate description of current practices in a language, including community opinion as to the social and regional associations of each practice it describes.

These premises and conclusions are no longer controversial among qualified students of language, including the best lexicographers. They require, however, that books which present information on the proper use of a language, including dictionaries, be ultimately based on observation of how that language is actually used. A statement on the meaning, pronunciation, or status of a word must derive from observation of what meaning it is customarily used to convey, of how it is customarily pronounced (provided the pronunciation has community approval), and of community opinion as to its appropriateness in a variety of contexts. These matters must be observed from actual occurrences in the speech or writing of persons who represent their respective communities. It follows, then, that whoever produces a book on language must himself observe the use of that language—either unsystematically as he encounters speech and writing, or at second hand from statements made in other books, or systematically by gathering and classifying samples of the language in use.

The entries in *Webster's Third New International Dictionary* are based on three major sources. One, which is used by every reputable lexicographer, is the *Oxford English Dictionary,* an historical record of the English language which occupies about four feet of shelf space and is no longer in print. It was compiled from over four million quotations illustrating the use of English words since the language was first written. The second major source is earlier Merriam-Webster dictionaries, especially the *Second Edition.* The third and most important source is a file of about four and a half million quotations from recent and contemporary writing and speech, each one illustrating some use of some word. If the word is rare, the collection of citations will be small; but if it is a very common one, the collection of citations may be several inches thick.

Accumulating this enormous file of instances showing the language in use required many years of reading by a great many persons. In making sure that the file contained an adequate sampling of the language in use, the editorial staff has systematically read such publications as the *Dictionary of American Biography,* the books of the American Guide Series, dozens of college catalogs, a comprehensive selection of popular and technical periodicals and of major newspapers, and innumerable government and business reports and journals. This file is the greatest single record of how English has actually been used, the most comprehensive sample of the current, living language. It is not a set of statements about English but a collection of instances of English as it has been used by real individuals in real situations for the primary purpose of saying something to other real individuals. It is, then, the English language itself, the language of the English-speaking peoples, and the profound changes in English which were mentioned earlier are recorded in it. If a dictionary is reliable only insofar as it is a true description of actual practices by actual persons using their native tongue, here is a definitive sample of these practices.

On the authority of this file *Webster's Third New International Dictionary* contains about 50,000 words which have not appeared before in an unabridged Merriam-Webster and about 50,000 new meanings for words which have previously been so recorded.

Such an enormous body of evidence on the present state of English is a fundamental requirement to recording the changing language in a new dictionary according to modern principles of language description. It constitutes a record of practices which reveals the evolution of the language and contains the only kind of raw data from which a truly authoritative description of actual practices can be put together. Although there is general agreement on this basic principle of dictionary responsibility, it can be implemented only if a comprehensive sample of practices is available and only if the editorial staff displays a high degree of professional skill and integrity. Since our intellectual climate includes some notion that dictionaries and handbooks somehow arbitrate usage with some kind of superior wisdom and somehow strive to maintain the "purity" of English against the corrupting influence of popular use, even dictionary editors and handbook writers may be infected to some extent by the virus of this notion. To one who is familiar with the difficulties in this area, the consistency and fidelity with which the editors of *Webster's Third New International* have objectively described rather than arbitrarily prescribed is impressive.

And after all, this is what the average purchaser of a dictionary wants. As a reader he wants to know what meaning an author really intended when he used the word in question (not what, by some theory, he should have intended); and as a writer or speaker he wants to know what meaning his audience is most likely to understand from his use of the word in question (not what, by some theory, they should understand). Thus, his primary concern is what meaning the word has customarily conveyed in a given context—what its semantic value has been in the verbal marketplace.

In addition to the establishment of current meanings, fidelity to the conclusions of modern linguistic study is manifest in the establishment of current status and in the representation of current pronunciation. One of the responsibilities of a dictionary is to indicate when a word or use is nonstandard and to show, by some label or restrictive comment, the kind of limitation there is on its employment. The distinction between standard and nonstandard usage is different from the distinction between formal and informal styles and from that between written and conversational styles. The popular but false notion that standards drop in a series of levels from formal written (high level) to informal conversational (low level) has confused the issue, and a great many persons have taken the label "colloquial" to indicate some departure from the highest standards, contrary to the intention of the editors who affixed this label. Hence, *Webster's Third New International* does not use this label.

A great many persons are properly concerned with whether their English is "good" English, but there is some confusion as to what "good" English actually is. The whole force of what is known about this question by scholars—and incidentally of the intuitive opinion held by most who use the language—indicates that "good" English is that which most effectively accomplishes the purpose of the author (or speaker) without drawing irrelevant attention from the purpose to the words or constructions by which this purpose is accomplished. Thus, for ordinary purposes, "good" English is that which is customary and familiar in a given context and in the pursuit of a given objective. In other words, the language which should be used is that which is currently being used, provided this current use does not bring unwelcome attention. This conclusion throws the issue directly back to the available record of actual practices, the aforementioned citation file.

In *Webster's Third New International Dictionary* usages standard for all purposes are not labeled; nonstandard usages are given some label to indicate the kind of restriction which the evidence implies. An individual word or meaning may be nonstandard because it is restricted as to region, regarded as typical of uneducated speech or writing, out of date either as too old or as not fully established, or considered to be offensive to public decency. A few words or meanings are standard usage only under certain circumstances. For instance, *dolly* to mean "doll" is a child's term but is hardly wrong when used by a child or to a child. A special category of words and usages which stands beside standard English as a kind of facetious extension is slang: for instance, *horse* to mean "heroin," *score* to mean "a successful theft or its proceeds," and *liberate* to mean "steal." On the other hand, some former slang has passed into the standard language, e.g., *hard sell,* and some words which are occasionally regarded as slang really should not be so regarded, for they are the proper terms for the meanings, e.g., *coonjine.* Decisions in this area are especially difficult, for such words do not occur as often in writing as in speech, and no one can have a firsthand speaking acquaintance with everything of this type. At the same time, any speaker of American English is likely to encounter slang, if only in a paperback mystery story, and on occasion may find it useful.

Webster's Third New International represents pronunciation in terms of regional standards. In that respect it follows the conclusions of responsible scholarship in American English—and, in fact, the conclusions of anyone who listens to the voices of national leaders over radio or television. One can hardly pretend that each word has but one pronunciation, or even one preferred pronunciation, when he finds that members of the faculties of the greatest universities, national leaders in business and the professions, and holders of the highest offices speak with a great variety of accents. In order to accommodate this variety, the pronunciation editors have developed an adaptation of the older symbolization. They did not adopt one of the symbolizations used by scholars; rather they modified their own by adding some symbols and dropping others.

The objective was a set of symbols which would represent each speech sound which distinguishes one word from another and each difference in sound which is associated with some large region of the country. For example, a word like *foreign* is pronounced with different vowels by persons with equal education and community prestige but from different sections, and the same vowel in *bag* is pronounced differently in different sections. The pronunciations in this dictionary are based on records gathered by members of the pronunciation staff, supplemented somewhat from materials published by certain nationally recognized authorities in American English. In using these pronunciation guides, one selects the representation which fits most naturally into his own pattern of speech. He is thus not encouraged to adopt a pronunciation which will appear to be an affectation. Also, variations which arise from the amount of prominence a word has in different contexts are listed. The usual dictionary practice has been to list pronunciations of words like *he* and *to* as they would be pronounced in a list. Use of such pronunciations in all contexts leads to a kind of pseudo-correctness which is as noticeable, and as revealing, as a substandard pronunciation. This dictionary thus represents the normal pronunciation of English as it is spoken by cultured persons in each major section of the country—the "language of well-bred ease," regionally determined.

The matters which have been discussed so far have importance for everyone who uses a dictionary, but the extent to which this dictionary records current progress in academic fields should be of particular interest to everyone who is engaged in education. The general policy has been to include those terms which are employed in academic fields up to the graduate level. Thus a student on any lower level is likely to find every word that appears in his normal academic pursuits. One who has completed his formal education can expect to find the terms which have come into these fields of study as a result of recent advances. And as progress in scholarship and research is passed into lower academic channels, these terms move further into the public domain, for today we live rather close to the laboratory and the research center.

Since the study of the language and its use is central to the curriculum on practically every level below college, the results of scholarship in this area have a peculiarly broad significance. There is a considerable body of printed material on language in general and English in particular which, for one reason or another, is not widely familiar to teachers, even those in the language arts. Some of this deals with a general understanding of language as a medium of communication, some with the nature of language standards, and some with the details of English pronunciation and their relation to spelling, with the categories and processes in English grammar, and with the relation between vocabulary and meaning. Thus a teacher of English can find the meanings of such terms as *function word, head,* and *nominal,* which are being used in modern descriptions of English grammar. An elementary school teacher can see the true shape of the language more clearly in this dictionary than in any but a small part of the material on English which she is given to teach, and she can find better definitions of basic terms in this dictionary than in the majority of current textbooks. Any educated person who wishes to read the results of qualified scholarship in language can understand it more readily with this dictionary at hand. For *Webster's Third New International* displays a professional knowledge of modern scholarship in language, and, frankly, the greatest part of school textbooks on language do not, although this condition is slowly being corrected.

The preceding remarks have applied to those aspects of this dictionary which reflect two of the major developments mentioned in the introduction—the changing shape of the language, and the progress in the scholarly study of language. What remains now is to consider the application of better lexicographic procedures, including those which are possible only in a dictionary of similar size. These involve, you may recall, refinement in discriminating senses, precision and grace in wording entries, and devices for making entries clear and informative. The preparation of a single entry involves all three matters simultaneously.

As in all Merriam-Webster dictionaries the order of senses is historical. These senses are worked out into classes and subclasses, and the order of listing shows the development of meaning the word has undergone. In this way one sees the flow of semantic evolution which has produced the current meaning or meanings. Often some residue of meaning will remain as a subtle nuance which a very skillful writer will have in mind as he uses the word, even though a word's first recorded meaning is not necessarily permanent. In any event, regardless of the order of listing, anyone using a dictionary must search through the listed definitions until he finds the one which fits most harmoniously into the word's immediate context.

The innovation in dictionary style which is most quickly seen is the sharp distinction between a definition and a synonym. A definition is "a statement of the meaning of a word or word group"; a synonym is a word or word group with nearly equivalent meaning. Thus a definition breaks down a word's meaning into its semantic ingredients. It is analytical in that it reduces a single hard word into a phrase made up of simpler ones, or it expresses a meaning in terms of the components of that meaning. For instance, *courageous* is not defined by associating it with a synonym like brave, but it is defined by the phrase "marked by bold resolution in withstanding the dangerous, alarming, or difficult." In this dictionary each synonym in an entry is printed in small capitals to distinguish it as such. Each word in small capitals is also a cross-reference, for it is itself defined where it is listed as an entry.

Each definition and each set of one or more synonyms is marked by a boldface colon, which is used for no other purpose. The material following each boldface colon is a single definition for one sense of the word or a set of one or more synonyms for one sense of the word, with or without a label, explanatory note, illustrative context, or illustrative quotation. In effect, then, each such colon introduces a word or phrase which is one semantic equivalent of the entry word and could be substituted for it in some normal context. This device serves as a prominent mark for the eye to catch in scanning an entry and frees marks of punctuation in the same typeface as the text for ordinary punctuation uses. In consulting a long entry, one looks for the numbers and letters in boldface which break it down into classes and subclasses of senses and picks up definitions or synonyms until he finds a general meaning which he thinks will fit his context. Then he tries each phrasal definition, considering any explanatory material which accompanies it, until he is satisfied.

Of other means of giving the required information about an entry word, the one which is most worthy of mention is the use of quotations. *Webster's Third New International Dictionary* supplies over 200,000 quotations and verbal illustrations from over 14,000 individuals and several hundred publications. Each quotation is followed by a designation of author or source. Sometimes a nuance of meaning is not reducible to a verbal statement, and sometimes an entry word or one of its uses is associated primarily with a particular style. Quotations illustrating the proper use of an entry word demonstrate these matters which are not easily or briefly stated. When, for example, *crash the gate* is illustrated by the quotation "all the kids used to sneak in . . . they had a million ways of crashing the gate," one can see what style it is appropriate to.

Anyone who is familiar with dictionaries knows that their style is frequently cryptic and associative rather than clear and precise. In other words, there seems to be a dictionary jargon as recognizable as a government or business jargon. Entries are often grotesque as writing and merely suggestive as expressions of meaning. Probably the greatest offender in this respect is the phrase "of or pertaining to," in which the participle means little more than "in some general way associated with." The editors of this dictionary have simply eliminated this phrase from their defining vocabulary. Likewise, *or* is sometimes less than clear. In English generally it may be used between elements with similar meanings or, as here, between elements which are mutually excluding alternates. In ordinary writing one depends on the context to indicate which meaning it has, but a dictionary is consulted by someone who is in doubt as to a context. For this reason this dictionary does not use *or* as a divider between synonymous or equivalent words— only when the members of the series are alternatives or when one members adds to another.

The preceding paragraphs discuss a few of the more obvious refinements in lexicography which appear in *Webster's Third New International Dictionary*. It is less easy to display or to describe the quality of professionalism which is likewise evident in it. There is a level of professionalism at which results seem to be both inevitable and effortless. In its best definitions this dictionary has this quality, and it is generally free of clumsiness resulting from massing word on word without regard for stylistic virtue and of triteness resulting from carelessly employing general formulas rather than specific and individually appropriate phrases. Its style is, in the main, analytic rather than suggestive. In other words, the editors have tried to write as well as to define, and the best definitions are portions of good expository prose rather than mere verbal formulas. There is, in their choice of words, the awareness of semantic values and associations which one expects from thoroughly competent writers, and, in their discriminations, the meticulous respect for nuances of meaning which one expects from precise and orderly minds.

One can be completely sincere in saying that this latest dictionary to bear the Merriam-Webster label is an intellectual achievement of the very highest order. It is not easy, in fact it is extraordinarily difficult, to conduct a major intellectual project, involving dozens of persons and requiring many years of effort, in keeping with fundamental principles which are not part of the common intellectual background shared by everyone. To the scholar in language, who knows something of the difficulties in such a project, the consistent skill which has been displayed is most impressive. To one who simply wishes to use a dictionary, it is of primary importance that this dictionary has been produced by a staff of professionals roughly equivalent to the faculty of a small college, that it embodies the best and most thoroughly established principles of current scholarship in language, and that it is based on the largest available collection of evidence showing what current English actually is. Whatever authority these attributes give, it has.

~ C ~

suggestions for discussion

1. What is a good term to describe the logical order of the sentences in the first paragraph in Miss Bryant's treatment of the history of the dictionary? Try reading these sentences in a haphazard order. For example read the fourth sentence first; then read the second sentence, etc. What would be the effects of such reading?

2. In the same selection, the second paragraph has a more complex order than does the first. How can you describe this order? Is the same order followed in the first paragraph of the second selection?

3. Traditionally, some of these logical sentence patterns which develop coherence have been described as "space," "time," "general

to the particular," "particular to the general," "rising to a climax," and many others. Analyze some of the other paragraphs in this chapter and try to describe the patterns of development.

4. Pick out the words and phrases in Mortimer Adler's essay which seem to remind the reader, to make him move on, to point out, or in general which seem not to be making a statement. Compare the frequency of these transitions in his essay with those of Margaret Bryant's. What conclusions do you draw? Which seems to be easier reading?

5. Give a practical definition of the pronoun part of speech. How can a pronoun serve to connect or link sentences in a paragraph? Pick out the pronouns in the first paragraph of Margaret Bryant's essay and show how they develop coherence. Compare the use of pronouns in Mortimer Adler's essay with those in Margaret Bryant's. Which pronoun used frequently by Adler is never used by Miss Bryant? Can you make any comment on this difference in the practice of the two writers?

6. Refer to several paragraphs of the review of *Webster's Third New International Dictionary* by Sumner Ives. Notice that the author makes frequent use of the repetition of key words within paragraphs and among paragraphs. For example, in the first paragraph the word "language" occurs several times. Pick out other words that Professor Ives uses often to gain coherence. (Notice also that skillful repetition gives emphasis by making the repeated words and the ideas they represent prominent and, hence, memorable.)

~ D ~

suggestions for writing

1. Let us consider a matter that may be subject to dispute.

Refer, briefly, to the four selections reprinted in this chapter; all of them, of course, deal with dictionaries and lexicography. Which of them is, in your opinion, most clearly designed to present a great deal of factual information, with the least intrusion of the author's personality? Which most clearly reveals the author's personality?

Write a paper of four to six paragraphs, with ample reference to specific passages, to give your views on these questions.

2. Identify several (4 to 6) words in Dr. Johnson's Preface that to the author and, presumably, his readers in 1755 had meanings different from those meanings that you associate with them. Use your observation of these words, and use the knowledge of lexicography that you have gained in this chapter to demonstrate why a dictionary must be revised from time to time. Try to keep your statement to about six paragraphs. (A suggestion to set you off to a good beginning in your search for words: consider the word "primitive" as it is used in the second paragraph of our excerpt from Johnson's Preface. In your preparations for writing on this topic, be sure that you do not settle too easily on words that merely look strange to you; look the words up in your dictionary to make certain that they do indeed have current meanings that are different from their meanings in the Preface.)

3. Look back over Dr. Johnson's Preface and Sumner Ives' review of *Webster's Third International*. (Of the selections in this chapter, they differ from the other two in that they are intended to refer to single, specific works, and not to dictionaries in a general way.) What are some problems facing Johnson that the editor and staff of the Webster's did not have? Did they have special problems that Johnson was spared? Consider these questions, and any related ones that may occur to you, in a paper of about six paragraphs.

4. From your study of the readings in this chapter, write a paper aimed at your classmates' level of experience for the purpose of giving advice on the uses of a good dictionary to the student.

~ E ~

additional readings

Whitehall, Harold, "The Development of the English Dictionary," *Webster's New World Dictionary of the English Language* (College Edition) (Cleveland and New York: The World Publishing Company, 1960), pp. xxxii-xxxiv.

Gove, Philip B., "Preface," *Webster's Third New International Dictionary* (Springfield, Mass.: G. & C. Merriam Company, 1961), pp. 6a-7a.

Roberts, Paul, *Understanding English* (New York: Harper & Row, Publishers, 1958), Ch. 26, "How to Find Fault with a Dictionary."

Quirk, Randolph, *The Use of English* (New York: St. Martin's Press, Inc., 1962), Ch. 9, "What Do You Read, My Lord?"

Chapter Three

~ A ~

the effective paragraph

The paragraph helps to indicate to the reader how ideas are organized. You, therefore, must be responsible for judging how much to put into a paragraph, how to give the paragraph coherence, and for knowing why you have incorporated a certain body of material into a paragraph. In other words, from what you know about your purpose, you should make conscious decisions about the length and content of the paragraphs that you write.

For example, a newspaper will usually begin news stories with a paragraph of but a single sentence. Then a second paragraph with maybe two or three sentences will follow. A third paragraph with three or four sentences may come next. If the story is a long one, the last paragraphs will have many sentences in them. In almost all these paragraphs the main idea of the story will be repeated. And as the paragraphs get longer, this main idea will be given fuller and fuller expression. This method of paragraph development is called the "pyramid"; it is a journalistic device planned to appeal to the reader who must get his news in a hurry. But, if he has time to get all the facts, he will read all the way through the news article. The following news story is an example of the pyramid style:

The search for international understanding has led the United Nations to the glyph.

Glyphs are little symbols, such as the plus and minus signs used in mathematics. Since they are "independent of language and culture," glyphs have been stressed as a means of breaking down the language barrier.

With this in mind, the 113 United Nations member states are being asked to promote glyph development, invent new glyphs and standardize old ones, use more glyphs as road signs and widen the use of glyphs generally.

Since 1965 has been designated as International Cooperation Year, it is being suggested that developing the glyph is one of the useful tasks that could be encouraged.

The idea of promoting glyphs was first mentioned in United Nations circles by Dr. Margaret Mead, the anthropologist.

Suggestions from individuals are not customarily received or acted on. The idea was not pursued until the Canadian delegation saw its merits and sponsored it in the 12-nation committee planning the 1965 observance, which will coincide with the 20th anniversary of the founding of the United Nations.

The committee has given the glyph go-ahead. It has said it regards the idea of promoting glyphs as in complete harmony with the International Cooperation Year but is leaving it to the member governments to discover their own ways of using the symbols.

One obvious field, the committee suggests, would be in foreign travel, where identical road signs with universal acceptance would be a safety measure. The whole communication field stands to gain from the glyph—*le glyph* to the French, *glifko* to the Spanish, and *znak* to the Russians.

The official glyph (the origin of the term is a Greek word meaning "carving") for the 1965 international year is almost certain to be the insignia for the United Nations celebration. Artists at work on preliminary sketches have selected as their theme hands clasped in brotherhood. If the committee approves, the design will go on postage stamps and posters, as the first United Nations glyph.*

But that is journalism, and since you are interested in practical expository prose, you will recognize the fact that there may be other purposes and reasons for paragraph size. Still, in your writing, as in the news story, the essential reason for paragraph length and content is to satisfy the reader's desire to understand. In other words, the length and content of your paragraph depends entirely on your judgment of what you must supply your reader about your topic idea to satisfy him. Remember, the reader doesn't know what you

---

* Kathleen Tiltsch, *The New York Times*, Sunday, March 29, 1964, Sec. 1, p. 21.

have in mind. He depends entirely on what you present to him in writing to know what it is you are trying to communicate.

In the following selections you will notice that the paragraph lengths differ and that they differ because the authors have had different purposes and, therefore, different kinds of obligations to satisfy their readers.

~ B ~

dialect

Explanatory *

Mark Twain

In this book a number of dialects are used, to wit: the Missouri Negro dialect; the extremest form of the backwoods Southwestern dialect; the ordinary "Pike County" dialect; and four modified varieties of this last. The shadings have not been done in a haphazard fashion, or by guesswork; but painstakingly, and with the trustworthy guidance and support of personal familiarity with these several forms of speech.

I make this explanation for the reason that without it many readers would suppose that all these characters were trying to talk alike and not succeeding.

Introduction to the Adventures of Huckleberry Finn †

Lionel Trilling

As for the style of the book, it is not less than definitive in American Literature. The prose of *Huckleberry Finn* established for written prose the virtues of American colloquial speech. This has nothing to do with pronunciation or grammar. It has something to

---

* *Huckleberry Finn.*

† From Lionel Trilling's Introduction to Mark Twain's *The Adventures of Huckleberry Finn*, Rinehart Editions. Copyright © 1948 by Lionel Trilling. Reprinted by permission of the publishers, Holt, Rinehart and Winston, Inc.

do with ease and freedom in the use of language. Most of all it has to do with the structure of the sentence, which is simple, direct, and fluent, maintaining the rhythm of the word-groups of speech and the intonations of the speaking voice.

In the matter of language, American literature had a special problem. The young nation was inclined to think that the mark of the truly literary product was a grandiosity and elegance not to be found in the common speech. It therefore encouraged a greater breach between its vernacular and its literary language than, say, English literature of the same period ever allowed. This accounts for the hollow ring one now and then hears even in the work of our best writers in the first half of the last century. English writers of equal stature would never have made the lapses into rhetorical excess that are common in Cooper and Poe and that are to be found even in Melville and Hawthorne.

Yet at the same time that the language of ambitious literature was high and thus always in danger of falseness, the American reader was keenly interested in the actualities of daily speech. No literature, indeed, was ever so taken up with matters of speech as ours was. "Dialect," which attracted even our serious writers, was the accepted common ground of our popular humorous writing. Nothing in social life seemed so remarkable as the different forms which speech could take—the brogue of the immigrant Irish or the mispronunciation of the German, the "affectation" of the English, the reputed precision of the Bostonian, the legendary twang of the Yankee farmer, and the drawl of the Pike County man. Mark Twain, of course, was in the tradition of humor that exploited this interest, and no one could play with it nearly so well. Although today the carefully spelled-out dialects of nineteenth-century American humor are likely to seem dull enough, the subtle variations of speech of *Huckleberry Finn,* of which Mark Twain was justly proud, are still part of the liveliness and flavor of the book.

Out of his knowledge of the actual speech of America Mark Twain forged a classic prose. The adjective may seem a strange one, yet it is apt. Forget the misspellings and the faults of grammar, and the prose will be seen to move with the greatest simplicity, directness, lucidity, and grace. These qualities are by no means accidental. Mark Twain, who read widely, was passionately interested in the problems of style; the mark of the strictest literary sensibility is everywhere to be found in the prose of *Huckleberry Finn.*

It is this prose that Ernest Hemingway had chiefly in mind when he said that "all modern American literature comes from one book by Mark Twain called *Huckleberry Finn*." Hemingway's own prose stems from it directly and consciously; so does the prose of the two modern writers who most influenced Hemingway's early style, Gertrude Stein and Sherwood Anderson (although neither of them could maintain the robust purity of their model); so, too, does the best of William Faulkner's prose, which, like Mark Twain's own, reinforces the colloquial tradition with the literary tradition. Indeed, it may be said that almost every contemporary writer who deals conscientiously with the problems and possibility of prose must feel, directly or indirectly, the influence of Mark Twain. He is the master of the style that escapes the fixity of the printed page, that sounds in our ears with the immediacy of the heard voice, the very voice of unpretentious truth.

NB

From THE DEVELOPMENT OF MODERN ENGLISH *

Stuart Robertson
Frederic Cassidy

Everybody is aware that differences both geographic and social exist in our language. Even those of us who have not traveled, or who have lived in a limited area, will have had this fact thrust upon us by comic strips, movies, radio, and television—usually, it is true, in a form distorted and conventionalized for humorous effect, but once in a while more truthfully represented. Thus we are made conscious of "hillbilly talk," or "cowboy talk," "Brooklynese," "gangster talk," and so on. And each of us has surely made for himself certain connections between particular parts of the country and the more striking varieties of pronunciation and vocabulary found in those localities. The linguistic geographer seeks to make such correlations systematically, and when he has done his work in any area he is able to draw maps showing the distribution of the significant variations, and thus, in effect, setting off the regional subdivisions of the language.

---

* *Second Edition* (Englewood Cliffs, N.J.: Prentice-Hall, Inc., 1954), pp. 386-390.

Linguistic geography began in Germany in the nineteenth century with the work of Georg Wenker, who sent out to over 44,000 village schoolmasters a list of forty sentences containing words and sounds known to vary locally. He asked them to translate these into the form of pronunciation used in their part of the country. Unfortunately they were not trained for accurate listening or recording of small differences, so the experiment was not wholly successful. The first successful full-scale linguistic atlas of a whole country was produced in France by Jules Gillieron and Edmond Edmont (1902-09), the evidence on 2000 items being gathered at first hand by Edmont in 600 localities throughout the area. Further improvements in method were made by Karl Jaberg and Jakob Jud in their atlas of Italy and southern Switzerland, and still others have been added in the work of the *Linguistic Atlas of the United States and Canada,* still in progress.

The linguistic geographer today first studies the settlement-history of the area he is to work in. Upon this basis, guided often by some preliminary sampling of the area's speech habits, he chooses a number of communities which, in aggregate, will represent the whole area. Some of these must be rural, some urban; some must be long-established, others relatively new; some must be along the routes of population movement, others isolated; they must also represent proportionally the national or ethnic backgrounds of the population. Next, in these communities he seeks people who have been there all their lives (and their forebears too if possible, though in recently settled areas of the United States, the latter is obviously impossible); they must also be of various generations, occupations, and degrees of education. To all of these people the investigator puts the same series of questions. The sum of their answers (which he records in careful phonetic transcription) allows him to compare for local variations, and since he knows the appropriate facts about each of the answerers (or "informants"), he is in a position to correlate the differences of language with geography, education, and social status. Furthermore, by a comparison of the generations he can judge the direction of change—what things are old-fashioned or new-fangled. Ultimately he can set off on the map what are called "focal areas" (those which are being imitated, and whose influence is therefore spreading), "relic areas" (those which conserve language forms longer than others do), and "transition areas" (those in which outside influences are more striking than local characteristics). . . .

Regional Differences in American Pronunciation. The main divisions that used to be set forth were three: New England or Eastern, Southern, and General American, the latter two conceived of as reflecting more or less the political boundary of the Civil War. Now, however, these labels must be abandoned or revised, for it is clear that the New England area is by no means homogeneous, and that there is no north-south boundary following political lines. Indeed, we must recognize that there are three more-or-less horizontal bands, linguistically distinct, running from east to west across the United States: the Northern, the Midland, and the Southern (the term "Southern" being redefined). New England east of the Connecticut River forms a small separate area allied to the northern but differing in certain respects. The Northern includes Western New England, upstate New York, a narrow strip of Pennsylvania along Lake Erie, the northern third of Ohio, Indiana, and Illinois, and the states to the north of them. Beyond the Mississippi the evidence has not yet been sufficiently gathered, but the divisions between the areas appear to run generally westward, with regional boundaries becoming less sharply defined as one approaches the Rocky Mountains and the Pacific coast.

REGIONAL AND SOCIAL VARIATIONS *

Albert Marckwardt

The English language is spoken natively in America by no less than 145 million persons over an area of some three million square miles. Various parts of the United States differ considerably from each other with respect to climate, topography, plant and animal life, economic conditions, and social structure. Sociologists and historians recognize at least six regional cultures within the continental borders of the country. The same a priori grounds that led us to assume the existence of a series of differences between British and American English at the outset of this work will justify the inference that the language is likely not to be uniform throughout the

---

* From *American English* by Albert H. Marckwardt. Copyright © 1958 by Oxford University Press, Inc. Reprinted by permission.

country. The American novelist John Steinbeck in his *Grapes of Wrath* offers convincing evidence of the plausibility of this assumption:

> 'I knowed you wasn't Oklahomy folks. You talk queer kinda—That ain't no blame, you understan'.'
>
> 'Ever'body says words different,' said Ivy. 'Arkansas folks says 'em different, and Oklahomy folks says 'em different. And we seen a lady from Massachusetts, an' she said 'em differentest of all. Couldn' hardly make out what she was sayin'.'

Early travelers to America and native commentators on the language agree on the existence of regional differences at an early period in our national history. Mrs. Anne Royal called attention to various Southernisms in the works which she wrote during the second quarter of the nineteenth century, and as early as 1829, Dr. Robley Dunglison had identified many of the Americanisms, in the glossary he compiled, with particular portions of the country. Charles Dickens recognized regional differences in the English he encountered in his first tour of the United States, and William Howard Russell, reporting on Abraham Lincoln's first state banquet, at which he was a guest, mentions his astonishment at finding 'a diversity of accent almost as great as if a number of foreigners had been speaking English.'

A number of other observers, however, were sufficiently impressed by the uniformity of the language throughout the country to make this a matter of comment. De Tocqueville, in a rather extended treatment of the language of the young republic, flatly declared, 'There is no patois in the New World,' and John Pickering, along with Noah Webster easily the most distinguished of our early philologists, also remarked on the great uniformity of dialect through the United States, 'in consequence,' as he said, 'of the frequent removals of people from one part of our country to another.'

There is truth in both types of comment. People in various parts of the United States do not all speak alike, but there is greater uniformity here than in England or in the countries of Western Europe, and this makes the collection of a trustworthy body of information upon the regional variations in American English a somewhat difficult and delicate matter.

The gathering of authentic data on the dialects of many of the countries of Western Europe began in the latter decades of the nineteenth century. The *Atlas linguistique de la France* followed closely upon the heels of the *Sprachatlas des deutschen Reichs,* and the activities of the English Dialect Society were initiated about the same time. In 1889 a group of American scholars organized the American Dialect Society, hoping that the activities of this organization might result in a body of material from which either a dialect dictionary or a series of linguistic maps, or both, might be compiled. The society remained relatively small, however, and although some valuable information appeared in its journal *Dialect Notes,* a systematic survey of the regional varieties of American English has not yet resulted from its activities.

The past quarter of a century, however, has seen the development of such a survey. Beginning in 1928, a group of researchers under the direction of Professor Hans Kurath, now of the University of Michigan, undertook the compilation of a *Linguistic Atlas of New England* as the first unit of a projected *Linguistic Atlas of the United States and Canada.* The New England atlas, comprising a collection of some 600 maps, each showing the distribution of a single language feature throughout the area, was published over the period from 1939 to 1943. Since that time, field work for comparable atlases of the Middle Atlantic and of the South Atlantic states has been completed, and the materials are awaiting editing and publication. Field records for atlases of the North Central states and the Upper Middle West are virtually complete, and significant beginnings have been made in the Rocky Mountain and the Pacific Coast areas. Surveys in Louisiana, in Texas, and in Ontario are also under way. It is perhaps not too optimistic to predict that within the next twenty-five years all of the United States and Canada as well will have been covered in at least an initial survey.

For a number of reasons it is not easy to collect a body of valid and reliable information on American dialects. The wide spread of education, the virtual extinction of illiteracy, the extreme mobility of the population—both geographically and from one social class to another—and the tremendous development of a number of media of mass communication have all contributed to the recession of local speech forms. Moreover, the cultural insecurity of a large portion of the American people has caused them to feel apologetic about their language. Consequently, they seldom display the same degree of pride or affection that many an English or a European speaker has for his particular patois. Since all dialect research is essentially a sampling process, this means that the investigator must take particular pains to secure representative and comparable samples from the areas which are studied. Happily, the very care which this demands has had the result of developing the methodology of linguistic geography in this country to a very high level.

In general, the material for a linguistic atlas is based upon the natural responses of a number of carefully selected individuals representing certain carefully chosen communities, which in themselves reflect the principal strains of settlement and facets of cultural development in the area as a whole. Since the spread of education generally results in the disappearance of local or regional speech forms, and since the extension of schooling to virtually all of the population has been an achievement of the past seventy-five years, it became necessary for the American investigator to differentiate between the oldest generation, for whom schooling beyond the elementary level is not usual, and a middle-aged group who is likely to have had some experience with secondary schools. In addition, it is highly desirable to include some representatives of the standard or cultivated speech in each region, that their language may serve as a basis of comparison with the folk speech. Accordingly, in the American atlases, from each community represented, the field worker will choose at least two, and sometimes three representatives, in contrast to the usual practice of European researchers, who may safely content themselves with one. Moreover, it is equally necessary to make certain that the persons chosen in any community have not been subject to alien linguistic influences; consequently, only those who have lived there all of their lives, and preferably those who represent families who have long been identified with the area in question, are interviewed, although as one moves westward into the more recently settled areas this is not always possible.

Since complete materials are available only for the eastern seaboard and for the area north of the Ohio River as far west as the Mississippi, tentative conclusions relative to the regional variations in American English can be presented only for the eastern half of the country. The principal dialect areas presented in Kurath's *Word Geography of the Eastern United States* are indicated on the accompanying map.

The three major dialect boundaries, it will be noted, cut the country into lateral strips and are labeled by Professor Kurath *Northern, Midland,* and *Southern* respectively. The line which

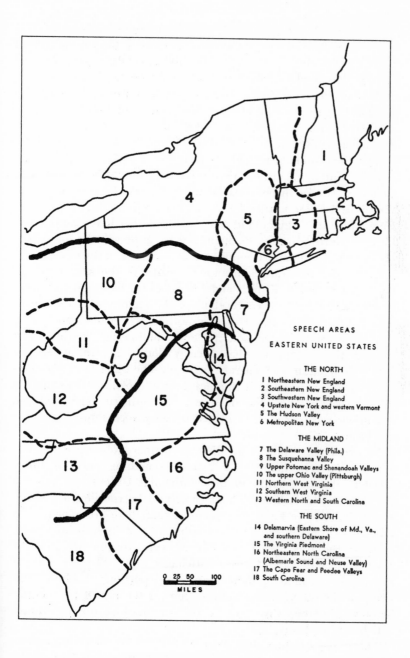

SPEECH AREAS

EASTERN UNITED STATES

THE NORTH

1 Northeastern New England
2 Southeastern New England
3 Southwestern New England
4 Upstate New York and western Vermont
5 The Hudson Valley
6 Metropolitan New York

THE MIDLAND

7 The Delaware Valley (Phila.)
8 The Susquehanna Valley
9 Upper Potomac and Shenandoah Valleys
10 The upper Ohio Valley (Pittsburgh)
11 Northern West Virginia
12 Southern West Virginia
13 Western North and South Carolina

THE SOUTH

14 Delamarvia (Eastern Shore of Md., Va.,
    and southern Delaware)
15 The Virginia Piedmont
16 Northeastern North Carolina
    (Albemarle Sound and Neuse Valley)
17 The Cape Fear and Peedee Valleys
18 South Carolina

0 25 50   100
MILES

separates the Northern and Midland areas begins in New Jersey a little below Sandy Hook, proceeds northwest to the east branch of the Susquehanna near Scranton, Pennsylvania, then goes westward through Pennsylvania just below the northern tier of counties. In Ohio the boundary dips below the Western Reserve, then turns northwest again, passing above Fort Wayne, Indiana. When it approaches South Bend it dips slightly to the southwest and cuts through Illinois, reaching the Mississippi at a point slightly above Quincy. The other principal boundary, that separating the Southern and Midland areas, begins at a point somewhat below Dover in Delaware, sweeps through Baltimore in something of an arc, turns sharply southwest north of the Potomac, follows the crest of the Blue Ridge in Virginia, and south of the James River swerves out into the North Carolina Piedmont. As we approach the lower part of South Carolina and Georgia, the boundary is as yet unknown.

Even these necessarily incomplete results of the survey carried on under Professor Kurath and his associates have modified considerably our previous conceptions of the regional distribution of American speech forms. This modification is brought about principally by adding one concept and eliminating another. The concept thus eliminated has been variously known as Middle Western, Western, or General American. The older view of American dialects, reduced to its simplest terms, recognized the existence of a New England type of speech, a Southern type, and the remainder was generally blanketed by some such term as General American.

It seems clear now that what is neither New England nor Southern—which includes, of course, something between three-quarters and nine-tenths of the continental United States—is far too diverse and lacking in homogeneity to be considered a single major dialect. We know, for example, that there are a significant number of differences, both in vocabulary and in verb inflections, between the folk speech of most of Pennsylvania and that of New York state, and between Michigan and Wisconsin on the one hand, and most of Indiana and large portions of Illinois and Ohio on the other. As our information for the rest of the country becomes available, there can be little doubt that this conclusion will be strengthened.

The concept which has been added is the recognition of a Midland type of speech as distinct from both North and South.

An examination of the evidence which Professor Kurath presents in his *Word Geography* leaves no doubt that the speech of this area, though it is by no means uniform, is sufficiently differentiated from both North and South to justify its classification as a major dialect area. This conclusion is supported not only by Atwood's study of the verb forms in the eastern portion of the country but by the available materials from the North Central States. The map shown on page 69 includes also a few, but not all, of the sub-dialect areas which merit recognition. In the North the principal area is that which separates coastal New England from western New England, New Nork state, and the territory to the west. In general, this boundary follows the line of the Green Mountains, the Berkshire Hills, and the Connecticut River. The Metropolitan New York area consists of a broad circle with the city itself at the center; the Hudson Valley area encompasses the original Dutch settlements in New York and northern New Jersey, spreading into northeastern Pennsylvania. The Midland area is divided into northern and southern sub-areas, the line of demarcation being just a little south of the Old National Road in Ohio, Indiana, and Illinois. Within the Southern dialect region, the Virginia Piedmont and the Delmarva peninsula constitute distinct sub-areas.

Thus far it is the lexical materials gathered in connection with the various atlas projects which have been analyzed most extensively, and as the title of Professor Kurath's work indicates, his plotting of the major dialect areas is based upon vocabulary evidence. For example, characteristic Northern expressions that are current throughout the area include *pail, swill, whiffletree* or *whippletree, comforter* or *comfortable* for a thick quilt, *brook, co-boss* or *come-boss* as a cow call, *johnnycake, salt pork,* and *darning needle* for a dragonfly. In the Midland area we find *blinds* for roller shades, *skillet, spouting* or *spouts* for eaves, a *piece* for food taken between meals, *snake feeder* for a dragonfly, *sook* as the call to calves, *armload* for an armful of wood; and one *hulls* beans when he takes off the shells. A quarter *till* the hour is a typical Midland expression, as is the elliptical to *want off,* or *out,* or *in.* The South has *lightwood* as the term for kindling, a *turn* of wood for an armful; stringbeans are generally *snap beans; hasslet* is the term for the edible inner organs of a pig, *chittlins* for the small intestine; and in this area cows are said to *low* at feeding time.

The sub-dialect areas also have their characteristic forms. In coastal New England, for instance, *pigsty* is the normal term for pig-pen, *bonny clapper* for curdled sour milk, *buttonwood* for a sycamore, and *pandowdy* for a cobbler type of dessert. Eastern Virginia has *cuppin* for a cowpen, *corn house* for a crib. *Lumber room* survives as the term for a storeroom. A grasshopper is known as a *hopper grass,* and *batter bread* is used for a soft cornbread containing egg.

As far as the sectors of the American lexicon which reflect regional differences are concerned, the matter is trenchantly sum-maried in Kurath's *Word Geography,* where the author points out first of all that the vocabularies of the arts and sciences, of industries, commercial enterprises, social and political institutions, and even many of the crafts, are national in scope because the activities they reflect are organized on a national basis. He then goes on to say:

> Enterprises and activities that are regionally restricted have, on the other hand, a considerable body of regional vocabulary which, to be sure, may be known in other parts of the country, even if it is not in active use. The cotton planter of the South, the tobacco grower, the dairy farmer, the wheat grower, the miner, the lumberman, and the rancher of the West have many words and expressions that are strictly regional and sometimes local in their currency.
>
> Regional and local expressions are most common in the vocabulary of the intimate everyday life of the home and the farm—not only among the simple folk and the middle class but also among the cultured . . . Food, clothing, shelter, health, the day's work, play, mating, social gatherings, the land, the farm buildings, implements, the farm stocks and crops, the weather, the fauna and flora—these are the intimate concern of the common folk in the countryside, and for these things expressions are handed down in the family and the neighborhood that schooling and reading and a familiarity with regional or national usage do not blot out.

It is not only in the vocabulary that one finds regional differ-ences in American speech. There are pronunciation features as well. Throughout the Northern area, for example, the distinction between [o] and [ɔ] in such word pairs as *hoarse* and *horse, mourning* and *morning* is generally maintained; [s] regularly occurs in *grease* (verb) and *greasy,* and *root* is pronounced by many with the vowel of *wood*. Within the Northern area such sub-dialects as coastal New England and Metropolitan New York also show many characteristic forms; the treatment of the vowel of *bird* is only one of these, and words of the *calf, pass, path, dance* group constitute another. In the Midland area speakers fail to distinguish between *hoarse* and *horse*. Rounding is characteristic of the vowels of *hog, frog, log, wasp* and *wash,* and in the last of these words an *r* often intrudes in the speech of the not too highly educated. The vowels of *due* and *new* will resemble that of *food* rather than *feud*. In the South, *r* is 'lost' except before vowels, as it is in eastern New England and New York City but not in the Northern area generally. Words like *Tuesday, due,* and *new* have a y-like glide preceding the vowel, and final [z] in *Mrs.* is the normal form.

Among the older, relatively uneducated group and even to some extent among the middle-aged informants who have had some secondary schooling there are also regional differences in inflectional forms and syntax. For example, *hadn't ought* for 'oughtn't,' *see* as a past tense form, *clim* for 'climbed' among the oldest sector of the population, *wan't* for 'wasn't,' *be* in such expressions as *How be you?,* and the choice of the preposition *to* in *sick to his stomach* are all characteristic of the Northern area. *Clum* for 'climbed,' *seen* for 'saw,' *all the further* and *I'll wait on you* are to be found in the Midlands, whereas *belongs to be, heern* for 'heard,' *seed* as the past tense of 'to see,' *holp* for 'helped,' *might could* and *mought have* are characteristic of the South.

All of this raises the question as to how the regional forms of American English developed in our three and one-half centuries of linguistic history. The first factor which must be taken into account is settlement history. Where did our earliest settlers come from, and what dialects did they speak? At the time of the earliest settlements, English local and regional dialects were in a stronger position than they are today in that they constituted the natural speech of a greater portion of the English-speaking population and were in customary use farther up the social scale.

Moreover, it is quite unlikely that any single local settlement, even at the outset, ever consisted entirely of speakers of the same dialect. Of ten families of settlers gathered in any one place, two might well have spoken London English, three or four others one of the southern or southeastern county dialects. There would be in addition a couple of families speaking northern English and another two or three employing a western dialect. In the course of their being in constant contact with each other, compromises for the everyday terms in which their dialects differed would normally have developed, and one could reasonably expect to find a southern English term for a water receptacle, a northern word for earthworm, and a western designation for sour milk. Matters of pronunciation would eventually, perhaps after a slightly longer time, be compromised in much the same manner. Moreover, the resultant compromises for various localities would be different. In the first place, no two localities would have had exactly the same proportions of speakers of the various English dialects, and even if they had, the two localities would not have arrived at precisely the same set of compromises. Thus, early in our history we developed, at various points on the Atlantic seaboard, a number of local cultures, each with distinctive social characteristics of its own—including a dialect which was basically a unique blend of British types of speech, supplemented in its vocabulary by borrowings from the Indians and from Dutch and German neighbors.

With the beginning of the nineteenth century, three changes occurred which were to have a profound effect upon the language situation in America. First, the industrial revolution resulted in the growth of a number of industrial centers, uprooting a considerable proportion of the farm population and concentrating it in the cities. The development of the railroad and other mechanical means of travel increased greatly the mobility of the average person. The large-scale migrations westward also resulted in some resettlement and shifting, even among those who did not set out on the long trek. All of this resulted in a general abandonment of narrowly local speech forms in favor of fewer, more or less general, regional types. Some local speech forms have remained even to the present day. These are usually known as relics, particularly when they are distributed in isolated spots over an area rather than in concentration. *Open stone peach,* for example, is a relic for freestone peach, occurring in Maryland. *Smurring up,* 'getting foggy,' survives as a relic in eastern Maine and more rarely on Cape Cod and Martha's Vineyard.

Even prior to the shifts in population and changes in the culture pattern, certain colonial cities such as Boston, Philadelphia, and Charleston had acquired prestige by developing as centers of trade and foci of immigration. They became socially and culturally outstanding, as well as economically powerful, thus dominating the areas surrounding them. As a consequence, local expressions and pronunciations peculiar to the countryside came to be replaced by new forms of speech emanating from these centers. A fairly recent instance of this is to be found in the New England term *tonic* for soda water, practically co-extensive with the area served by Boston wholesalers. Professor Kurath considers the influence of these centers as second only to the influence of the original settlement in shaping the regional types of speech on the Atlantic seaboard and in determining their geographic boundaries.

Nor was the general process of dialect formation by any means completed with the settlement of the Atlantic seaboard. As the land to the west came to be taken up in successive stages (for example, western New York, Michigan, Wisconsin in the North; southern Ohio, Indiana, and southern Illinois in the Midland area) the same mixtures of speech forms among the settlers were present at first, and the same linguistic compromises had to be worked out. The same processes occurred in the interior South, in Texas, and later on in the Far West. Consequently, the complete linguistic history, particularly with respect to regional forms, of the United States will not be known until all of the facts concerning the present regional distribution of speech forms have been collected, and until these facts have been collated with the settlement history of the various areas and the speech types employed by the settlers at the time they moved in. In its entirety this would necessitate a greater knowledge of the local dialects of seventeenth-century England than we have at present.

Moreover, such environmental factors as topography, climate, and plant and animal life also play their parts in influencing the dialect of an area, just as they did in the general transplanting of the English language to America. The complexity and size of the network of fresh-water streams will affect the distribution and meaning of such terms as *brook, creek, branch,* and *river.* In parts of Ohio and Pennsylvania, for example, the term *creek* is applied to a much larger body of water than in Michigan. It is even more obvious that in those parts of the country where snow is a rarity or does not fall at all, there will be no necessity for a battery of terms to indicate coasting face down on a sled. It is not surprising that those areas of the country where cows can be milked outside, for at least part of the year, will develop a specific term for the place where this is done: witness *milk gap* or *milking gap* current in the Appalachians south of the James River. The wealth of terms for various types of fences throughout the country is again dependent, in part at least, on the material which is available for building them, be it stones, stumps, or wooden rails.

Different types of institutions and practices which developed in various parts of the country also had their effect upon regional vocabulary. Those settlements which did not follow the practice of setting aside a parcel of land for common grazing purposes had little use for such terms as *green* or *common*. The meaning of *town* will vary according to the place and importance of township and county respectively in the organization of local government. The same principle applies equally well to foods of various kinds, which reflect not only materials which are readily available but folk practices as well. The German custom of preparing raised doughnuts as Lenten fare survives in the Pennsylvania term *fossnocks,* shortened from *Fastnachtskuchen.*

Finally, a new invention or development introduced into several parts of the country at the same time will acquire different names in various places. The baby carriage, for example, seems to have been a development of the 1830's and '40's, and this is the term which developed in New England. Within the Philadelphia trade area, however, the article became known as a *baby coach,* whereas *baby buggy* was adopted west of the Alleghenies and *baby cab* in other regions throughout the country. Nor have we necessarily seen an end to this process. Within the last two decades the building of large, double-lane, limited-access automobile highways has been undertaken in various parts of the country, yet the terminology for them differs considerably. In eastern New York, Connecticut, and Rhode Island these are *parkways,* but *turnpikes* in Pennsylvania, New Jersey, New Hampshire, Maine, Massachusetts, Ohio, and Indiana. In New York *thruway* is used, and they are *expressways* in Michigan and *freeways* in California. These would seem to be regionalisms in the making.

It is of interest also to look at the dialect situation from the point of view of various words which are employed in various parts of the country for the same concept. One of the most interesting and instructive distributions is to be found in connection with the terms used for *earthworm*. This word is used by cultivated speakers in the metropolitan centers. *Angleworm* is the regional term in the North, *fishworm* in the Midland area, and *fishing worm* in the coastal South. *Fish bait* and *bait worm* occupy smaller areas within the extensive *fishworm* region, but are also distributed over a wide territory.

In addition, there is a large number of local terms, many of which are used principally by the older and less-educated inhabitants. The Merrimack Valley, in New Hampshire, and Essex County, Massachusetts, have *mud worm*. *Eace worm* is used in Rhode Island. *Angle dog* appears in upper Connecticut, and *ground worm* on the Eastern Shore of Virginia. *Red worm* is used in the mountains of North Carolina, and an area around Toledo, Ohio, uses *dew worm*. Scattered instances of *rainworm* appear on Buzzards Bay in Massachusetts, throughout the Pennsylvania German area, and in German settlements in North Carolina, Maine, and Wisconsin. We have, thus, a wealth of older local terms, three distinct regional words, and the cultivated *earthworm* appearing in addition as a folk word in South Carolina and along the North Carolina and Virginia coast. Where and how did the various terms originate, and what can be determined about their subsequent history?

Earthworm itself is not an old word; it appears to have been compounded only shortly before the earliest English migrations to America. The earliest *Oxford English Dictionary* citation of the word in its present form is 1591; it appears also as *yearth worm* some thirty years earlier. The various regional terms all seem to have been coined in America; the dictionaries either record no British citations or fail to include the words at all.

The local terms have a varied and interesting history. *Mud worm* seems to occur in standard British English from the beginning of the nineteenth century on. *Eace worm*, as a combined form, goes back at least to Middle English; the first element was a term for 'bait' as early as Aelfric; it is used today in a number of southern counties in England from Kent to Gloucester. *Angle dog* is used currently in Devonshire. *Ground worm*, though coined in England, was transferred to North Carolina and Maryland in the eighteenth century. *Red worm* appears first in England in 1450 and continues through to the mid-nineteenth century, though chiefly in books on fishing, as does *dew worm,* which goes back even farther, to the late Old English period. *Rainworm,* though it appears in Aelfric as *renwyrm,* may be a reformation, even in British English, on the pattern of *Regenwurm* in German, for there is a gap of seven centuries in the citations in the *Oxford English Dictionary* and there is reason to believe that its revival in 1731 was influenced by the German form. Moreover, with but one exception, it has been cited for the United States only in areas settled by Germans.

Thus we have in the standard cultivated term one of relatively recent British formation. Apparently the regional terms were compounded in America, whereas the local terms represent survivals either of dialect usage or anglers' jargon and one loan translation. It is worth noting that the common Old English term, *angle twicce,* surviving as *angle twitch* in Cornwall and Devon, seems not to have found its way to America, and there are, furthermore, such other English formations as *tag worm, marsh worm,* and *garden worm* which have not been recorded in America.

At times, too, changes in meaning seem to have entered into the dialect situation, as is illustrated by the development of the regional terms *skillet* and *spider,* the former current in the Midland and the Virginia Piedmont, the latter in the North and in the Southern tidewater area. *Frying pan* is the urban term and is slowly supplanting the others. *Spider* was originally applied to the cast-iron pan with short legs, from which the name was presumably derived, but it was ultimately transferred to the flat-bottomed pan as well. This would seem also to explain the local term *creeper,* used in Marblehead, Massachusetts. *Skillet,* a term of doubtful etymology, first appears in English in 1403, when it was applied to a long-handled brass or copper vessel used for boiling liquids or stewing meat. It is still so used in dialects throughout England. The shift in meaning to a frying pan took place only in America, but an advertisement of 1790, offering for sale 'bakepans, spiders, skillets,' would suggest that even as late as this a distinction between the two was recognized. The examples above have been offered only as a suggestion of the various language processes which have played a part in the distribution and meaning of some of our dialect terms. It is quite obvious that no definitive conclusions about these matters can be reached until the actual facts of dialect distribution are better known than they are at present.

Thus far our concern has been only with regional dialects or speech differences, although we have recognized these as occurring particularly on certain social levels. This raises the question of the extent to which social dialects occur in American English. Is there a so-called vulgate which has reasonably uniform characteristics throughout the country, and if so, what is it?

For the most part, the language of the uncultivated will be recognized in terms of its inflectional characteristics, or at any rate it is this aspect of the language for which the most authentic information is available. Before these matters are taken up in detail, therefore, one or two points about the operation of inflections should be clearly understood.

First, we must recognize that our inflectional endings are in reality a series of patterns which are applied quite automatically whenever a situation demanding their use occurs. Even in highly inflected languages, such as Modern Finnish or Ciceronian Latin, the speaker does or did not find it necessary to recite a paradigm to determine the proper case ending. Second, throughout the history of the language, there are two forces constantly at work upon the inflectional system: sound change, which often introduces irregularities or disturbances in the system, and analogy, which tends to simplify or to straighten these out by extending the scope of the already existing pattern. As we look at some of the features of present-day substandard English, we shall see how these forces operate.

Possibly the one inflectional form most characteristic of the nouns in substandard American English is the unchanged plural after numbers: *six mile down the road, five foot tall,* and similarly applied to *month, year,* and *gallon.* Actually this is the preservation of an old partitive genitive plural after numbers, which resisted the analogical extension of the *-s* inflection to cases other than the nominative and accusative. The lesson to be learned from this is that the substandard language frequently preserves linguistically older forms than Standard English, a fact not too surprising when it is recalled that substandard English depends entirely on oral transmission from one generation to another.

Certain of the pronoun inflections, however, demonstrate precisely the contrary tendency: the development of innovations or new forms and patterns in substandard English. This is true, for example, of the possessive pronoun in its so-called absolute form, which in the standard language represents a strange and inconsistent mixture of patterns indeed. *Mine* and the archaic *thine* are formed from the adjectival form by adding *-n*. *Hers, ours, yours,* and *theirs,* on the other hand, add *-s* to the adjectival form, probably on the pattern of the noun genitive. *His* and *its* are indistinguishable so far as their secondary and absolute forms are concerned. In contrast, the substandard *mine, yourn, hisn, hern, ourn, theirn* present a perfectly regular pattern formed by an analogical extension of *mine* and *thine* to the third person singular and to the plural forms. At one time or another, several of these forms appeared in Standard English, but they seem never to have caught on and were, as we have seen, replaced in part by the *-s* forms. But the substandard language carried out the innovation completely and consistently except for *its,* which is virtually never used in the absolute form anyway.

A further point worth mentioning is that although speakers of the substandard language are rarely trained in school grammar, their language observes its own laws—not those of Standard English—in a thoroughly rigorous manner. *Hisn,* for example, is the absolute, not the secondary or adjectival form, and the two are never confused. Most speakers of the substandard language might be expected to say *the book is hisn;* no speaker of substandard English would ever say *hisn book.*

The reflexive pronouns give us another instance of a more regular operation of analogy on the substandard level than on the standard. In Standard English, *myself, yourself, ourselves,* and *yourselves* are combinations of the genitive pronoun plus the singular or plural of the *-self* form; *himself,* and *themselves* employ the object form of the pronoun, whereas *herself* and *itself* could be either. Substandard English, in substituting *hisself* and *theirself* in the third person and adhering to the singular of *self* in *ourself* and *yourself* (plural), is not only more consistent but more economical in that the latter combinations signal the plural only once and avoid the tautology of the plural *-selves.* The only ambiguity is in the second person, but the second personal pronoun has lost its distinctions between singular and plural anyway, except for the Southern form *you all.*

One curious feature of the substandard pronoun is the substitution of the object for the subjective form in such sentences as

Us girls went home, John and her was married, Me and him was late. This seems to occur principally when the subject is compound or when one or more words intervene between the pronominal subject and verb, as in *us girls.* Postverbally the reverse type of substitution (subject for object form) is often found, as in *She gave it to mother and I, She took all of we children.* Since these locutions are found considerably higher up the social and educational scale than those previously mentioned, it is possible, at least, that they are the result of overcorrection.

Space does not permit an exhaustive treatment of all the inflectional forms of substandard English, but a few that are typical deserve brief mention. *Them* as a demonstrative adjective *(them books)* probably harks back to the days when the English article and the demonstrative *that* (dative ðæm) were one and the same form. The multiple negative was also a regular and accepted feature of older English, as was the so-called flat adverb, without the *-ly* derivative suffix. However, since the standard and substandard languages are undoubtedly farthest apart with respect to verb forms, some features of the verbs of the vulgate, as they were once called by the late Robert Menner, should be described.

First of all, with respect to the present tense, there is some tendency to dispose of the distinctive inflection for the third person singular, either by eliminating it in such forms as *he want, she write,* etc., or by extending the peculiar form of the third person to the first and second—*I has some good friends, You is in lots of trouble.*

It is in the preterit and past participle forms, chiefly of those verbs which are somewhat irregular in Standard English, that the widest deviations occur. Again one may recognize here the two opposing tendencies: the retention of older forms and the simplification of irregularities through analogical processes.

The older forms retained in the substandard language owe their origin chiefly to the fact that the so-called strong verb in earlier stages of the language had four principal parts, a past tense singular as well as a past tense plural, in addition to the infinitive and present participle. Thus *writ* as a past tense of *write* represents an older preterit plural form, as do *begun* and *swum.*

On the other hand, the overwhelming tendency in English verb development throughout the last seven or eight centuries has been toward an aggrandizement of the regular or weak inflection at the expense of the older minor conjugations. This is in effect a tendency toward a two-part verb, the infinitive or present stem opposed to an identical past tense and past participle. In general, this has been brought about through analogical processes. Deviant substandard forms are usually the result of analogies which have not operated in Standard English and which take one of two directions: either the extension of the weak past inflections to such irregular verbs as *know* and *see* (*knowed, seed*) or the amalgamation of the strong preterit or past participle with the complementary form (*I taken, he done* as preterits; *have gave, have wrote, has went* as past participial forms).

In one sense, therefore, the differences between the grammatical systems of standard and substandard English represent a difference in the direction and rapidity of inflectional changes. Unquestionably the easy transition from one social class to another in the United States has resulted in a very hazy line of demarcation between what is acceptable and what is considered illiterate. According to the most rigorous schoolbook standard, some of the language employed in American legislative councils and in business life would not pass muster. The awareness of this, combined with an unrealistic treatment of language in our schools, has resulted at times in a defiance of these questionable standards. More often it has given people a guilt complex about the language they use. James West, in his community study entitled *Plainville, U.S.A.* makes a pertinent comment upon this very point:

> 'Inferior' English has been selected as a primary and almost universal trait for apology because the school teacher, the press, and the radio have all cooperated to arouse self-consciousness concerning dialect forms, phrases, and phonetics. All but the 'most backwoodsy' speakers frequently ridicule and parody the stratum or strata of speech beneath or older than their own, and at the same time feel uncertain about their own usages.

Consequently, few Americans, even among the well-educated, are confident and assured of the essential aptness and correctness of their speech. It will take at least a half-century of a more enlightened attitude toward language in the public schools to bring about any perceptible change in this state of affairs. In the meantime, what is sadly needed is an entertaining, yet scientific, treatment of vulgate speech to demonstrate how interesting a phenomenon it really is.

THE TOWER OF BABEL *

And the whole earth was of one language, and of one speech.

And it came to pass, as they journeyed from the east, that they found a plain in the land of Shinar; and they dwelt there.

And they said one to another, Go to, let us make brick, and burn them throughly. And they had brick for stone, and slime had they for morter.

And they said, Go to, let us build us a city and a tower, whose top may reach unto heaven; and let us make us a name, lest we be scattered abroad upon the face of the whole earth.

And the Lord came down to see the city and the tower, which the children of men builded.

And the Lord said Behold, the people is one, and they have all one language; and this they begin to do: and now nothing will be restrained from them, which they have imagined to do.

Go to, let us go down, and there confound their language, that they may not understand one another's speech.

So the Lord scattered them abroad from thence upon the face of all the earth: and they left off to build the city.

Therefore is the name of it called Babel; because the Lord did there confound the language of all the earth: and from thence did the Lord scatter them abroad upon the face of all the earth.

~ C ~

suggestions for discussion

1. Reread Lionel Trilling's remarks on the style of *Huckleberry Finn*. Do you think that these remarks would be adaptable to a pyramid style? You might try writing, say, three paragraphs of

---

* Gen. 11:1-9. King James Version.

such an adaptation. (For a starter, let the following sentence be the first paragraph: "The prose of *Huckleberry Finn* established for written prose the virtues of American colloquial speech.") If you think the task difficult, try to account for the difficulty.

Make sure that you know what is meant by "colloquial speech."

2. Try to put yourself for a moment into the position of the author of Mark Twain's "Explanatory," and give one good reason for having the second paragraph consist of only one sentence. (Most readers of Twain would feel that the length of the paragraph was not accidental but that its author would have had a purpose in mind.)

3. What would happen to a reader's impression of the organization of Professor Marckwardt's thought if his remarks on dialects were arranged as a series of one-sentence paragraphs? To get some idea of the effect of such an arrangement, take a paragraph and arbitrarily represent each sentence as a separate paragraph. What change do you notice in the organization of the author's thoughts once his own demonstrated sense of paragraph development has been thus violated?

4. As you look back over the selections reprinted in this chapter, why do you suppose that the paragraph length in the excerpts from Trilling's comments on *Huckleberry Finn*, Robertson and Cassidy on dialect, and Marckwardt's "Regional and Social Differences" tends to be more varied than does the length of paragraphs in newspaper writing?

~ D ~

suggestions for writing

1. Using the "pyramid" style of development, write a story of four to six paragraphs on some recent occurrence, say a school election or a ball game or any other matter that will be familiar to you and your classmates.

2. Using Mark Twain's "Explanatory" and Trilling's work, and

after looking into your dictionary, how would you define *dialect?* Write a paragraph of four or five sentences in which you present your definition and amplify it for clarity. Stay especially alert to the demands of coherence in your paragraph.

3. After a careful review of the selection by Albert H. Marckwardt, write a paper of about six paragraphs on regional and social usages that an alert stranger might notice in the kinds of speech heard in your home town (or state, if you wish).

4. Using your own language—with whatever reference to your dictionary that you need to make—rewrite the story of the tower of Babel in as many paragraphs as you think are justified by the material. Compare your version with the text reproduced above. What do you think may have been the purpose of the division into short verses? (You may be interested in comparing your version also with the modernized text in Genesis, Chapter 11, of the Revised Standard Version of the Bible (published by Thomas Nelson and Sons, 1953).

~ E ~

additional readings

Pei, Mario, *The Story of English* (Philadelphia: J. B. Lippincott Co., 1953), Part II, Ch. 1, "The Geography of English."

Pyles, Thomas, *Words and Ways of American English* (New York: Random House, 1952), Ch. 3, "Some characteristics of American English and their Backgrounds."

Robertson, Stuart, and Frederic G. Cassidy, *The Development of Modern English* (Englewood Cliffs, N.J.: Prentice-Hall, Inc., 1954), Ch. 12, "The Modern Period-Pronunciation, Variations and Standards."

Chapter Four

~ A ~

variety in the paragraph

In the last chapter we discussed the quantitative development of paragraphs by trying to answer the question: How does one decide on the content of a paragraph? In this chapter our concern will be with the qualitative aspects of the paragraph.

In the main, our objective is to communicate as effectively as possible. To help us communicate clearly, sometimes we resort to psychological devices. For instance, we all know that we are more receptive if what we are learning is interesting or if what we are trying to learn has been treated so that the facts are palatable. Therefore, we construct each paragraph with sentences put together in as interesting a fashion as possible. We do this most commonly through sentence variety, and so we must learn to vary the form of sentences. If all sentences in every paragraph look exactly alike—if all begin with the subject followed by the verb and then the object or if all have approximately the same number of words in them—soon our readers will notice the similarity in pattern in spite of the difference in words and thoughts in these sentences. Then we shall have bored readers on our hands no matter how inherently fascinating our ideas are.

To keep from boring our readers with monotonous sentence patterns, we must vary sentences. The simplest way would be to

change the length of the sentences. Another way, a more sophisti-
cated method, is to change the sentence patterns. In the following selections variety in sentence patterns will become apparent to
you with some close analysis.

~ B ~

the history of the english language

THE PERIODS OF THE ENGLISH LANGUAGE *

Albert Marckwardt

By the middle of the fifth century, Britain was ripe for conquest.
The Roman legions were no longer there to discourage invaders.
Wars between Celts, Picts, and Scots kept the island in a turmoil.
In the period from 450 to 550, the Jutes, Angles, and Saxons, tribes
speaking mutually intelligible dialects, moved from the Danish
peninsula and the land at its base to establish permanent settlements on the island which they later came to call *Engla Land* or
England. As the Celtic speaking Britons were driven to the west and
north, the language of the invaders became dominant. Thus
English set out upon its career of 1500 years of continuous use on
the island and its later dissemination to every continent on the
globe.

Because the language has had such a long and uninterrupted
existence, students of English find it convenient to divide this
continuum into periods. Just as the origins of English have their
roots in a social dislocation—emigration and conquest—similar
events may be recognized as the points of division in the history of
the language. Thus, the span of years from the invasion of the
Anglo-Saxons to the invasion of the Normans, roughly from 450

---

* From *Standard College Dictionary*, copyright © 1963, by Funk & Wagnalls
Company, Inc. Reprinted by permission of Harcourt, Brace & World, Inc.

to 1050, may be thought of as the oldest period of the language. We call the language of the island during these six hundred years Old English. Old English is the language of *Beowulf,* of Caedmon and Cynewulf, of King Alfred, Aelfric, and Wulstan.

Shortly before the end of the fifteenth century, life in England again faced a profound change. By 1475 the Wars of the Roses were over; England was united under a Tudor monarch, soon to embark upon the political and intellectual adventures of the Renaissance. In addition the invention of printing was about to make its profound impact upon the social life of the nation as well as the language. Therefore, we recognize a mid-period extending from 1050 to 1475 and call the language of that time Middle English. This is the language of Chaucer, of *Sir Gawain and the Green Knights,* of *Piers Plowman,* and of the romances.

After 1475 we consider the language to have entered upon its modern phase. But even so, it is evident that the language of Shakespeare and of the Authorized Version of the Bible differs in many respects from that of the nineteenth and twentieth centuries. Accordingly, we are led to distinguish between Early Modern English, which we define as the period from 1475 to 1700, and Late Modern English, extending over the eighteenth and nineteenth centuries to the present. Here the difference lies chiefly in the temper of the times, with the ebullience of the Renaissance contrasting with the symmetry, order, and respect for authority characteristic of the time of Pope and Johnson.

THE YEAR 1066 *

Albert C. Baugh

When in January, 1066, after a reign of twenty-four years, Edward the Confessor died childless, England was again faced with the choice of a successor. And there was not much doubt as to where the choice would fall. At his succession Edward had found

---

* From *A History of the English Language,* 2nd edition, by Albert C. Baugh. Copyright © 1957, Appleton-Century-Crofts, Inc. Reprinted by permission of Appleton-Century-Crofts.

England divided into a few large districts, each under the control of a powerful earl. The most influential of these nobles was Godwin, earl of the West Saxon earldom. He was a shrewd, capable man and was soon Edward's principal adviser. Except for one brief interval he was the virtual ruler of England until the time of his death. His eldest son Harold succeeded to his title and influence, and during the last twelve years of Edward's reign exercised a firm and capable influence over national affairs. The day after Edward's death Harold was elected king.

His election did not long go unchallenged. William, the duke of Normandy at this time, was a second cousin to the late king. While this relationship did not give him any right of inheritance to the English throne, he had nevertheless been living in expectation of becoming Edward's successor. Edward seems to have encouraged him in this hope. While William was on a brief visit in England Edward had assured him that he should succeed him. Even Harold had been led, though unwillingly, to acknowledge his claim. Having on one occasion fallen into William's hands, he had, it seems, been forced to swear, as the price of his freedom, not to become a candidate or oppose William's election. But the English had had enough of French favorites, and when the time came Harold did not consider himself bound by his former pledge.

Only by force could William hope to obtain the crown to which he believed himself entitled. Perhaps the difficulty involved in an armed invasion of England would have discouraged a less determined claimant. But William was an exceptionally able man. From infancy he had surmounted difficulties. Handicapped by the taint of illegitimacy, the son of his father by a tanner's daughter of Falaise, he had succeeded to the dukedom of Normandy at the age of six. He was the object of repeated attempts upon his life, and only the devoted care of his regents enabled him to reach maturity. In early manhood he had had to face a number of crucial contests with rebellious barons, powerful neighbors, and even his overlord, the French king. But he had emerged triumphantly from them all, greatly strengthened in position and admirably schooled for the final test of his fortune. William the Great, as the chroniclers called him, was not the man to relinquish a kingdom without a struggle.

Having determined upon his course of action, he lost no time in beginning preparations. He secured the cooperation of his vassals by the promise of liberal rewards, once England was his to dispose of. He came to terms with his rivals and enemies on the continent. He appealed to the pope for the sanction of his enterprise and received the blessing of the Church. As a result of these inducements the ambitious, the adventurous, and the greedy flocked to his banner from all over France and even other parts of Europe. In September he landed at Pevensey, on the south coast of England, with a formidable force.

His landing was unopposed. Harold was occupied in the north of England meeting an invasion by the king of Norway, another claimant to the throne, who had been joined by a brother of Harold's Tostig, returning from exile. Hardly had Harold triumphed in battle over the invaders when word reached him of William's landing. The news was scarcely unexpected, but the English were not fully prepared for it. It was difficult to keep a medieval army together over a protracted period. William's departure had been delayed, and with the coming of the harvest season, many of those whom Harold had assembled a few months before, in anticipation of an attack, had been sent home. Harold was forced to meet the invader with such forces as he had. He called upon his brothers in the earldoms of Mercia and Northumbria to join him and repel the foreigner by a united effort. But they hung back. Nevertheless, hurrying south with his army, Harold finally reached a point between the Norman host and London. He drew up his forces on a broad hill at Senlac, not far from Hastings, and awaited William's attack. The battle began about nine o'clock in the morning. So advantageous was Harold's position and so well did the English defend themselves that in the afternoon they still held their ground. For William the situation was becoming desperate and he resorted to a desperate stratagem. His only hope lay in getting the English out of their advantageous position on the hill. Since he could not drive them off, he determined to try to lure them off, and ordered a feigned retreat. The English fell into the trap. Thinking the Normans were really fleeing, a part of the English army started in pursuit, intending to cut them down in their flight. But the Normans made a stand and the battle was renewed on more even terms. Then happened one of those accidents more easily possible in medieval than in modern warfare. Harold, always in the thick of the fight, was pierced in the eye by a Norman arrow. His death was intantaneous. Two of his brothers had already fallen. Deprived of their leaders, the English became disorganized. The confusion spread. The Normans were quick to profit by the situation and the English were soon in full retreat. When night fell they were fleeing in all directions, seeking safety under the cover of darkness, and William was left in possession of the field.

While William had won the battle of Hastings and eliminated his rival, he had not yet attained the English crown. It was only after he had burnt and pillaged the southeast of England that the citizens of London decided that further resistance would be useless. Accordingly they capitulated, and on Christmas day, 1066, William was crowned king of England.

From IVANHOE

Sir Walter Scott

In that pleasant district of merry England which is watered by the river Don there extended in ancient times a large forest, covering the greater part of the beautiful hills and valleys which lie between Sheffield and the pleasant town of Doncaster. The remains of this extensive wood are still to be seen at the noble seats of Wentworth, of Wharncliffe Park, and around Rotherham. Here haunted of yore the fabulous Dragon of Wantley; here were fought many of the most desperate battles during the Civil Wars of the Roses; and here also flourished in ancient times those bands of gallant outlaws whose deeds have been rendered so popular in English song.

Such being our chief scene, the date of our story refers to a period toward the end of the reign of Richard I, when his return from his long captivity had become an event rather wished than hoped for by his despairing subjects, who were in the meantime subjected to every species of subordinate oppression. The nobles, whose power had become exorbitant during the reign of Stephen, and whom the prudence of Henry the Second had scarce reduced into some degree of subjection to the crown, had now resumed their ancient license in its utmost extent; despising the feeble interference of the English Consul of State. fortifying their castles, increas-

ing the number of their dependents, reducing all around them
to a state of vassalage, and striving, by every means in their power,
to place themselves each at the head of such forces as might
enable him to make a figure in the national convulsions which
appeared to be impending.

The situation of the inferior gentry, or Franklins, as they were
called, who by the law and spirit of the English constitution were
entitled to hold themselves independent of feudal tyranny, became now unusually precarious. If, as was most generally the case,
they placed themselves under the protection of any of the petty
kings in their vicinity, accepted of feudal offices in his household,
or bound themselves, by mutual treaties of alliance and protection to support him in his enterprises, they might indeed pur-
chase temporary repose; but it must be with the sacrifice of that
independence which was so dear to every English bosom, and at
the certain hazard of being involved as a party in whatever rash
expedition the ambition of their protector might lead him to
undertake. On the other hand, such and so multiplied were the
means of vexation and oppression possessed by the great Barons,
that they never wanted the pretext, and seldom the will, to harass
and pursue, even to the very edge of destruction, any of their less
powerful neighbors who attempted to separate themselves from
their authority, and to trust for their protection, during the
dangers of the times, to their own inoffensive conduct, and to the
laws of the land.

A circumstance which greatly tended to enhance the tyranny of
the nobility, and the sufferings of the inferior classes, arose from
the consequences of the Conquest by Duke William of Normandy.
Four generations had not sufficed to blend the hostile blood of the
Normans and Anglo-Saxons, or to unite, by common language and
mutual interests, two hostile races, one of which still felt the elation
of triumph, while the other groaned under all the consequences
of defeat. The power had been completely placed in the hands of
the Norman nobility by the event of the battle of Hastings, and
it had been used, as our histories assure us, with no moderate hand.
The whole race of Saxon princes and nobles had been extirpated
or disinherited, with few or no exceptions; nor were the numbers
great who possessed land in the country of their fathers, even as
proprietors of the second, or of yet inferior classes. The royal
policy had long been to weaken, by every means, legal or illegal,

the strength of a part of the population which was justly considered as nourishing the most inveterate antipathy to their victor. All the monarchs of the Norman race had shown the most marked predilection for their Norman subjects; the laws of the chase, and many others equally unknown to the milder and more free spirit of the Saxon constitution, had been fixed upon the necks of the subjugated inhabitants, to add weight, as it were, to the feudal chains with which they were loaded. At court, and in the castles of the great nobles, where the pomp and state of a court was emulated, Norman-French was the only language employed; in courts of law, the pleadings and judgments were delivered in the same tongue. In short, French was the language of honor, of chivalry, and even of justice, while the far more manly and expressive Anglo-Saxon was abandoned to the use of rustics and hinds, who knew no other. Still, however, the necessary intercourse between the lords of the soil, and those oppressed inferior beings by whom the soil was cultivated, occasioned the gradual formation of a dialect, compounded betwixt the French and Anglo-Saxon, in which they could render themselves mutually intelligible to each other; and from this necessity arose by degrees the structure of our present English language, in which the speech of the victors and the vanquished have been so happily blended together; and which has since been so richly improved by importations from the classical languages, and from those spoken by the southern nations of Europe.

NB

WHY THE LANGUAGE HAS CHANGED *

J. N. Hook
E. G. Mathews

A language changes because things happen to people. If we could imagine the impossible—a society in which nothing happened—there would be no changes in language. But except possibly in a cemetery, things are constantly happening to people:

---

* J. N. Hook and E. G. Mathews, *Modern American Grammar and Usage.* Copyright © 1956 The Ronald Press Company.

they eat, drink, sleep, talk, make love, meet strangers, struggle against natural perils, and fight against one another. They slowly adapt their language to meet the changing conditions of their lives. Although the changes made in one generation may be small, those made in a dozen generations may enormously affect the language. The big and little phases of history—fashions, fads, inventions, the influence of a leader, a war or two, an invasion or two, travel to a foreign land, the demands of business intercourse —may alter a language so much that a Rip Van Winkle who slept two or three hundred years might have trouble in making himself understood when he awoke. Even in a relatively quiet society, linguistic change proceeds inexorably.

Think, if you will, of the English language as a river. Its headwaters are the closely interrelated Teutonic languages of the Angles, Saxons, and Jutes, who lived mainly in the northern part of what is now Germany. They provided the basic grammatical structure of the language that we call English; they provided most of its linguistic heritage; they provided its basic words, the common everyday words that still are the most important in our simple communications. But to the basic elements brought in by these Teutonic peoples many additions have been made.

When the Teutons began invading and settling in the British Isles in 449 A.D., they found in possession the Celts, who previously had been pushed about by Roman soldiers for several centuries. The Teutons pushed the Celts about some more, finally tending to localize them in what we now call Ireland, Wales, and parts of Scotland. But the Teutonic language was influenced somewhat by the Celtic and indirectly by the Latin which the Celts had fragmentarily learned. So in English we have words of Celtic ancestry such as *brat, cairn,* and *crag,* and the place names *Aberdeen* (*Aber* = river mouth), *Avon* (river), *Caerleon, Cardiff, Carlyle* (*caer* or *car* = fortress), *Dundee, Dunbarton, Dunbar* (*dun* = hill), *Inchcape* (*inch* = island), *Kildare, Kilpatrick* (*kill* = church). And as a result of the early and indirect Latin tributary (which existed on the Continent even before the invasions of Britain), we have *wall* and *street* and *port,* words that give promise of enduring even longer than the Roman constructions that they name; and we have place names: Roman *Londinium* (originally Celtic) is now *London,* Eboracum (also once Celtic) has undergone considerable transformation to appear as *York,* and Latin *castra,* a military camp, appears both in England and the United States in *Lancaster, Worcester, Leicester, Gloucester, Chester, Dorchester, Rochester.* Thus Latin and Celtic are early tributaries of English.

By the end of the sixth century Latin was to renew its influence upon English. In 597 Roman missionaries began coming to the British Isles in an attempt to Christianize the inhabitants. They introduced such church words as *altar, creed, mass,* and *nun* and some homely words such as *beet, pine, cheese,* and *cup.* Some of the words that the priests brought over had been borrowed by Latin from Greek: *bishop, deacon, martyr, church, devil, priest, monk, pope, psalm, dish,* and *plum.* So once more a double tributary entered the river of the English language.

In the seventh and most of the eighth centuries the Anglo-Saxon inhabitants of the British Isles lived a relatively peaceful existence —simple by modern standards, but maybe happier than a more complex society can be. But starting in about 790, "Northmen" or Danes began to invade the islands. They were rough and vigorous; in 793, "the heathen men miserably destroyed God's church at Lindisfarne with rapine and slaughter," a contemporary account says. The forays grew into expeditions; the Danes began to colonize; Alfred the Great for a while paid them tribute but then organized military forces and compelled the invaders to sign a peace treaty. One of the terms of the treaty was that the Danes accept Christianity. Since the chief difference between the Danes and the Anglo-Saxons had been in religion, this concession meant that the two groups, already speaking kindred and often mutually intelligible languages, would merge. However, attacks by new groups of Danes, not covered by the treaty, continued, and early in the eleventh century a Danish king, Cnut, ruled in England.

It is often difficult to separate the linguistic contributions of the Danes from the closely related Anglo-Saxon, but apparently we owe to Danish such words as *fellow, husband, law, wrong,* and a number of words with an *sk* sound, as *skill, scale, scare, skirt* (*shirt,* a cognate form, is from Anglo-Saxon), *skin, sky, score,* and *bask.* Numerous English place names are Danish in origin. Danish *thwaite* (piece of ground) appears in many names such as *Stonethwaite, Hallthwaite; thorp* (village) is in names like *Lowthorpe* and *Northorpe; by* (town) is in *Derby, Kirby, Selby, Whitby,* etc.; *toft* (a clearing) is in *Lowestoft.*

The next big tributary came from north via east, Northmen,

later called Normans, had begun moving into France at about the time that the Danes invaded England. They were flexible people who adopted French as their language, changing it somewhat in the process. They made of Normandy one of the most vigorous and ambitious states of Europe. In 1066, after the death of England's Edward the Confessor, the Duke of Normandy decided that he would attempt to gain the crown of his late cousin, and at Hastings he earned the more glorious title of William the Conqueror. His people moved into the British Isles, relegated natives to the rank of second-class citizens, and eventually concentrated their grip upon England as they lost their continental footholds.

Now began the period of greatest linguistic turmoil that English has known. England was a country of two languages: the Norman French of the ruling classes and the English of the conquered. The Bishop of Worcester was deposed in 1095 because he was "an idiot who did not know French." French was used in the churches, in the courts, in important business transactions, and in the schools. But inevitably the two groups had to meet. A French landowner had to give instructions to his tenants; an English farmer or smith had to try to sell his goods or his skills; intermarriage became frequent. Each group picked up words from the other. However, just as American occupation troops learned only the rudiments of German, Italian, and Japanese after World War II, the Normans did not learn the intricacies of English nor did the English learn the intricacies of Norman French. Each group learned only the fundamentals.

Before the Norman conquest there had been signs that grammatical inflections were being reduced—the dative and accusative cases, for instance, were blending their forms. But the coming of the Normans seems to have expedited such change. At any rate, after the Normans had been in England for about three centuries, English inflections were not nearly so numerous.

The two groups gradually blended. So did their vocabularies, and to a much smaller extent their grammar, although the impact of Norman French upon English was less than one might think. But partly as a result of that impact, and more largely as a result of other, less tangible causes, grammatical gender was replaced by natural gender, word order became less free as inflections were reduced, pronunciations changed, and many words from Norman French, French, and Latin entered the language.

Chaucer's contemporary, John Gower, in the fourteenth century wrote three major works—one in English, one in French, and one in Latin. He chose three languages because he was not sure which language would become standard in England, and he wanted one of his works to be in the language that endured. Had he lived fifty years later, he would have had no difficulty in seeing that English was going to be the winner.

During the Renaissance two more large tributaries entered English. These, of course, were in the form of additional Latin and Greek contributions. Thousands of words came into the English vocabulary during this period, including huge numbers of relatively useless terms that lived briefly and were then buried in soon-to-be-forgotten graves. English spellings were also influenced by the new interest in the Classical languages. Learned men perhaps foolishly proclaimed that the orthography of English words should reveal their Latin backgrounds. They therefore recommended the spellings *debt* and *doubt,* even though the *b's* in these words were not pronounced, and even though the French, from whom the English had borrowed both words, had already dropped the *b's* that existed in Latin. A number of words with *tio,* like nation, had also been taken from the French, which often used a phonetically accurate *c* instead of *t;* in English the sound in question was pronounced as *s* or *sh,* but Renaissance scholars insisted that the Latin *t* be retained. Many other of our present illogical spellings may be attributed to the scholars of the Renaissance.

During the Renaissance period and later, the feeling grew that English grammar should be described in the terminology of Latin grammar. Sometimes that procedure was not objectionable, for many elements of the two languages were similar. But when the grammarians insisted upon finding in English everything that existed in Latin, when they made of Latin a procrustean bed into which English must be in some way fitted, and when they ignored the fact that English was basically a Teutonic and not an Italic language, they did irreparable harm to many generations of persons who wanted to acquire a clear understanding of the structure and peculiarities of the language.

Since the Renaissance, many small tributaries have enlarged the stream of English. These cannot be listed in chronological order. Latin has kept appearing, as have French and Greek. Italian has contributed many of the technical terms of music. Dutch has given sailing terms like *ahoy, boom, deck, hoist, skipper, sloop,* and *yacht.* Spanish has given, directly or indirectly, miscellaneous words like *matador, vanilla, armada, alligator,* and *mosquito.* North American Indian has contributed such words as *hominy, Mississippi* (an Algonquin word meaning "big river," not "Father of Waters"), *moccasin, moose, opossum, papoose, pemmican, raccoon, skunk, squaw, toboggan, tomahawk, wampum,* and *wigwam.* Among other contributing languages, with one or two representative words from each, have been Bengali (*bungalow*); Persian (*azure*); Slavic (*polka, vampire, mammoth*); Hebrew (*amen, hallelujah, behemoth*); Hungarian (*goulash*); Tartar (*khan*); Malay (*amuck, gong, cockatoo*); Indian (*rajah, nabob, khaki, yogi*); Australian (*boomerang, kangaroo*); South American Indian (*alpaca, condor, jaguar, quinine*); Polynesian (*taboo, tattoo*); African (*gumbo, mumbo jumbo, okra*). Even Chinese has given us some words (*tea, typhoon, chop suey,* and *chow mein*); Chinese Pidgin English has contributed the familiar *chopstick;* Japanese has given us *tycoon, kimono, judo,* and *ju-jitsu.*

The borrowing has of course gone the other way, also, although the details need not concern us here. English and American gastronomic and athletic terms, for instance, have been incorporated in many European languages. An American can use the terms *cocktail* and *beefsteak* with satisfactory results in almost any European restaurant.

Why did English change? Simply because many things happened to many people in many countries. Had the Angles, Saxons, and Jutes moved southeast instead of southwest, the language of the British Isles might never have been Teutonic. Had Harold defeated William the Conqueror at Hastings in 1066, the language of today might have been considerably different, perhaps more complicated in morphology, more simple in syntax. Had the English been stay-at-homes, their language might have lacked some of the versatility, the expressiveness, and the color that we believe it now has.

~ C ~

suggestions for discussion

1. The sentence is a grammatical structure that is susceptible to almost infinite variations. Yet, in the modern form of our language, the sentence has a fairly small number of patterns or types that recur over and over. And even the variations tend to be more or less predictable. Consider, for example, the first sentence in the selection from the *Standard College Dictionary;* it is a good one for our purposes now, because it shows one of the most basic and fixed principles of sentence building and, at the same time, one of our favorite ways of varying the structure of sentences.

The typical feature—one could almost say the *standard* feature— of the sentence lies in the fact that the subject ("Britain") comes before the predicate ("was ripe for conquests"). The opportunity for variation lies chiefly in the fact that the modifier consisting of "by the middle of the fifth century" may be put where it is, before the subject, or at the end of the predicate so that the whole sentence *could* have read: "Britain was ripe for conquest by the middle of the fifth century." *sic*

Reading rapidly through this same selection, see how many sentences you can identify that contain elements that may be moved with no change in the practical meaning of the sentences. Be careful to notice also that some changes will obscure the meaning, change it, or produce an uncommon and disagreeable arrangement of words.

2. The sentence that is discussed above, in its original form, is called a periodic sentence, a sentence, that is, of which the grammatical organization and the sense are concluded together. As rewritten, "Britain was ripe for conquest by the middle of the fifth century," it is a *loose sentence* or one in which a movable element of the grammar comes after the point when the sense is concluded. In conversation we use both sentence types freely; in

writing, however, many teachers prefer that their students use more periodic than loose sentences.

Again, glance through the selection from the *Standard College Dictionary*. Does its author show any sign of preferring one of these sentence types over the other?

3. Another valuable way of altering the structure of sentences is by using sentences of varying lengths. There are no rules that, strictly followed, will guide us at all times. Still, a few principles are clear enough. For one, the short sentence, especially when placed among longer ones, is an excellent way to emphasize a single thought. Too, it gives a pleasing effect when read. A second principle is that a fairly long sentence provides the writer a chance to express subtle contrasts or comparisons, or cause and effect, or a series of related thoughts.

Now, glance back over the selections above. In proportion to its length, which one shows the greatest number of short sentences (say, sentences of not more than eight words)? Which uses the largest number of noticeably long sentences (say, sentences of more than fifteen words)? Do you think that the different purposes of the writers had any effect on their using a good number of short— or long—sentences?

4. Observe that all three of the selections contain sentences that begin with such words as *but, therefore, still,* and the like. Could most of these sentences have been joined to the preceding sentences? Considering your earlier lessons in coherence, are you able to suggest any reason or reasons for the writers' opening sentences with these words?

~ D ~

suggestions for writing

1. The following passage is from Shakespeare's *Othello* where (in Act III, Scene iii) it is spoken hypocritically by that chief of villains, Iago. Your assignment is to rewrite it as a paragraph;

make changes only to modernize the language but do not alter the meaning. Of course, you will not retain the verse form but will write the paragraph as if it were your own prose.

> Good name in man and woman, dear my lord,
> Is the immediate jewel of their souls.
> Who steals my purse steals trash: 'tis something, nothing;
> 'Twas mine, 'tis his, and has been slave to thousands;
> But he that filches from me my good name
> Robs me of that which not enriches him
> And makes me poor indeed.

2. Read at least one full act of a play by Shakespeare, and then write a paragraph or so in which you show some important contrasts that are apparent between his brand of English and yours. You might arrange your thoughts, and your paragraphs, if you will, by observing first the words that you would not use or that you would not use to mean what Shakespeare meant. (For example, you probably would not say that anything is the *immediate* jewel of one's soul.) Next you might look for change of word order or arrangement and for other grammatical changes. (For example, in the passage quoted above, the clause "which not enriches him" is not your way of saying things.)

3. The third of the selections that you have read in this chapter is from Scott's novel *Ivanhoe;* the fourth is a modern view of the history of the English language.

Write a paper of four to six paragraphs in which you compare the two readings. In your preparations for writing, notice that the two selections are not intended for the same purposes; notice also that the writers have different information (with Scott's the less reliable). In your paper, be sure to pay attention to the variety of sentence patterns that you employ. Keep in mind, too, the requirements of unity and coherence.

~ E ~

additional readings

Pei, Mario, *The Story of English* (Philadelphia: J. B. Lippincott Co., 1953), Part I, Ch. 1, "The Prehistory of English"; Ch. 2, "The Tongue of the Anglo-Saxons"; Ch. 3, "The Coming of the Normans"; Ch. 4, "The Chaucerian Era."

Robertson, Stuart, and Frederic G. Cassidy, *The Development of Modern English* (Englewood Cliffs, N.J.: Prentice-Hall, Inc., 1954), Ch. 2, "The Ancestry of English."

Pyles, Thomas, *The Origins and Development of the English Language* (New York: Harcourt, Brace & World, Inc., 1964), Ch. 5, "The Backgrounds of English."

Bryant, Margaret M., *Modern English and Its Heritage,* 2nd ed. (New York: The Macmillan Company, 1962), Ch. 1, "The Indo-European Heritage"; Ch. 2, "Germanic Heritage"; Ch. 3, "Old English Heritage."

Chapter Five

~ A ~

emphasis in the sentence

In the first four chapters we have discussed the organization of paragraphs. In this chapter we shall need to pay attention to the important ideas within the sentence.

It is possible, and, in fact, it is characteristic of bad writing, to obscure the ideas in sentences to the point where the reader will be completely confused. Or, at times, the reader may be led, through misplaced emphasis, to draw an erroneous conclusion from the sentence he has read.

The writer must try to form sentences so as to keep the emphasis on what *he* wishes to have prominence. It is not enough to leave matters up to the reader. Luckily, the writer has some ready and easy devices to use. He may use the periodic sentences and occasionally the loose sentences described in Chapter Four. He may arrange a series so that there is a progression from the less to the more important idea—a climactic arrangement. (Or he may proceed from the more to the less important idea—an anticlimactic order that is especially useful in comic writing.) He may repeat key words and ideas. He may use striking comparisons or contrasts. He may intersperse very short sentences among long ones. And, of course, he must always seek the precise word, the best of all words, for the meaning he wishes to convey.

In the following essays, you will be reminded of some of these methods for attaining emphasis.

~ B ~

social problems in the language

SOCIAL ASPECTS: CLASS, TABOO, AND POLITICS *

Margaret Schlauch

Speculating on the function of clothes in society, and what they have done to us, Carlyle at one point of *Sartor Resartus* asks us to imagine the functioning of "government, legislation, property, police, and civilized society" if all persons were abruptly forced to appear in public without any clothing whatsoever. We are so accustomed to reliance on badges, buttons, styles, and materials in judging our fellowmen, he argues, that august institutions would dissolve in "wails and howls" without them. These are the signs of rank and class; we deplore their artificiality, but we need them. "Lives the man," he asks, "that can figure a naked Duke of Windlestraw addressing a naked House of Lords? Imagination, choked as in mephitic air, recoils on itself, and will not forward with the picture. . . ." It is the wig, squirrel-skins, and plush gown that announce the judge; without them he would be no more by day that he is by night, only "a forked Radish with a head fantastically carved."

But Carlyle is wrong. Even with the badges and uniforms stripped away, something would remain as a guide, as sure if less ponderable, to the social position of each forked radish. Even a naked Duke of Windlestraw, upon opening his mouth, would speak the English

---

* From *The Gift of Tongues* by Margaret Schlauch. Copyright 1942 by Margaret Schlauch. Reprinted by permission of The Viking Press, Inc.

language with a certain air, an accent and intonation inextricably associated with his rank and authority. An untrained imposter from the lower levels of society would be detected by his speech, although appearing as one nude radish among many. Of course his speech could be faked for this occasion; but so could his clothes, for other occasions. Both types of deception have been practiced. It is a pity that Carlyle did not turn his attention to language as a metaphorical clothing of man in society.

The existence of different manners of speech for persons in various ranks is a familiar fact. We are constantly sorting and classifying people according to them. A variation of any national language according to social levels is called a *class dialect*. Even within the class dialect there may be many variations and minor divisions. For instance, the younger members of a privileged class who attend special schools sometimes develop a special jargon among themselves which is almost incomprehensible to outsiders. Yet it is clearly an offshoot of the general "upper-class" dialect of their parents. Poorer youngsters also develop a kind of tribal school jargon as local and esoteric as the other. Even families and other restricted groups develop special jargons mystifying to an outsider. But these are even more clearly recognized and assigned to the general class dialects to which they belong.

When we talk, then, we tell much more about ourselves than the factual statements we are making. The sum total of small nuances will indicate much about our training, environment, economic position, and even profession. In conversation we are unconsciously providing a rich commentary about ourselves which supplements the clothing and outward possessions we gather.

The existence of an accepted upper-class dialect associated with those who govern a country and man its professions has some amusing consequences. The sociological implications have never been adequately explored. For one thing, the levels will not be clearly preserved if historical change is moving rapidly, as at the time of the French Revolution. And even where change has been slow and barriers are clearly marked, the rise and fall of individuals brings about incongruities—a lack of harmony, let us say, between the physical clothing and the garment of speech.

It is only human for people in a stratified society to want to appear more smart and elegant than they are by birth and training.

This is true if the society does leave some opportunities for personal advancement from the lower ranks. When people are over-eager to climb, they adopt a speech of uneasy and self-conscious gentility. One of its obvious characteristics in an excess of zeal for correctness: zeal to "talk good grammar," as it is sometimes called. This solicitude produces what we call hypercorrect forms.

For instance, a person may have been drilled in school to correct his native speech in the matter of present participles: to "pronounce the final g," as the unscientific saying is, in words like "ringing, singing, eating." The drill embarrasses him into self-consciousness, and he tends, for safety's sake to substitute the syllable [ɪŋ] for *all* final [n]'s in his speech. So he says "curting," "garding," "ruing" for "curtain," "garden," "ruin." Or it may be that in triumph at having corrected errors like "Him and me get along fine" into "He and I get along well," the rising individual produces sentences like "It's a secret between him (he) and I."

The *arriviste* in language is also apt to gloat in the use of perfect tenses and to overdo them. "It was a great pleasure *to have met you.*" Excessive self-consciousness about adverbial endings produces "finely" or "fastly" if the speaker has recently learned to avoid "He works good." A preposition is doubled in sentences like "It's the man for whom I was waiting for" when the speaker is just unlearning "who I was waiting for."

Another more refined vice of the self-consciously correct person is the refusal to use unstressed forms of articles or prepositions, as if they were always vulgar. He pronounces "the man and the girl" with painful distinctness, as if he were still in first grade struggling over individual words under a teacher's strict eye. He says [ði: mæn ænd ði: gəɪl], pedantically; and yet it is the best speakers, those at home in cultured English, who say: [ðə mæn ən ðə gəːl]. In accepted English, too, there is a clear difference between "to" [tə] and "too" [tuː]. The man at ease in society says: "I'm about to come too" as [əɪm ə'baut tə 'kʌm 'tuː] not the hypercorrect [əɪ 'æm ə'baut 'tuː 'kʌm 'tuː], which is in fact a bad self-betrayal. A mistaken snobbishness prompts this schoolroom isolation of words. Yet the most snobbish of snobs, the man poised with inherited confidence, is the one who freely permits slurred forms—provided, of course, they are the "right" slurred forms, hallowed by general usage in his "set."

PROVOCATIVE PRONOUNS FOR PRECISE PEOPLE *

Lodwick Hartley

A little grammar, like a little learning, is a dangerous thing. And people who know least about how the language really operates are often those who are most positive about the way in which it should be spoken and written.

Incidentally, in my very first paragraph I have already violated a principle (syntactical, it is true, rather than grammatical) that is dear to some pretenders to competence in the language. "Never, begin a sentence with *and, but,* or *for,*" the assumed rule runs. And it may even be extended to *because* and other conjunctions. But is there any reason or authority for such a rule? Not so far as I can tell. Because there is no authority, then, I think that we can quickly rid our minds of another taboo.

Clearly, this kind of false notion is in the class of the taboo about ending the sentence with a preposition. Both are classic examples of ideas promulgated by people who think that they know grammar and syntax but who in reality have only a smattering of each.

There is another class of people (or is it merely a subclass?) who have a strong faith in the "niceties" of grammar and who insist upon demonstrating their familiarity with them on every possible occasion. These include, I am afraid, the same people who think it elegant to hold a tea cup with the small finger of the right hand in a delicate curve outward.

For them the linguistic equivalent of the curved little finger is —among other things—a devotion to constructions involving the auxiliary verb *shall,* as well as to an overuse of the pronoun *one.*

Now *shall* and *will* have for so long been baffling to speakers of the English language that many people have despaired of making any distinction in their use. (Some valid distinctions do exist, of course.)

Observe the friend of yours who says with what used to be called

* Raleigh (N.C.), *News and Observer,* Sunday, January 4, 1959, Section III, p. 2.

old-maidish primness, "Yes, I shall be at home when you call," and "I shall do what you have requested," and "I shall see you later."

Naturally, all the handbooks of usage say (but instead of *say* should I not have used *state?*) that *shall* with the pronoun of the first person indicates simple futurity. At the same time, they do not give license for riding a good horse to death. Once in a while, *will* is much better, and even more accurate—as in "I will do what you have requested" and "I will certainly meet you for golf next Wednesday," indicating a willingness or promise to perform an act and not merely the likelihood of its being performed.

But the *shall* addict persists in thinking that there is something inherently fashionable about his consistency. Very few people, of course, confuse *shall* (indicating determination on the part of the speaker) and *will* (indicating simple futurity) when they are used with pronouns of the second and third persons: *you* or *he* or *they*.

The partisans of *one* are equally numerous; and, because they somehow think that they are fashionable, they are at least equally ridiculous. One has only to listen to one's pseudo-educated and superprecise friends to get one's ear full. However, *one*, like *shall*, can be perfectly proper when used like one's dress clothes with taste and discretion.

Perhaps, after all, the most flagrant offenders among people who have learned a little grammar are the *I* and the *whom* addicts.

For some undetermined reason, the average child doggedly insists on saying "me and Jim" rather than "Jim and I" regardless of the grammatical context of his statement. It seems to make little difference whether the youngster lives in the local Mortgage Hill area or in Shanty Town.

When the child goes to school, however, he is cajoled, admonished, and threatened enough to convince him that he has committed a mortal sin (pride leads the "Seven Deadly Sins") by naming himself before he names his playmate and that he has committed a grammatical sin by using a pronoun in the objective form as the subject of a sentence. So he learns to say "Jim and I are going to play together." Unfortunately, however, the experience becomes traumatic, and our young man is afflicted with a fixed idea for the rest of his life.

Listen to your friend who says "Mr. Jones invited my wife and I to his country place for a swim." Nine to one, he glows inwardly because of his altruism in putting his wife first and because of his discrimination in using *I* instead of *me*. He thinks, of course, that he has fully demonstrated his worthiness to move in the society of a man fashionable enough to have a private swimming pool. But he has a rude surprise awaiting him. Mr. Jones's wife will most assuredly know that he should have said "wife and me," since both words are the objects of *invited;* and she will have her own opinion of whether he deserves to associate with her set.

Our poor fellow will also be afraid to say, "You're being unfair to us Smiths. After all, we live in as good a part of town as you do." Hadn't he once been told that he could *not* say "Us boys are going" and that he should have said "we boys"? So he timidly says, "You're being unfair to we Smiths"; and he is ever so irretrievably back on the wrong side of the grammatical railroad tracks. After all, a preposition is relentless in requiring an object in all the socially acceptable parts of town.

The *whom* addicts are not in the same class only because there are not quite so many people who can catch them in their errors. But, like the *I* addicts—since they have learned through dint of considerable effort that *whom* is the right form for certain situations—they insist on getting more than their money's worth out of this hard-earned knowledge.

Thus they indulge in such constructions as "Whom do you think will be the next president of the Country Club?" Or "There has been a lively discussion as to whom will marry Mrs. Walsingham Cartwright next," or "She is the one whom we all suppose was slightly inebriated at our last club dance." Of course, the speaker who really knows his grammar—and does not merely think that he does—will see that "who" is the right form in all three sentences—as the subject of "will be," "will marry," or "was inebriated."

Very well, you may say, but some highly-placed people will be found in the above categories. Indeed, I remember something of the cold chill that ran over me when, in a newsreel of fairly recent issue, a very important personage said, "Thank you for all you've done for Esmeralda and I." (I have sufficiently disguised the name so that it should not possibly be attached to the wife of any great contemporary American political figure.)

And then there was John Milton (rest to his puritanical bones!) who referred to a hero (that some say he may have admired too much) as "Satan, than whom none sat higher." Why *whom?* Only Milton could answer. At any rate, one of the greatest English poets said it; and he did so in such a resounding way that "than whom" is the accepted idiom to this moment.

It is better to be president than right, as any sensible man knows. And poets have a special license of their own. But as for us ordinary human beings, we'd better not attempt to display learning that we do not have. Too many people will know just enough to catch us.

ON LANGUAGE *

James Fenimore Cooper

Language being the medium of thought, its use enters into our most familiar practices. A just, clear, and simple expression of our ideas is a necessary accomplishment for all who aspire to be classed with gentlemen and ladies. It renders all more respectable, besides making intercourse more intelligible, safer, and more agreeable.

NB

The common faults of American language are an ambition to effect, a want of simplicity, and a turgid abuse of terms. To these may be added ambiguity of expression. Many perversions of significations also exist, and a formality of speech, which, while it renders conversation ungraceful, and destroys its playfulness, seriously weakens the power of the language, by applying to ordinary ideas, words that are suited only to themes of gravity and dignity.

While it is true that the great body of the American people use their language more correctly than the mass of any other considerable nation, it is equally true that a smaller proportion than common attain to elegance in this accomplishment, especially in speech. Contrary to the general law in such matters, the women of the country have a less agreeable utterance than the men, a defect that great care should be taken to remedy, as the nursery is the birth-place of so many of our habits.

The limits of this work will not permit an enumeration of the popular abuses of significations, but a few shall be mentioned, in order that the student may possess a general clue to the faults. "Creek," a word that signifies an *inlet* of the sea, or of a lake, is misapplied to running streams, and frequently to the *outlets* of lakes. A "square," is called a "park;" "lakes," are often called "ponds;" and "arms of the sea," are sometimes termed "rivers."

In pronunciation, the faults are still more numerous, partaking decidedly of provincialisms. The letter *u,* sounded like double *o,* or *oo,* or like *i,* as in vir*too,* for*tin,* for*tinate;* and *ew,* pronounced also

---

* *The American Democrat* (Cooperstown: H. E. Phinney, 1838), pp. 117-124.

like *oo,* are common errors. This is an exceedingly vicious pronunciation, rendering the language mean and vulgar. "New," pronounced as *"noo,"* is an example, and "few," as *"foo;"* the true sounds are *"nu"* and *"fu,"* the *u* retaining its proper soft sound, and not that of *"oo."*

The attempt to reduce the pronunciation of the English language to a common rule, produces much confusion, and taking the usages of polite life as the standard, many uncouth innovations. All know the pronunciation of plough; but it will scarcely do to take this sound as the only power of the same combination of final letters, for we should be compelled to call though, thou; through, throu; and tough, tou.

False accentuation is a common American fault. Ensign (insin,) is called en*syne,* and engine (injin,) en*gyne.* Indeed, it is a common fault of narrow associations, to suppose that words are to be pronounced as they are spelled.

Many words are in a state of mutation, the pronunciation being unsettled even in the best society, a result that must often arise where language is as variable and undetermined as the English. To this class belong "clerk," "cucumber" and "gold," which are often pronounced as spelt, though it were better and more in conformity with polite usage to say "clark," "*cow*-cumber," (not cow*cum*ber,) and "goold." For *lootenant* (lieutenant) there is not sufficient authority, the true pronunciation being *"levten*ant." By making a familiar compound of this word, we see the uselessness of attempting to reduce the language to any other laws than those of the usages of polite life, for they who affect to say *looten*ant, do not say "*looten*ant-co-lo-nel," but "*looten*ant-kurnel."

The polite pronunciation of "either," and "neither," is "i-ther" and "ni-ther," and not "eether" and "neether." This is a case in which the better usage of the language has respected derivations, for *"ei,"* in German are pronounced as in "height" and "sleight," *"ie"* making the sound of *"ee."* We see the arbitrary usages of the English, however, by comparing these legitimate sounds with those of the words "lieutenant colonel," which are derived from the French, in which language the latter word is called *"co-lo-nel."*

Some changes of the language are to be regretted, as they lead to false inferences, and society is always a loser by mistaking names for things. Life is a fact, and it is seldom any good arises from a misapprehension of the real circumstances under which we exist. The word "gentleman" has a positive and limited signification. It means one elevated above the mass of society by his birth, manners, attainments, character, and social condition. As no civilized society can exist without these social differences, nothing is gained by denying the use of the term. If blackguards were to be *called* "gentlemen," and gentlemen, "blackguards," the difference between them would be as obvious as it is today.

The word "gentleman," is derived from the French *gentilhomme,* which originally signified one of noble birth. This was at a time when the characteristics of the condition were never found beyond a caste. As society advanced, ordinary men attained the qualifications of nobility, without that of birth, and the meaning of the word was extended. It is now possible to be a gentleman without birth, though, even in America, where such distinctions are purely conditional, they who have birth, except in extraordinary instances, are classed with gentlemen. To call a laborer, one who has neither education, manners, accomplishments, tastes, associations, nor any one of the ordinary requisites, a gentleman, is just as absurd as to call one who is thus qualified, a fellow. The word must have some especial signification, or it would be synonymous with man. One may have gentlemanlike feelings, principles, and appearance, without possessing the liberal attainments that distinguish the gentleman. Least of all does money alone make a gentleman, though, as it becomes a means of obtaining the other requisites, it is usual to give it a place in the claims of the class. Men may be, and often are, very rich, without having the smallest title to be deemed a gentleman. A man may be a distinguished gentleman, and not possess as much money as his own footman.

This word, however, is sometimes used instead of the old terms, "sirs," "my masters," &c. &c., as in addressing bodies of men. Thus we say "gentlemen," in addressing a publick meeting in complaisance, and as, by possibility, some gentlemen may be present. This is a license that may be tolerated, though he who should insist that all present were, as individuals, gentlemen, would hardly escape ridicule.

What has just been said of the word gentleman, is equally true with that of lady. The standard of these two classes, rises as society becomes more civilized and refined; the man who might pass for a gentleman in one nation, or community, not being able to maintain the same position in another.

The inefficiency of the effort to subvert things by names, is shown in the fact that, in all civilized communities, there is a class of men, who silently and quietly recognize each other, as gentlemen; who associate together freely and without reserve, and who admit each other's claims without scruple or distrust. This class may be limited by prejudice and arbitrary enactments, as in Europe, or it may have no other rules than those of taste, sentiment, and the silent laws of usage, as in America.

The same observations may be made in relation to the words master and servant. He who employs laborers, with the right to command, is a master, and he who lets himself to work, with an obligation to obey, a servant. Thus there are house, or domestic servants, farm servants, shop servants, and various other servants; the term master being in all these cases the correlative.

In consequence of the domestic servants of America having once been negro-slaves, a prejudice has arisen among the laboring classes of the whites, who not only dislike the term servant, but have also rejected that of master. So far has this prejudice gone, that in lieu of the latter, they have resorted to the use of the word *boss,* which has precisely the same meaning in Dutch! How far a subterfuge of this nature is worthy of a manly and common sense people, will admit of question.

A similar objection may be made to the use of the word "help," which is not only an innovation on a just and established term, but which does not properly convey the meaning intended. They who aid their masters in the toil may be deemed "helps," but they who perform all the labor do not assist, or help to do the thing, but they do it themselves. A man does not usually hire his cook to *help* him cook his dinner, but to cook it herself. Nothing is therefore gained, while something is lost in simplicity and clearness by the substitution of new and imperfect terms, for the long established words of the language. In all cases in which the people of America have retained the *things* of their ancestors, they should not be ashamed to keep the *names.*

The love of turgid expressions is gaining ground, and ought to be corrected. One of the most certain evidences of a man of high breeding, is his simplicity of speech; a simplicity that is equally removed from vulgarity and exaggeration. He calls a spade, a "spade." His enunciation, while clear, deliberate, and dignified, is totally without strut, showing his familiarity with the world, and, in some degree, reflecting the qualities of his mind, which is polished without being addicted to sentimentalism, or any other bloated feeling. He never calls his wife, "his lady," but "his wife," and he is not afraid of lessening the dignity of the human race, by styling the most elevated and refined of his fellow creatures, "men and women." He does not say, in speaking of a dance, that "the attire of ladies was exceedingly elegant and peculiarly becoming at the late assembly," but that "the women were well dressed at the last ball;" nor is he apt to remark, "that the Rev. Mr. G_____ gave us an elegant and searching discourse the past sabbath," but, that "the parson preached a good sermon last Sunday."

The utterance of a gentleman ought to be deliberate and clear, without being measured. All idea of effort should be banished, though nothing lost for want of distinctness. His emphasis ought to be almost imperceptible; never halting, or abrupt; and least of all, so placed as to give an idea of his own sense of cleverness; but regulated by those slight intonations that give point to wit, and force to reason. His language should rise with the subject, and, as he must be an educated and accomplished man, he cannot but know that the highest quality of eloquence, and all sublimity, is in the thought, rather than in the words, though there must be an adaption of the one to the other.

This is still more true of women than of men, since the former are the natural agents in maintaining the refinement of a people.

All cannot reach the highest standard in such matters, for it depends on early habit, and particularly on early associations. The children of gentlemen are as readily distinguished from other children by these peculiarities, as by the greater delicacy of their minds, and higher tact in breeding. But we are not to abandon all improvement, because perfection is reached but by few. Simplicity should be the first aim, after one is removed from vulgarity, and let the finer shades of accomplishment be acquired as they can be attained. In no case, however, can one who aims at turgid language, exaggerated sentiment, or pedantic utterance, lay claim to be either a man or woman of the world.

~ C ~

suggestions for discussion

1. The selections in this chapter are intended to help you recognize an important fact about your language: That fashions in it change as certainly as they do in clothing, table manners, and other

forms of social behavior. Also, while they were not written as exercises in emphasis, they do represent the work of authors who wanted to make a point and, furthermore, to make it emphatically. That point is that we should attempt to use a fashion of speech that is suitable to our rearing and that makes communication as easy as it can be but that we should avoid what Cooper calls "an ambition to effect" and "a want of simplicity." (Professor Hartley and Miss Schlauch deal specifically with several objectional hypercorrect usages.)

Review all three selections and observe how many times each author restated or suggested this main point. What has repetition of an idea to do with emphasis?

2. Still thinking of repetition, examine one or more of the selections to see how repeating a word or phrase contributes to emphasis. (For example, what is the effect of Miss Schlauch's picking up Thomas Carlyle's "forked radish" and repeating it?)

3. In one or more of the selections, look for short sentences, especially when they come right after or right before long ones. Observe their effectiveness in giving prominence to the ideas they express. (You might begin your consideration of short sentences with Miss Schlauch's saying "But Carlyle is wrong." Would she have made her disagreement with Carlyle as clear and forceful had she said "That Carlyle is erroneous in this opinion is readily seen in the fact that . . . "?)

4. Instead of "You have only to listen to your pseudo-educated and superprecise friends to get your earful," Hartley wrote, "One has only to listen to one's pseudo-educated and superprecise friends to get one's ear full." His purpose was to emphasize the absurdity of overusing the word "one." The same author also used alliteration, as in "pride and pronouns" and as in the title of his article, to draw attention to the concepts represented by the words. Can you identify other occurrences of these devices for emphasis in this or in any other of the selections that you have just read?

5. The "forked radish" that we have already noted and Carlyle's "Duke of Windlestraw" represent an important practice of good writers: the use of concrete detail instead of general allusion. (Consider the difference between what Carlyle actually wrote, as Miss Schlauch quoted him, and "Lives the man that can figure (or visualize) a naked person addressing a naked congregation?" The difference is precisely the difference between the memorable, emphatic original and the merely preposterous restatement.) Elsewhere in

the selections in this chapter, identify particular or specific details
that contribute to emphasis.

~ D ~

suggestions for writing

1. Reread Lodwick Hartley's article and the selection from Margaret Schlauch's book, *Gift of Tongues*. Write two or three paragraphs on their explanations of such constructions as "between
you and I" and "he told Henry and I." Notice that persons who say
such things as these would never say "he told I"; what do you suppose causes them to say "he told Henry and I"? Do you agree with
the explanations of Hartley and Miss Schlauch?

2. If you judge from "On Language," the second of the selections
you have read in this chapter, do you think that James Fenimore
Cooper would have agreed with Miss Schlauch that language is as
clearly a badge as is clothing? Express your response in two or three
paragraphs, with a revealing quotation or two to support your view.
(You may have had some experience in which a well-dressed person
might have given up an advantage once he began to speak or in
which, conversely, a shabbily dressed one surprised you by speaking
better than you had expected.)

3. With the aid of your dictionary, identify several points of
usage or pronunciation objected to—or approved, if you wish—by
Cooper with respect to which fashions have changed between his
time and ours. Write a paragraph or two on changes in language
with your observations on Cooper's preferences as examples.

4. Would Hartley's statement that "we'd better not attempt to
display learning that we do not have" be in agreement with Miss
Schlauch's attitude toward the social aspects of language? Would it
be in agreement with Cooper's concluding paragraph? Write a short
paper of three or four paragraphs to make your answer clear and
defensible.

~ E ~

additional readings

Roberts, Paul, *Understanding English* (New York: Harper & Row, Publishers, 1958), Ch. 23, "Split Infinitives and Such."

Myers, L. M., *Guide to American English,* 3rd ed. (Englewood Cliffs, N.J.: Prentice-Hall, Inc., 1962), Ch. 2, "Areas of Usage."

Pyles, Thomas, *The Origins and Development of the English Language* (New York: Harcourt, Brace & World, Inc., 1964), Ch. 1, "Facts, Assumptions, and Misconceptions About Language."

Bloomfield, Morton W., and Leonard Newmark, *A Linguistic Introduction to the History of English* (New York: Alfred A. Knopf, Inc., 1963), Ch. VII, "The Problem of Correctness and Good Usage, 1600-1850."

Chapter Six

~ A ~

diction

In the preceding chapters we have discussed effectively organized units of words: paragraphs and sentences. It is time now to talk briefly about the effective choice of words. This choice, skillfully made, is usually described as "good diction." Bad diction, on the other hand, even well-organized bad diction, gets the same results as a beautifully packaged but mediocre food product. In both cases one wonders why so much effort had been wasted on so poor a product.

The selection of the exact word then is the essence of communication. In general, this process of selection will require consideration of two kinds of meanings that words have, the exact meaning of the word, its *denotation*, and the accrued meanings of the word, its *connotations*. The careful selection of the word to fit the exact idea you have in mind depends on the meaning that both you and your reader ascribe to it. It comes as a surprise to many young writers that it is possible to select a word that seems exactly right only to have the reader see his own meanings in the word.

In the following selections you will be able to analyze the process of word selection and, at the same time, learn something about words and their meanings.

~ B ~

the meaning of words

WHAT DOES A WORD STAND FOR? *

L. M. Myers

Most of us think we know what "meaning" means. We may say, for instance, that the word "stool" *means* a chair with no back. If anybody asks us what we mean by "means," we probably say that the word "stands for" the piece of furniture. In a way this is true, but it needs more examination. Just how is the word connected with the thing?

What happens when you look at a stool? Light waves reflected from it strike your eyes and stimulate a flow of electrical currents over nerve-paths leading to your brain. It is in the brain, not in the eye itself, that the effective seeing takes place. If your optical nerve is cut, your eye becomes completely useless. And what you see in your brain is a *partial and not particularly accurate image of the stool.* The people who developed our language did not know this. They "believed what they saw," and they had good reason to, because the human eye was the keenest instrument of perception available. Anything that it could not see could only be guessed at, not measured. But you know that at best your eyes have missed the cell structure, not to mention the spacing and motion of the particles of which the cells are composed. How much else they have missed depends partly on the accuracy of your vision and partly on the *influence of your previous experiences.*

Suppose, for example, that a carpenter and a typist, both with 20-20 vision, look at a stool in a lunchroom. The carpenter may notice the grain of the wood and the way the rungs are joined to the legs—details of which the typist is completely unconscious. But she may notice a roughness that would be likely to snag her stock-

---

* *Guide to American English* (Englewood Cliffs, N.J.: Prentice-Hall, Inc., 1963), pp. 138-47.

ings—a different detail that the carpenter might not see at all. There is no use saying that they both *saw* it all but only *noticed* parts. We have a phrase for that: certain details "failed to register." We can talk and act only about what does register, accurately or inaccurately. If you don't think this is important, consider the hunters who have shot cows and even wives after clearly "seeing" bucks complete with spreading antlers.

Even the bare act of seeing is not as simple as the passing of a current through an electric circuit. *Secondary* nerve circuits are brought into the action, and these inevitably affect the mental picture that is formed. *Which* secondary circuits are brought in depends on previous experience—that is why the carpenter and the typist see different stools. When you speak of the stool you may think, and even insist, that you mean "the whole stool," but you cannot mean more than you are conscious of meaning (though what you say may mean more to somebody else than it does to you). If you sit on the stool without noticing that the paint is wet, you are not likely to admit that the stickiness of the surface was included in your meaning. The "object" that you see and talk about is a *unique abstraction,* created by a reaction between your nervous system and the physical process.

You may find it hard to grasp the idea in the last sentence, because you have almost certainly been trained to believe that objects have a reality of their own, independent of observers. But the reality of objects is a theory that will not hold in the light of modern science. What exists is a *process*—an arrangement of dancing particles. The object that the carpenter sees and feels and calls a stool is derived from this process by the impressions made on his sense and modified by his previous experiences. The object that the typist sees is at least slightly different because her senses and her previous experiences are different. Naturally there are similarities as well as differences in our nervous systems; and if our backgrounds are also similar, we may derive objects that are very much alike. But no two of us ever see quite the same things.

The stool you talk about, then, is an abstraction—that is, a selection of some of the characteristics of the underlying process. When you speak the word "stool" you almost certainly use it to refer to even less than you have seen. You may, for instance, have noticed a knot in the grain of the seat, a small crack in one leg, a smear of grease on another. But when you say "Hand me that stool," you have no idea of calling your companion's attention to any of these details. In fact you may already have dismissed them from your own mind. You use the word merely to indicate those characteristics which you assume that he has also noticed and is likely to connect with the word. The word "stool" is therefore a second-level abstraction from the object already abstracted by your senses.

If you use the word to refer to a number of different objects, as in "I don't like to sit on a *stool*," you are using a third level of abstraction; and if you use other words like "seats" or "furniture" or "property," you go higher still—you include more and more different objects with less and less in common. Every time you go up a level you leave out more of the characteristics of the individual object. As a result, the higher you go, the less chance you have of getting your hearer to duplicate the impression in your own mind. If you say "Hand me that stool," you will probably be adequately understood. If you say "Get me a stool," he may bring one half or twice as high as you wanted. And if you give him some money and ask him to buy some "attractive furniture," it may mean the end of a friendship.

You may be used to thinking of words as divided into two classes, abstract and concrete; but the evidence shows that all words are abstract on one level or another. Moreover, the difference in levels is not a permanent characteristic of the words, but varies with the way they are used. Thus *wealth* is likely to represent a higher level of abstraction than *dollar*. But if I reach in my pocket, pull out a few coins, and say "Here is my entire *wealth* at the moment," I am using *wealth* on the lowest possible verbal level. On the other hand, if I say, "He is always anxious to pick up an honest *dollar*," I am using *dollar* on a fairly high level. Nevertheless, since *dollar* is usually a low-level word, it will probably make a more direct and forceful impression on your hearer in most circumstances than *wealth* would.

Thinking of *levels of abstraction* may seem much more complicated than the simple division into abstract and concrete words. But it is a great deal more accurate; and once you get used to it, you will find that it straightens out a good many difficulties.

As we have just seen, when a man speaks, he uses words as symbols to indicate something that is going on *in his own mind*. His words are directly connected not with the processes in the outer world, but with his own abstractions from those processes. It is this private mental activity that the words mean to him, and we may call it *meaning 1*.

When another man listens, the words stimulate some activity in *his* mind. We may call this activity *meaning 2*. If it is very similar to that of the speaker, we say he understands. In other words, *meaning 1* and *meaning 2* are so similar that no noticeable difference appears; but the two meanings can never be absolutely identical.

When there is an obvious difference between the two meanings it is rather silly to argue about which is the "right" one, but it may be useful to consider which is closer to our *general habits of association,* which we may call *meaning 3*. For instance, if you ask a child for a chisel and he hands you a screwdriver, you may explain the difference between the two kinds of tools, and tell him which label is usually applied to each. He will probably accept your explanation; and since you now use these labels in very similar ways, you may avoid future misunderstandings. You have not, however, established the "real" meaning of the word, because *words in themselves have no meanings at all*. It takes a mind to develop a meaning by associating a symbol with something else, and no two minds work in quite the same way.

If you ask for a stool you can expect other people to know *roughly* what you mean. They are not likely to associate the word with a bed or a cat or a chisel. Our habits are enough alike so that a given word *limits* the possible associations within a certain range. But we must be prepared for borderline cases; a low-backed seat, for example, might be called either a chair or a stool. And we must realize that even when there is a complete *verbal* agreement there is still a little misunderstanding, because no two of us see exactly the same stool.

It is also important to realize that *meaning 3* or the "dictionary meaning" is merely a generalization derived from the *meanings 1* and *meanings 2* that occur in everyday communication. If you find a puzzling word in a sentence and look it up, a dictionary can tell you something about *how other people have used this word in the past*. This information may give you a definite impression (*meaning 2*) about what the writer means by the word in this sentence (*meaning 1*). You may therefore learn something from the writer that you might otherwise have missed. But you cannot find the true and permanent meaning of the word, because there is no such thing.

The idea that we can all learn to speak exactly alike and use words with only their universally agreed "correct" meanings is therefore a delusion that we might as well abandon. But we can profitably try to learn: (1) to speak more nearly alike; (2) to become conscious of the probable differences in our meanings.

If you say that a stone weighs ten pounds, a friend may argue with you or want to bet with you. Such an argument or bet may be settled by weighing the stone. When you read the scales you will probably agree about what the stone weighs. On the other hand, if you argue about which of two girls is prettier, there is no way to settle the question satisfactorily.

There is nothing mysterious about this. Some matters affect all of us so frequently that we have had to develop standards of measurement that are as impersonal as possible. We recognize that no scale and no measuring stick is absolutely perfect, and that it is possible to measure inaccurately either by cheating or by carelessness. However, both our commonest measuring devices and our methods of using them are so nearly uniform that most of us will ordinarily accept their readings without protest. Moreover, we are generally conscious of these standards. Consequently, when we say that a stone weighs ten pounds or that a man is six feet tall, the information conveyed to all our hearers will be remarkably similar. Such statements as these may be said to have public meanings. Anybody knows how to test them; and anybody who does test them will get very similar results. *All statements that have public meanings involve some kind of measurement by generally accepted standards.* The standards need not be universally known, but they must be agreed upon by an appropriate group. Thus the statement that "Roberts suffered second-degree burns" has a public meaning. Anybody with such medical training will know that Roberts had blisters resulting from heat. And anybody who does *not* understand the statement will probably accept the explanation of those who do.

At the other extreme there are meanings which are purely private because there are no acceptable ways of measuring them. You don't know how cauliflower tastes to your brother, and you won't get very far by explaining that it is "really delicious" if he finds it nauseating.

In between these extremes lies the area of most of our difficulties. You cannot prove that one girl is prettier than another as easily or as definitely as you can prove that she is taller; but there is likely to be a good deal of similarity in the opinions of a given group of people who have lived in the same atmosphere and have interchanged ideas. If we don't exaggerate the permanence or the "universality" of our local and temporary standards of measurement, they can be very useful for communication. Find an illustrated magazine of thirty years ago and admire the glamorous beauties—those streamlined girls with the fascinating helmet-liner hats, their waistlines artfully arranged below their hips. It may be hard to believe it now, but they were beautiful once (I was there); and they may be beautiful again.

Some people cannot believe that their relative standards are less than absolute. Others feel that if they are not absolute they are no standards at all. But we must use what we have. We can now measure rather accurately many things at which our fathers could only guess; and as time goes on we may learn to do even better.

If we consider the question of meaning in this light, we arrive at the conclusion that *a meaningful statement should suggest a measurement,* considering "measurement" in its widest sense. If somebody says "It's cold outside," you may want to know what the thermometer reads, or you may simply ask "Should I wear my heavy coat?" The thermometer reading is a more public type of measurement, but you may not be skilled in interpreting it. Besides, it covers only the factor of temperature, and leaves out wind and humidity. You may find a less precise measurement more useful—for example, an estimate of how thick your clothing should be to keep you comfortable.

There is a widespread belief that some things are subject to measurement and others are not. It seems more accurate to say that some things are more *accessible* to measurement than others. We have been able to measure height and weight for a long time. Only recently have we begun to find ways of measuring the strength of brainwaves and the secretions of the ductless glands. Some of the measurements we should like to make are so complicated and difficult that we may never arrive at a satisfactory method of making them, or reach general agreement about a scale. But unless we can measure a thing—by at least a rough estimate—well, we can make noises about it, but how are we to say anything that has a discoverable meaning?

Alfred Korzybski has compared our statements about things to maps of territories. A good map is drawn to scale: that is, the structure of the map corresponds to the structure of the territory. And a meaningful statement should also correspond in structure to the territory that it describes. This is a very useful comparison, because on the whole we deal with maps rather more sensibly than we do with words. We know, for instance, that a man cannot draw a map of a place he has not measured, whether accurately with surveying instruments or roughly with his eye, and whether directly or by using somebody else's map. And before we depend on a map we want to have some idea of how it came to be made and what kind of measurements were used in making it. Of course we might be deceived by an inaccurate or dishonest map, but we wouldn't believe one that showed rivers running uphill or palm trees growing out of a glacier. When it comes to verbal maps, however, some of us are ready to believe almost anything, because we have never thought of applying the structural test.

For instance, a politician promises to act "in the best interests of all the people," and thereby attracts a number of votes. This sounds like a fine way to act; and it would be, too, if water could run uphill. Unfortunately, some people would gain by having the income tax raised so the sales tax could be eliminated; others would be better off with the sales tax raised and the income tax reduced. If we want to know what the candidate actually plans to do about this issue, we'd better try to get him to talk in map language, so we can examine the structure of the events for which his words stand. He may be unwilling to do this, because as soon as he indicates what things and activities his words refer to he will probably lose some votes; but until he does, his words have no measurable meaning.

Sometimes the relation of a good verbal map to the territory it represents is direct and obvious—for instance, "John is six foot two and weighs over two hundred pounds." Sometimes it is less direct, but still possible to follow with confidence if you know something about the territory. "Murphy sparks the Panthers" might not convey much to some people, but almost any follower of baseball would read it as meaning not only that Murphy fields well and gets his hits when they count most, but that his teammates play better when he is in there. This is a very slight sketch of a complicated situation, but it is map language because the words stand for things that happen.

But when language is related *only to other language,* it has no value as a map of events, no matter how impressive it sounds. A faculty does not get anywhere by defining "liberal education" as "the kind of education that develops a broad cultural background."

Neither phrase has any map value until the speaker decides what activities it represents. You can't just study "culture." You have to make up your mind whether to learn French verbs or differential equations or appropriate remarks to make after listening to Beethoven's quartets. It is sometimes convenient to have ambiguous map language, so that we may "agree in principle" and then make whatever interpretations we please. But when we want to convey or receive information, we'd better examine the relation between the words and the events they represent.

We must remember, however, that this relation between words and events is not something that can be transferred whole from one mind to another. It can only be suggested, though sometimes (when all the measurements involved are public) very directly. At other times it has to be done indirectly or even with considerable distortion of details in order to make the main points clear to somebody with a very different background of experience. A young chauffeur once summed up a Conference on Communication so compactly that he left the experts who had been holding it wondering if they hadn't been wasting their time. "As I see it," he remarked, "what all this adds up to is: if you want to get a message across to somebody, you'd better tune in on his wavelength, and not just broadcast."

A great many people never do anything but broadcast. This is partly because they are too self-centered to think about adjusting to the other fellow's wavelength; but perhaps it is also partly because they have never been taught about wavelengths. In most of our schools no mention is made of *meaning 1* and *meaning 2*. Students are taught to find the "true meaning" of words, to use them "correctly and accurately," and to "say exactly what they mean." There is a clear assumption that if they do these things, everybody will understand them—or at least that everybody ought to.

Of course they are taught some other things too, such as "using language appropriate to the occasion" and even "establishing rapport with the audience." But the two sets of theories are in conflict, and they usually hear much more about the first set. They should not be blamed too much if, especially in writing, they tend to work on what they assume is a universal broadcast band.

A radio message conveys nothing unless both sender and receiver are tuned in, and it is useless to argue about which has the "primary responsibility" for the tuning. It may seem unfair to ask you to tune in to the writer when you read, and then tune in to the reader when you write—the other fellows ought to do some of the work. But if you think a little more about it you will probably decide that the writers that give you the most satisfaction are the ones that have managed to find your wavelength. It is not entirely one-sided. Besides, even from a purely selfish standpoint there are more important things than dividing the work into exactly even parts. If you want to learn something from a book that is already written, you have to make the adjustment or you will miss the message. And if you think it is at all important for your own writing to be understood and appreciated, you'd better tune your transmitter too. It may be extra work, but you will learn a lot more and exert a good deal more influence than your lazy neighbor.

It takes some imagination to adjust a paper to an audience. You must figure out not only what words they are likely to know, but what experiences they have probably had. You can't expect your estimates to be perfect, especially if you are writing for a number of different people, but you should make them carefully. You begin by thinking of what you and your audience have in common. When you go beyond this area, try to make your explanations in terms of these common holdings.

This may seem perfectly obvious, but a great many writers, not all of them freshmen, either never think of it or deliberately disregard it. The haughty ones take the attitude that people who don't know what *they* know are not worth considering. The overhumble ones assume that anything they know must be known to everybody else. In between are the people who are not really attempting to communicate—they are just running off at the mouth.

It is very helpful to pick a specific audience for every paper you write. This audience may be either real or imaginary, and it may be either a single person or a fairly uniform group. But don't try to write to everybody at once. It can't be done, and any attempt to do it is likely to be either very dull or ridiculously inconsistent. Jimmy Brown writes an explanation of baseball. In the first paragraph he explains carefully that there are nine men on a team. But in the third paragraph he uses such terms as "squeeze play" and "drag bunt" with no explanation at all. It is rather hard to imagine anybody who would need the information in the first paragraph and at the same time understand the terms in the third.

Of course you may say that your real audience is your instructor, who is the only reason you are writing the paper. It is perfectly legitimate to aim your paper at him if you take the trouble actually to aim it—to figure out what he probably knows about the subject and how his mind works—and to hold steady throughout the paper. But don't expect to make a hit by displaying your ignorance on his favorite subject. And don't treat him like a specialist in animal husbandry in one paragraph and an idiot boy in the next. In any case, he is not likely to insist that you aim directly at him. He won't even insist that you tell him exactly who you are aiming at. But he will probably notice it if you are trying to aim in all directions at once.

Perhaps the easiest way to aim a paper is to imagine that you are writing it for a particular friend. You have some idea of what he already knows, not only about your subject, but about other subjects that you can relate it to. You therefore have a basis for deciding what you can reasonably leave out, as well as what you should put in. If you want other people to read it too, you can make a few explanations that he might not need; but keep him in mind as a guide to the general direction.

Changing Meanings and Values of Words *

Stuart Robertson
Frederick Cassidy

The study of meaning in language is called semasiology or semantics. The latter term, however, has recently been used widely to refer to what is properly called general semantics, a study allied more closely to the field of philosophy than to that of linguistics, and which therefore will not be dealt with in this book. The term *semantics* nevertheless has application within the field of linguistics; there it is limited at present to the description of the meanings which words or other units of language convey, and, when these are seen historically, also to the various types of meaning-change that occur.

---

* *The Development of Modern English* (Englewood Cliffs, N.J.: Prentice-Hall, Inc., 1954), pp. 232-36.

But the word "meaning" itself poses difficult problems. What is the meaning of "meaning"? We all recognize that language is a give-and-take of speech-signals, a series of stimuli by speakers and responses by hearers; also that some non-linguistic stimuli produce linguistic responses, and *vice versa*. (Thus a kiss may produce the response "Darling!"—and *vice versa*.) When the hearer of a linguistic stimulus responds to it in some predictable way, we say, in common parlance, that he has "understood" the speaker. But we are by no means certain—here we must throw ourselves upon the psychologists—what goes on inside the hearer's nervous system between his hearing of the words and his response to them. The student of language therefore limits himself to an investigation of the parts of the process which are clearly accessible, and with which he can deal with some degree of objectivity. Less and less do linguists raise the question of "ideas" or "concepts" in the mind; today they generally define meaning as simply the situation out of which language comes and the response that it elicits.

If this is meaning, how does it change? It is clear that, for speakers of the same language, there must be a large measure of consistency in the response to linguistic signals—otherwise, communication would be impossible. Nevertheless, since no two situations can ever be exactly alike, there is always some area of variation, and over a period of time the increment of slight variations will alter the reference of the linguistic signal. Let us take an example. Since meaning involves both the situation out of which a word comes (which makes the speaker say it) and the hearer's response, every speech situation is complex, with many components. But the relative prominence of these components will not always be the same. When the word *green* is first said it ordinarily brings a response in terms of color; but if the context concerns a fruit, this primary element of color may become associated with a secondary element—unripeness. Repetition may then establish this association until the element of unripeness becomes more prominent than that of color—so much so that it becomes possible to say, without fear of misunderstanding, "Blackberries are red when they are green."

Every new focus of prominence, once established, may beget others: when fruit and young people are associated, the element of unripeness may be paralleled with inexperience, and the latter may then assume primary prominence in such a statement as, "Those freshmen are pretty green." Thus a series of shifts in focus, from one element in a situation to others, will produce shifts in meaning —or "new meanings" for words. In this example, *green* has acquired two new meanings and lost none; but many a word, after shifting, has lost its first meaning entirely. Indeed, over the centuries meanings grow and decay in a surprising variety of ways, the chief of which we are to examine in this chapter.

Yet before proceeding we must give attention to one more point. Even though it is generally recognized that meanings change, many people still cling, curiously enough, to the quite contradictory notion that words all have "true" meanings, that changes somehow take us away from the "true" meaning, and that the way to find out what a word "really means" is to find out what it once meant. This is particularly true in respect to borrowed words in English, the belief evidently being that the meaning of the word in contemporary English and the meaning of the Latin or Greek word from which the English word is derived must be one and the same. A little reflection should show that an appeal to etymology in order to establish the present meaning of the word is as untrustworthy as an appeal to spelling in order to establish its present pronunciation. And for a reason that is almost exactly parallel: change of *meaning* is likely to have altered the etymological sense, which is thereby rendered archaic or obsolete, just as change of *sound* is likely to be unrecorded in the "antiquarian" spelling that so frequently characterizes Modern English. The study of etymology has great value and interest . . . but its usefulness in settling the question of what a word means is subject to considerable qualification.

Let us see what results when one ignores the idea that a word may change its meaning and appeals to its etymology in order to determine its present meaning. A handbook of only twenty-odd years ago on "correct English" sets forth the following dictum: "*Dilapidated* . . . Said of a building or other structure. But the word is from the Latin *lapis,* a stone, and cannot properly be used of any but a stone structure." One might just as reasonably argue that because *candidate* is related to the Latin *candidus* (white), it cannot properly be used of an aspirant for political office unless he is clothed in a suit of white material. More clearly even, one might protest that *holiday* properly describes Christmas or Easter, but should never be used of Independence Day or Labor Day; or that *bonfire* should not be applied except where the combustible material is bone. These arguments are not much more grotesque than some that have been seriously maintained in defense of an etymological crotchet, while ignoring the fact of change of meaning. Indeed, one who argues on this basis is a victim of the "etymological fallacy." The fact is that what a word once meant is not necessarily what it now means; the etymological meaning has often died out, and a quite new development is the living descendant. This is particularly true of words in common or popular use. Words, after all, are for the most part purely conventional symbols. They mean only what those who are using them agree to make them mean. Exactly the same principles apply to "learned" words, but because their traditional users have generally known the language from which they were borrowed, or of whose elements they were composed, they have tended to preserve the etymological meaning—indeed, it is conventional to use such words with an eye to their source; thus they are less prone to alterations of meaning than are popular words. It is in this way, incidentally, that a cultural tradition holds in check, to some extent, the constant tendency of language to change.

Change of meaning, however, though usually unpredictable, is not utterly arbitrary; as we shall see in a moment, it often proceeds along familiar paths. Furthermore, though it takes place in all languages, it does not proceed at the same rate even in related ones. If we look at cognate words in English and German, for example, which might have been expected to have the same meaning, we often find them widely different, and the difference is most commonly the result of some radical change of sense in the English word. Opposite instances can be found, admittedly, in which the English word has stood still and the German one changed; yet it is usually the latter which is conservative. Examples of this characteristic English shift in meaning are the following: *Schlagen* and *slay* are originally the same word, but the German word retains the general meaning of "smite" or "strike" while the English word has become narrowed to mean "strike with fatal consequences" or "kill." *Knabe* is the cognate in German of Old English *cnapa* or *cnafa,* and has the same meaning "boy"; but Modern English *knave* has a radically different one; the German *Tier* means any kind of animal, as did the cognate Old English *deor,* but in Modern English *deer* means one particular kind of animal.

CATS AND BABIES *

Stuart Chase

Here beside me on the table as I write, occasionally running a tentative paw through the littered sheets of manuscript and notes, is Hobie Baker, a tawny yellow tomcat, named for a great hockey-player. Hobie will never learn to talk. He can learn to respond to my talk, as he responds to other signs—sounds, smells, sights in his environment. He can utter cries indicating pain, pleasure, or excitement. He can announce that he wants to go out of doors, and let there be no delay about it. But he cannot master words and language. This in some respects is fortunate for Hobie, for he will not suffer from hallucinations provoked by bad language. He will remain a realist all his life, interpreting real things on the macroscopic level with appropriate responses, and having no traffic with philosophy or formal logic. It is highly improbable that he will ever suffer from a nervous breakdown. He is certainly able to think after a fashion, interpreting signs in the light of past experience, deliberately deciding his course of action, the survival value of which is high.

Instead of words, Hobie occasionally uses a crude gesture language. We know that he has a nervous system corresponding to that in man, with messages coming in to the receptors in skin, ear, and eye and going over the wires to the cortex, where memories are duly filed for reference. There are fewer switchboards in his cortex than in mine, which may be one reason why he cannot learn to talk. Relatively more of his behavior is under the direction of the lower nervous centers.

Apparently he thinks, connects referents with memory, proceeds to many actions as a result of contemplation evoking a decision. He deals in abstractions of a low order. After he has encountered enough individual objects showing a rough similarity, his filing sys-

---

* From *The Tyranny of Words,* copyright, 1938, by Stuart Chase. Reprinted by permission of Harcourt, Brace & World, Inc.

tem informs him of the equivalent of "Hell, there's another man!" or "Great Zeus, a mouse!" It is no longer necessary to investigate every man and mouse, for he has achieved an abstract idea of men and mice in general. Similarly with beds, sofas, doors, chairs, and other things he uses frequently. He finds meaning in doors-in-general, and proves it by going to a door in a strange house to be let out. This is probably as far as his abstraction process goes and probably as far as any animal can go without language. Hobie's idea of causality is not profound. If he objects to being combed, he spits and claws at the comb, not at the human being who wields it.

The higher in the animal scale one goes, the longer may be the time before reaction to a given situation is completed. The amoeba reacts almost immediately. Hobie sees a field mouse, but he does not spring. He crouches and stalks. A man may deliberately turn his back on the prey, and go into the barn for a gun.

Meaning comes to Hobie as it comes to me, through past experience. If my experience has been only with gentle dogs and I identify gentleness with dogs-in-general, I am likely to be shocked and pained some day when I mistake a savage barn-defender for a "dog." There are no dogs-in-general in the world of experience, but only Rover$_1$, Rover$_2$, Rover$_3$, some gentle, some neutral, and some vicious. Similarly, Hobie may form a concept of snakes-in-general from acquaintance with harmless black snakes, and some day— God forbid—meet a copperhead in the swamp. Cattle sometimes die of poisonous weeds because they have wrongly identified all young green growing things with good edible grass.

Generally speaking, animals tend to learn cumulatively through experience. The old elephant is the wisest of the herd. This selective process does not always operate in the case of human beings. The old are sometimes wise, but more often they are stuffed above the average with superstitions, misconceptions, and irrational dogmas. The window of the Union League Club comes to mind. Philosophers and medicine men are normally past the prime of life. Why is this? One may hazard the guess that erroneous identifications in human beings are pickled and preserved in words, and so not subject to the constant check of the environment, as in the case of cats and elephants. In the end, of course, a day of reckoning arrives. We are not permitted to misinterpret the environment indefinitely.

Pavlov's laboratory can cause $Rover_1$ to identify food with sound, switching the association pattern from smell to sound by ringing a bell whenever food is ready. When he hears the bell he comes a-running. This creates an artificial identification. By repeated switchings and counterswitchings, a fine case of nervous collapse can be induced in Rover. One must go to considerable trouble in a laboratory to make an animal crazy by building up erroneous identifications. The route to craziness for human beings is practically effortless.

Hobie cannot talk, but a parrot can. Is a parrot, then, the higher animal? Obviously not. Parrot talk is imitation of sound, and has no connection with thought or meaning. The symbols have no referents, either real or imagined. He just likes to hear himself talk. Little boys learn lines of Latin verse by a similar mindless process, though I never heard of one who liked it. Sailors sometimes acquire a few words of a foreign language just for sound effects, and are grieved to learn by brisk physical assault that they have insulted somebody's grandmother in unmentionable ways. Speaking without knowing is called "psittacism," but is a practice not confined to parrots.

I find Hobie a useful exhibit along this difficult trail of semantics. What "meaning" connotes to him is often so clear and simple that I have no trouble in following it. I come from a like evolutionary matrix. "Meaning" to me has like roots, and a like mechanism of apprehension. I have a six-cylinder brain and he has a one-lunger, but they operate on like principles. (I am having difficulty avoiding the word "same." No two things in this world are ever the same, or completely identical.) When I grow bewildered in the jungles of language, I return to observation of Hobie as a kind of compass line. "What do you mean?" one asks. Well, what does a cat mean? Then I try to build up from that foundation, so fresh and close to the boundary where inside meets outside.

BABIES An adult may have characteristics in common with a cat, but the infant has more. He arrives from warm, safe shelter to what William James called a big, blooming, buzzing confusion. He brings with him only two instinctive fears, if Watson is to be credited, fear of falling, and fear of some loud sounds. He is quite indifferent to snakes, bears, spiders, lions. During his first few months millions of signs strike the sensitive receptors in his skin and trace patterns in his nervous system. To them he reacts unconsciously at first, then gradually, marvelously, with dawning consciousness. Most sounds made by an infant are expressions of some emotional state correlated with a definite *situation*—a moving object in the outside world, hunger or pain inside. These sounds have significance to those who tend and care for him. Presently cries and gurgles give way to articulated syllables—"goo," "ma," "ba"—mixed and blurred with plain squawks and yells.

Then comes the exciting moment—the beginning of human language, the point which Hobie Baker can never reach! Syllables come out of the blur of noises; objects come out of the blur of the world outside. Mother or nurse encourages the imitation of certain sounds. Presently syllable and object take on a rough correlation. The word and the thing merge. Remember this, for it is at once the beginning of genuine humanity and the beginning of one of humanity's greatest trials. *The word and the thing merge.* All wearers of pants become "Dah-dee," but after a little, only the father himself.

For a considerable period, word and gesture language develop together. The child asks to be taken up, or more simply, holds up his arms. He points to what he wants, even as Hobie sits up and begs for food. Gesture language is clear and effective. After the child begins to go to school, word language rapidly takes precedence over gesture. Words, unlike pointing, have no meaning in themselves. Except for such imitative sounds as "buzz," "bang," "honk," "quack," "hiss," "purr," most words are as purely symbolic as $x, y,$ and z. But they can carry communication far beyond the limits of gesture, and children practice them with as much gusto as Hobie stalks a mouse. Failure to learn to speak is very rare. Only in some deaf-mutes, and in the last degree of imbecility, is speech impossible. The roots of vocal language run deep.

There is usually strong emotion with the infant's early syllables —the piercing joy of recognition; the sudden fear expressed by "No! No!"; the excitement of "See!"; the demand to handle and touch. The word "ma-ma," uttered in a piteous voice, possesses the miraculous power of materializing that person. Here, to follow Malinowski, we note the seeds of word magic, in which *the name gives power over the person or thing it signifies.* . . . The speech of a child is seldom reflective or thought-provoking; the files of the cortex are still relatively bare. Words are active forces which give a measure of control over the environment—attract this, repulse that. Words *mean* in so far as they *act*. With the passing of the years, the child learns to divorce words from direct action, but the close association at his most formative period makes him a potential candidate for word magic throughout his life.

"There's going to be a 'splosion!

"Boom!!

" 'Splosion's all over."

In this classic example, the word made an entirely satisfactory explosion. Little Willy may some day become Senator William A. Blower, to announce with passionate conviction:

> Are we ready to throw to the winds that age-old and revered principle derived from the great Magna Carta and engraved on our fundamental codes that no one shall be deprived of life, liberty, and property except by due process of law? If we are not, this is the time to arise in our might and fight, that our institutions shall not be ruthlessly violated. Our courts have been rendered servile. The entire government has been seized by one man. Here and now we must scotch the threat of dictatorship so that it may never again rear its ugly head. . . .

Boom! 'Splosion's all over.

Children are prone to uncritical identification. They appreciate resemblances more than differences. They love great big things and little tiny things, and are unmindful of the middle ground where most things lie. They see some elements in a situation but leave out many of its characteristics. They frequently generalize from one or two instances. "A million cats in the back yard last night!" boils down, on cross-examination, to "Well, there was our old cat and another one."

Thus it appears that most children do not long maintain Hobie Baker's realistic appraisal of the environment. Verbal identifications and confused abstractions begin at a tender age. Children are usually more realistic than adults in the matter of morals, however. Current notions of what constitutes right and wrong must be hammered into them, since they are born amoral. If a child is taught these lessons without also learning to abuse the verb "to be," he is fortunate. "Dirt *is* bad." "If your hands are dirty, you *are* a bad boy." "It *is* wrong to kick papa." "*Be* good." Such admonitions build up a massive chain of illegitimate identifications.

Language is no more than crudely acquired before children

begin to suffer from it, and to misinterpret the world by reason of it. Is the fault to be charged to the child, or to the language taught him?

Jerome Frank lists some results of asking children about the names of things: [1]

> The *sun* is so called because it behaves as if it were the sun.
> The *stars* are so called because they are that shape.
> A *table,* because it is used for writing.
> *Clouds,* because they are all gray.

How firmly the child believes in the reality of the word! It comes first; it is strong in its own right.

Some day children will be taught to a different pattern, perhaps like this:

> That bright ball up in the sky warms us and gives us light. It is a long, long way off. It is called "the sun." It might have been called "nus" or "dree" or anything. In Mexico they call it "sol." Where words come from is always interesting but not very important. Once somebody made them up out of his head, as you and Emma Jane made up a private language in the orchard the other day. You can take a ride in this metal machine here that I touch with my hand, but you can't take a ride in the word "autogiro." You can pretend to take a ride? Oh, yes, you can pretend. That's always fun. But if you want to fly with me to Nantucket to play in the sand this afternoon, we can't very well climb on the back of those letters, can we?

~ C ~

suggestions for discussion

1. One of the points—perhaps the most important point—for you to get from this lesson is that different people use words differently. For example, you may recall hearing radio or television announcers make such declarations as that the weather for the

---

[1] *The Law and the Modern Mind.*

week end will be "beautiful, with mild temperatures and no rain."
Obviously, forest rangers, farmers, and others whose vocations will
have been made difficult or even dangerous by protracted dry
weather will hardly agree that a continuation of this weather will
be "beautiful."

Now, call to mind two or three additional situations in which
speakers might disagree over a word.

2. Reread Myers' discussion of levels of abstraction; while keeping in mind that any word is likely to represent different levels
of abstraction from time to time, arrange the following series of
words in what would seem to you to be the most typical order
from the most particular (lowest level of abstraction) through the
various intermediate levels to the most general (highest level of
abstraction):

Sample: (1) Salmo gairdneri (the scientific name of the rainbow
trout), (2) trout, (3) fish, (4) aquatic animal, (5) fauna.

    A. Cow, domestic animal, Bossie, bovine.

    B. Bourbon, intoxicant, alcoholic beverage, Old Swashbuckle,
       whiskey.

    C. *Macbeth,* drama, tragedy, play.

3. Try to find at least one word that could be inserted into any
of the series in No. 2 above. For instance, in the sample, *game fish*
could be placed between *trout* and *fish.*

4. What Myers calls *meaning 3* is approximated by the term
denotation in the headnote to this lesson. When the *meanings 1*
and *2* that Myers talks about most predictably approach agreement,
meaning 3 or the *denotation* of a word is established for this particular situation. Terms for "measurable" concepts—*mile, inch,
pound, John Wilkes Booth*—represent nearly the same thing to all
of us so that we do not dispute their meanings. *Ridiculous, patriotic,
pious,* and *democratic* are words with less predictable agreement
between *meanings 1* and *2* and therefore with less certain *meaning 3*
or *denotation.* They are, however, words that stir us—they have
value connotations—that we either cherish or reject; and the arguments we have are over the values they represent. As an illustration, notice that under some conditions we might agree that the
statement "Jack took a loaf of bread without paying for it" is an
accurate, measurable, objective, i.e. unemotional, statement; at the
same time, we might immediately fall into dispute if one of us

proposed to say, "Jack is, therefore, a thief." The word *thief* is not one whose *meaning 3* or *denotation* stands without interference from its accrued shades of meaning or *connotation*.

There follow several statements that for our purposes here should be taken as acceptable to us; you should propose a restatement or an inference that we would probably disagree over.

Sample: "He kissed her on his first date with her" could be demonstrably true; "He trifled with her affections" or "He took liberties with her" might lead to argument.

A. He worked rapidly and left half of his chores undone.
B. He goes to a drag strip twice a week.
C. He had offers of athletic grants-in-aid from thirty colleges and universities.

5. The skillful writer and speaker will remember that statements suggesting measurement cause least disagreement, but he will know too that at times he will choose not to be precise or that sometimes he will use language to express ideas or emotions that he does not know how to state exactly. List three or four matters on which you may have ideas that, for one reason or another, you would not use or not be able to use words with clearly understood denotations.

6. Reread Robertson and Cassidy on the "etymological fallacy"— the idea that knowing the source of a word will lead one to its "correct" meaning. Now, in your dictionary, look up the etymologies and current meanings of these words: *girl, knave, sinister, harlot, pastor, passion.* Notice that the etymology of none of these is indicative of the way you would be most likely to use the word today.

7. Robertson and Cassidy point out that sometimes we associate two kinds of facts with the result that language used originally with respect to one thing becomes applicable to the other. Thus we say that the apples are green (unripe) and that the rookie ball-player is green (unripe or immature as a player). This transfer of meaning, the foundation of a figurative use of words, is often called a figure of speech. Much of the time the transfer is expressed openly, as in "My love is like a red, red rose." Often it is implied, and just as the writer must take pains to keep the figure of speech from being farfetched or absurd, the reader must apply his imagination to insure that he does not mistake or simply fail to perceive the meaning. For example, in talking about the beautiful girls of thirty years ago, Myers alludes to their "helmet-liner hats"; to a

man at least, this is a perfectly apt figure of speech. Make sure that you catch its meaning.

~ D ~

suggestions for writing

1. Look up the words *air, board, break,* and *pass;* consider their meanings as nouns only. Now, write a short paper (four to six paragraphs) in which you use these words and their meanings to demonstrate that one cannot accurately maintain that every word has its "correct" meaning.

2. Refer once more to the meanings of the words listed in question 1. Write a paper of four to six paragraphs in which you show how these words may represent different levels of abstraction.

3. In question 6 under *Suggestions for Discussion,* you were asked to look up several words (*girl, knave, harlot, pastor, sinister,* and *passion*) and to observe that their etymologies and their most common meanings today are different. Now write a paper of a few paragraphs explaining why the "etymological fallacy" is indeed a fallacy. Do not hesitate to use other words as additional examples.

4. Near the end of "Cats and Babies," Stuart Chase poses the question: "Language is no more than crudely acquired before children begin to suffer from it, and to misinterpret the world by reason of it. Is the fault to be charged to the child, or to the language taught him?"

Write a paper of four to six paragraphs in which you suggest an answer to Chase's question. The more of your own direct experience you can bring to your task, the better.

~ E ~

additional readings

Pyles, Thomas, *The Origins and Development of the English Language* (New York: Harcourt, Brace & World, Inc., 1964), Ch. XI, "Words and Meaning."

Hayakawa, S. I., *Language in Thought and Action,* 2nd ed. (New York: Harcourt, Brace & World, Inc., 1964), Ch. 2, "Symbols."

Perrin, Porter G., *Writer's Guide and Index to English,* 3rd ed. (Chicago: Scott, Foresman & Company, 1959), Ch. 8, "Words."

Chapter Seven

~ A ~

coherence in the theme or transitions between paragraphs

In Chapter Two we discussed the principle of coherence, pointing out that one should use transitions between sentences to develop the smoothness that is characteristic of a coherent paragraph. In this chapter emphasis will be placed upon the development of coherence throughout the entire composition. To be more specific, our concern is with moving from paragraph to paragraph in a smooth and logical manner.

The devices for coherence or transition between paragraphs are similar to those used to develop coherence within the paragraph. The most obvious of these devices is a word or phrase that simply states to the reader that he is to move from one paragraph to another. The repetition of key words or ideas from the preceding paragraph in an opening sentence is another familiar coherence device. The very fact that one paragraph follows another in an explicit order signifies coherence. The use of pronouns to refer to ideas in preceding paragraphs is another effective method for developing coherence. There is, however, one device that has not been mentioned in our discussion of coherence *within* the paragraph; this is the use of a complete transition paragraph. This paragraph generally sums up for the reader what has been said and prepares him for what lies ahead; as such it is effective when used in a long piece of writing—one longer than the student themes usually written in class. The selections to follow will enable you to see the practical application of some of these devices.

~ B ~

slang

NOW EVERYONE IS HIP ABOUT SLANG *

Bergen Evans

One of the most interesting changes taking place in our language today is the acceptance of an enormous amount of slang into standard English. Formerly it often took centuries for a piece of slang to gain such acceptance, if it ever gained it. Dr. Johnson, in 1755, insisted that words such as *frisky, gambler* and *conundrum* "ought not to be admitted to the language." But times have changed. So rapid, indeed, has the process of absorption become that there is a possibility that slang, as a clearly delimitable form of language in America, may be on the way out.

Square, for instance, in its slang meaning, has lost almost all of its original sting of irreverence (a characteristic of slang). It is no longer "secret" talk and its use certainly doesn't mark the user as one who is "in." It seems highly likely that it will soon be regarded as standard.

Hip, to choose another example from the beatnik talk which only yesterday seemed so wild and strange, is listed in Merriam-Webster's *Third International* merely as a variation of *hep,* and *hep* (though I would disagree) is not labeled slang. (That Merriam-Webster chose to define *hep* as the dominant form illustrates the

---

* *The New York Times,* March 22, 1964, *Magazine* section, p. 22 ff.

unavoidable lag of dictionaries; *hep* has been "out," decidedly un-
hip, for years!) Also not marked as slang is *gig*—a job, especially a
jazzman's job. *Dig, cool, chick, bug, bag* and *hung up* are labeled
slang but it is not unreasonable to assume that these will either
have disappeared from use, or will have been accepted as standard,
within a decade or two. (A good deal of British slang has apparently
already been accepted. A new edition of *The Concise Oxford Dictionary*, published last month, contains a number of "slang" expressions without indication in the text that they differ from
standard English.)

Those who get disturbed about slang as something "modern"
that is "corrupting" the language ought to know that it is as old
as language itself. Indeed, it *is* language, and one of the minor
pleasures of reading is to come across it in the literature of the
past. Chaucer, for instance, uses *gab* exactly as we use it today. A
desirable woman was a *piece* in the fourteenth century, and a *broad*
or a *frail* in the sixteenth. Bishop Latimer, in a sermon before
Edward VI (1547), said that those who had defrauded the King of
money ought to "make restitution . . . cough up." John Adams,
in a morning-after letter (1774) said, "We drank sentiments until
11 o'clock. Lee and Harrison were very high." Charlotte Brönte
referred to a foolish person as a sap—as others had been doing for
200 years before her.

From the difference between certain standard words in Latin and
in the Romance languages, we know that even the Romans used
slang. Thus, although the formal Latin word for head was *caput,*
the French is *la tete* and the Italian *la testa*—which obviously derive
from the Latin *testa,* an earthen pot. And where the formal Latin
word for leg was *crus,* the French is *la jambe* and the Italian *la
gamba* (whence "gams" and "gamboling"), derived from the Latin
gamba, hoof. The Romans wrote formally about the head and the
leg, but they apparently spoke of "the pot" and "the hoof."

One of the purposes of using slang, as with thieves' cant, from
which much of it has sprung, is to make it possible for certain
groups *not* to be understood by the uninitiated. Its use marks the
user as one of the knowing, a member of a prestigious in-group.
(And when the word is no longer good slang, its user is no longer
"in.") It is also used to shock and, if possible, irritate. Thus *neat*
is a term of approval with the younger set even though a labored
defiance of neatness is obligatory among them. Even more useful,

or more used, are expressions of contempt—*drip, clod, creep, dope, jerk* and *fink*—which reinforce status by rejecting the unworthy.

A large element in the creation of slang is sheer playfulness, an extension of the impulse that leads to such duplications of sound as *hotsy-totsy, heebie-jeebies* and *okeydoke.* The word *slang* is itself slang and embodies much of what it designates: it is breezy, catchy, eminently suitable, yet intriguing; we feel that we know its meaning but we find it hard to define and difficult to trace. It is probably language that is being slung about instead of being handled with stately consideration. In an early fifteenth-century poem we are told of one who "bold words did sling" and there *is* a boldness and a sling in slang. It risks daring metaphors and audacious allusions; it impudently defies propriety and dissolves with triumphant laughter into meaninglessness when solemnity indignantly demands that it explain itself.

Pomposity is slang's natural enemy, which may account for the fact that there are probably more slang words that describe drunkenness—the antithesis of dignity—than any other state or activity. Solemnity meets the condition with the plain *drunk,* the disapproving *drunken,* the scientific *intoxicated* and highfalutin *inebriated.* The Quakers, with gentle evasion, called it *tired.* But slang riots in every degree of its indignity, from the mild *lit,* through the hilarious *plastered,* to the terminal *stiff.*

Benjamin Franklin once compiled a Drinker's Dictionary containing 228 terms, but *The American Thesaurus of Slang* found it necessary 200 years later to list four times that number. And it is interesting, and perhaps significant, that modern slang seems to represent drunkenness less as a disreputable escapade, a breaking away from dull routine (as in *spree, toot, jag, bender, binge*) than as a sodden stasis (*loaded, pie-eyed, stewed, blotto*).

Much slang is humorously euphemistic. There are some situations so ghastly that one must ignore them or laugh at them. Airsickness, for example, is so outrageous an assault on our dignity (coupled, as it usually is, with humiliating fear) that it has come to be "one of those things we just don't talk about." The airlines—who can't ignore it—refer with ludicrous delicacy, to the equipment provided in the seat backs as "discomfort containers." But college students—who, at least in retrospect, seem to find the business amusing—call them "barff bags."

At one end of the gamut of slang's humor is the inane—what

Oliver Wendell Holmes called "the blank checks of a bankrupt mind"—such fatuities as "Sez you!", "Banana oil!", and "So's your old man!" But at the other are such concepts as "to join the majority" (to die), which goes back to ancient Rome, or the eighteenth century's "scandal broth," for tea, or the British lower classes' late nineteenth-century "nobby" (also "with knobs on") for smart, elegant or fashionable—a shrewder appraisal of Victorian design and decor than the upper classes were capable of making.

Grose, in his *Classical Dictionary of the Vulgar Tongue* (1796), tells us that "a forward girl, ready to oblige every man that shall ask her" was called an "Athanasian wench"—and is so flattering to his reader as not even to explain why. The explanation is that the first two words of the Athanasian creed are: "Whosoever desires. . . ."

If such allusiveness seems too recondite for anyone but dwellers in the groves of Academe, one must consider rhyming slang, which originated in the underworld, was developed by London Cockneys in the nineteenth century, enjoyed a vogue for several generations and is now disappearing.

Here the meaning lies in a word which is not spoken at all but which rhymes with the last of two or more words in a phrase. At first, similarity of sound was the sole connection—as *cherry ripe* for pipe or *apples and pears* for stairs. But Cockney wit and humor and linguistic imaginativeness (what ignorant nonsense in Shaw to assume that Professor Higgins's English was better, as speech, than was Eliza Doolittle's—Eliza's class danced linguistic circles around the gentry!) soon wove an implication of meaning into the allusion of sound. So a liar became a *holy friar;* a church, *chicken perch;* a lodger, an *artful dodger;* a gal, *rob my pal;* kids, *God forbids,* and so on—in one of the giddiest whirls language has ever been swept into.

And then, as though this were not involved and clever enough, the rhyming word itself was sometimes merely implied as a part of a well-known phrase. Thus *china* came to mean mate because "plate" rhymes with "mate"; and *Oliver* to mean fist because the unspoken "Twist" rhymes with "fist."

Now all of this surely marks slang, not as a degeneration of language, but rather as a sort of spume or spindrift of language riding its forward-surging wave; but, even so, language—as much a part of it as law or liturgy and shaped and controlled by the same forces that shape and control standard speech.

This is illustrated by the thousands of instances in which slang repeats the etymology of a standard word. Thus *to impose* is, literally, "to put something over on," *to excoriate* "to take the hide off," *to apprehend* "to catch on," *to converse* "to go round with" and *to exaggerate* "to pile it on." He who is *ecstatic* is "beside himself"; he has been driven out of himself, or "sent." He who is *replete* is "fed up" and that which is *superlative* has been "laid on thick." *Handsome* originally meant "pleasant to handle" or, as the young now say, "smooth." To be *recalcitrant* is to "kick" backwards (from Latin *calx, calvis*, heel).

To be *dependent* is to be a "hanger-on" and to be *enraptured* is to be "carried away"—gone, man, gone! Where the meticulous speaker of standard English might ask "What's fretting you?", a slangy speaker might ask, "What's eating you?" And where the standard speaker might stiffly aver that he was "not prone to accept" a certain imposition, the other might more vividly insist that he "would not take it lying down." Yet both have said the same thing: for *fretting* means voracious or gnawing eating, and *prone* means lying face downwards.

Many slang words pass into standard use and once they do, of course, they don't sound slangy at all. Among such now-sturdy-respectables are *club* (social), *dwindle, flout, foppish, freshman, fretful, glib, hubbub, nice, ribaldry, scoundrel, simper, swagger, tidy, tantrums, tarpaulin* and *trip* (journey).

Even more interesting is that many slang words stay in the language for centuries, but remain slang. *Booze,* once standard, became dialectal and then slang and has remained slang for centuries, spawning recently, in British slang, *boozer* (a pub). *Brass* (impudence) is also centuries old. So is to *chisel* (to use trickery), and so are *frisk* (to search a person for weapons), *corporation* (large belly), *leery, pad* (bed), *mum, blab, gag* (joke), *pigeon* (dupe), *hick* (rustic), *grub* (food) and hundreds of others.

A word can remain slang and undergo a semantic change just as if it were standard. Forty years ago a *nut* was a ludicrous eccentric; today he is one who is dangerously deranged. Like so many other things in the world, the word has acquired a menace.

Still other words pass from slang to standard within a few years of their creation. *Cello,* a nineteenth-century clipping of *violoncello,* and printed as 'cello up until a few years ago, is now standard. *Bleachers* was slang in 1904, but fully standard within two decades. *Sweater* was slang in 1880, but standard by 1914. These last two words, by the way, illustrate the way in which a slang word can lose its metaphorical vitality in the process of becoming a standard verbal symbol. We have to stop to think of the idea of bleaching in the *bleachers* and, offhand, would see nothing contradictory in a reference to a woman's wearing a dainty cashmere *sweater.*

Except through the caprice of usage, there's no accounting for the status of words. *Bored* (wearied by dullness), for instance, was listed as slang in 1722, but is now standard. But *flabbergast,* which was included in the same list, remains slang. The modern slang use of *dizzy* to mean foolish in a featherheaded way ("dizzy dame") recaptures the word's original standard meaning: a ninth-century West Saxon version of Matthew 25:1-3 says of the 10 virgins who went forth to meet the bridegroom, "Five of them were dizzy . . . and took lamps but they didn't take no oil with them."

It is, in fact, becoming increasingly difficult to draw a hard and fast line between slang and colloquial, and colloquial and standard, and thus to establish that this or that word is definitely not acceptable in dignified speech or writing. *Blues,* for instance, is still slang if it means low spirits. But if it means a genre of songs expressing low spirits, it is standard.

Jazz in its meaning of sexual intercourse is still low slang, very close to the underworld cant it originally was. As a description of a kind of music, however, it is standard. But in its recently acquired vogue meaning of fussy routine or nonsense ("and all that jazz") it is slang again.

Kid meaning a child was cant in the late sixteenth century, but had become slang by the mid-eighteenth century, and is now colloquial. The verb *to kid* (to tease by jesting, as with a child), remains slang. But *kidnap* has been standard for almost 300 years. *Gal* is slang only when a deliberate mispronunciation of *girl;* if it is the speaker's natural pronunciation, it is simply a social or regional variant. In 1748 Swift singled out *mob* (a clipping of *mobile vulgus,* the moving or fickle populace) for particular detestation as a corruption of the language. But despite the Dean's disapproval the word stuck and is now standard when it means a riotous assemblage.

A striking illustration of the extent to which even experts disagree in this matter of labeling is furnished by comparison of Wentworth and Flexner's *Dictionary of American Slang* (1960) with the Merriam-Webster *Third International* (1961). Of 2,355 words which Wentworth and Flexner list as slang, and with the meanings of which the *Third International* agrees, the *Third International* lists only 549 as slang.

In the face of such a divergence one must wonder if slang is not losing its identity. The increasing frankness of all expression has weakened its euphemistic value. The disappearance of fixed social classes has removed one of the chief motivations for its impertinence. And its universal use has destroyed its secrecy and reduced its value as an expression of in-group superiority.

There is also just too much of it around for it to be in any way esoteric. *The American Thesaurus of Slang* lists over 100,000 terms and the *Dictionary of American Slang* estimates that slang makes up perhaps one-fifth of the words we use. A single issue of *Time*—that of January 10, 1964—contains 266 words and phrases that in the days of *The Literary Digest* would have been considered sub-standard and unfit for serious writing. *The Washington Post* of the same date contains 152.

Very little contemporary slang has enough shock value left to tickle our fancy. The beatnik and teen-age jargon, of which so much has been made, is pretty unimaginative stuff when compared with, say, rhyming slang or the eighteenth-century slang in Grose's *Classical Dictionary of the Vulgar Tongue*. Impudence, impiety and indecency are now in the public domain and rarely startle. Greed, brutality and what passes for religion can still shock, but the mark of the in-group today is more the capacity to *be* shocked than the ability to shock.

American slang had a period of vigor and we were proud of it. "When Americans are through with the English language," Mr. Dooley boasted, "it will look as if it had been run over by a musical comedy." Perhaps our delight in slang was part of our traditional defiance of the British; after all, it was the *King's* English that we were tying in knots. But now that we are the senior partner, and it is the *President's* English, some of the fun may have gone out of twisting its tale. And perhaps there will be a renaissance of slang in British English—to mock and startle *us*.

The Nature of Slang *

H. L. Mencken

Slang is defined by the *Oxford Dictionary* as "language of a highly colloquial type, considered as below the level of standard educated speech, and consisting either of new words or of current words employed in some special sense." The origin of the word is unknown. Ernest Weekley, in his *Etymological Dictionary of Modern English*, 1921, suggests that it may have some relation to the verb *to sling*, and cites two Scandinavian dialect words, based upon the cognate verb *slenge* or *slengje*, that appear to be its brothers: *slengjeord*, a neologism, and *slengjenamn*, a nickname. But he is not sure, so he adds the note that "some regard it as an argotic perversion of the French *langue*, language." A German philologian, O. Ritter, believes that it may be derived, not from *langue*, but from *language* itself, most probably by a combination of blending and shortening, as in *thieve(s' lang)uage*, *beggar-(s' lang)uage* and so on. *Webster's New International*, 1934, follows somewhat haltingly after Weekley. The *Oxford Dictionary*, 1919, evades the question by dismissing *slang* as "a word of cant origin, the ultimate source of which is not apparent." When it first appeared in English, about the middle of the eighteenth century, it was employed as a synonym of *cant,* and so designated "the special vocabulary used by any set of persons of a low or disreputable character"; and half a century later it began to be used interchangeably with *argot*, which means the vocabulary special to any group, trade or profession. But during the past fifty years the three terms have tended to be more or less clearly distinguished. The jargon of criminals is both a kind of slang and a kind of argot, but it is best described as *cant,* a word derived from the Latin *cantus,* and going back, in its present sense to c. 1540. One of the principal aims of cant is to make what is said unintelligible to persons outside the group, a purpose that is absent from most forms of argot and slang. Argot often includes slang, as when a circus man calls his patrons *suckers* and speaks of refunding money to one full of complaints as *squaring the beef,* but when he calls the circus grounds the *lot* and the manager's quarters the *white wagon,* he is simply using the special language of his trade, and it is quite as respectable as the argot of lawyers or diplomats. The essence of slang is that it is of general dispersion, but still stands outside the accepted canon of the language. It is, says George H. McKnight, "a form of colloquial speech created in a spirit of defiance and aiming at freshness and novelty. . . . Its figures are consciously far-fetched and are intentionally drawn from the most ignoble of sources. Closely akin to profanity in its spirit, its aim is to shock." Among the impulses leading to its invention, adds Henry Bradley, "the two more important seem to be the desire to secure increased vivacity and the desire to secure increased sense of intimacy in the use of language." "It seldom attempts," says the London *Times,* "to supply deficiencies in conventional language; its object is nearly always to provide a new and different way of saying what can be perfectly well said without it." What chiefly lies behind it is simply a kind of linguistic exuberance, an excess of word-making energy. It relates itself to the standard language a great deal as dancing relates itself to music. But there is also something else. The best slang is not only ingenious and amusing; it also embodies a kind of social criticism. It not only provides new names for a series of everyday concepts, some new and some old; it also says something about them. "Words which produce the slang effect," observes Frank K. Sechrist, "arouse associations which are incongruous or incompatible with those of customary thinking."

Everyone including even the metaphysician in his study and the eremite in his cell, has a large vocabulary of slang, but the vocabulary of the vulgar is likely to be larger than that of the cultured, and it is harder worked. Its content may be divided into two categories: (a) old words, whether used singly or in combination, that have been put to new uses, usually metaphorical, and (b) new words that have not yet been admitted to the standard vocabulary. Examples of the first type are *rubberneck,* for a gaping and prying person, and *iceberg,* for a cold woman; examples of the second are *hoosegow, flim-flam, blurb, bazoo* and *blah.* There is a constant movement of slang terms into accepted usage. *Nice,* as an adjective of all work, signifying anything satisfactory, was once in slang use only, and the purists denounced it, but today no one would question "a *nice* day," "a *nice* time," or "a *nice* hotel." The French word *tete* has been a sound name for the human head for many centuries, but its origin was in *testa,* meaning a pot, a favorite slang word of the soldiers of the decaying Roman Empire, exactly analogous to our *block, nut* and *bean.* The verb-phrase *to hold up* is now perfectly good American, but so recently as 1901 the late Brander Matthews was sneering at it as slang. In the same way many other verb-phrases, e.g., *to cave in, to fill the bill* and to *fly off the handle,* once viewed askance, have gradually worked their way to a relatively high level of the standard speech. On some indeterminate tomorrow *to stick up* and *to take for a ride* may follow them. "Even the greatest purist," says Robert Lynd, "does not object today to the inclusion of the word *bogus* in a literary English vocabulary, though a hundred years ago *bogus* was an American slang word meaning an apparatus for coining false money. *Carpetbagger* and *bunkum* are other American slang words that have naturalized themselves in English speech, and *mob* is an example of English slang that was once as vulgar as *incog* or *photo.*" Sometimes a word comes in below the salt, gradually wins respectability, and then drops to the level of slang, and is worked to death. An example is offered by *strenuous.* It was first used by John Marston, the dramatist, in 1599, and apparently he invented it, as he invented *puffy, chilblained, spurious* and *clumsy.* As strange as it may seem to us today, all these words were frowned on by the purists of the time as uncouth and vulgar, and Ben Jonson attacked them with violence in his "Poetaster," written in 1601. In particular, Ben was upset by *strenuous.* But it made its way despite him, and during the next three centuries it was used by a multitude of impeccable authors, including Milton, Swift, Burke, Hazlitt, and Macaulay. And when Theodore Roosevelt invented and announced the "strenuous life," the adjective struck the American fancy and passed into slang, and in a little while it was so horribly threadbare that all persons of careful speech sickened of it, and to this day it bears the ridiculous connotation that hangs about most slang, and is seldom used seriously.

All neologisms, of course, are not slang. At about the time the word *hoosegow,* derived from the Spanish, came into American slang use, the word *rodeo,* also Spanish, came into the standard vocabulary. The distinction between the two is not hard to make out. *Hoosegow* was really not needed. We had plenty of words to designate a jail, and they were old and good words. *Hoosegow* came in simply because there was something arresting and out-landish about it—and the users of slang have a great liking for pungent novelties. *Rodeo,* on the other hand, designated something for which there was no other word in American—something, indeed, of which the generality of Americans had just become aware—and so it was accepted at once. Many neologisms have been the deliberate inventions of quite serious men, e.g., *gas, kodak, vaseline. Scientist* was concocted in 1840 by William Whewell, professor of moral theology and casuistical divinity at Cambridge. *Ampere* was proposed solemnly by the Electric Congress which met in Paris in 1881, and was taken into all civilized languages instantly. *Radio* was suggested for wireless telegrams by an international convention held in Berlin in 1906, and was extended to wireless broadcasts in the United States about 1920, though the English prefer *wireless* in the latter sense. But such words as these were never slang; they came into general and respectable use at once, along with *argon, x-ray, carburetor, stratosphere, bacillus,* and many another of the sort. These words were all sorely needed; it was impossible to convey the ideas behind them without them, save by clumsy circumlocutions. It is one of the functions of slang, also, to serve a short cut, but it is seldom if ever really necessary. Instead, as W. D. Whitney once said, it is only a wanton product of "the exuberance of mental activity, and the natural delight of language-making." This mental activity, of course, is the function of a relatively small class. "The unconscious genius of the people," said Paul Shorey, "no more invents slang than it invents epics. It is coined in the sweat of their brow by smart writers who, as they would say, are *out for the coin.*" Or, if not out for the coin, then at least out for notice, *kudos,* admiration, or maybe simply for satisfaction of the "natural delight of language-making." Some of the best slang emerges from the argot of college students, but everyone who has observed the process of its gestation knows that the general run of students have nothing to do with the matter, save maybe to provide an eager welcome for the novelties set before them. College slang is actually made by the campus wits, just as general slang is made by the wits of the newspapers and theaters. The idea of calling an engagement ring a *handcuff* did not occur to the young gentlemen of Harvard by mass inspiration; it occurred to a certain definite one of them, probably after long and deliberate cogitation, and he gave it to the rest and to his century.

Toward the end of 1933, W. J. Funk of the Funk and Wagnalls Company, publishers of the *Standard Dictionary* and the *Literary Digest,* undertook to supply the newspapers with the names of the ten most fecund makers of the American slang then current. He nominated T. A. (Tad) Dorgan, the cartoonist; Sime Silverman, editor of the theatrical weekly, *Variety;* Gene Buck, the song writer; Damon Runyon, the sports writer; Walter Winchell and Arthur (Bugs) Baer, newspaper columnists; George Ade, Ring Lardner and Gelett Burgess. He should have added Jack Conway and Johnny O'Connor of the staff of *Variety;* James Gleason author of *Is Zat So?* Rube Goldberg, the cartoonist; Johnny Stanley and Johnny Lyman, Broadway figures; Wilson Mizner and Milt Gross. Conway, who died in 1928, is credited with the invention of *palooka* (a third-rater), *belly-laugh, Arab* (for Jew), S. A. (sex appeal), *high-hat, push-over, boloney* (for buncombe, later adopted by Alfred E. Smith), *headache* (wife), and the verbs *to scram, to click* (meaning to succeed), and *to laugh that off.* Winchell, if he did not actually invent *whoopee,* at least gave it the popularity it enjoyed, c. 1930. He is also the father of *Chicagorilla, Joosh* (for Jewish), *pash* (for passion) and *shafts* (for legs), and he has devised a great many nonce words and phrases, some of them euphemistic and others far from it, e.g., for married: *welded, sealed, lohengrined, merged* and *middle-aisled;* for divorced: *Reno-vated;* for contemplating divorce: *telling it to a judge, soured, curdled, in husband trouble, this-and-that-way,* and *on the verge;* for love: *on the merge, on fire, uh-huh, that way, cupiding, Adam-and-Eveing* and *man-and-womaning it;* for expecting young: *infanticipating, baby-bound* and *storked.* I add a few other characteristic specimens of his art: *go-ghetto, debutramp, phffft, foofff* (a pest), *Wildeman* (a homosexual), *heheheh* (a mocking laugh), *Hard-Times Square* (Times Square), *blessed-event* (the birth of young), *the Hardened Artery* (Broadway), *radiodor* (a radio announcer), *moom-pitcher* (moving picture), *girl-mad, Park Rowgue* (a newspaper reporter) and *intelligentleman.* Most of these, of course, had only their brief days, but a few promise to survive. Dorgan, who died in 1929, was the begetter of *apple-sauce, twenty-three skiddoo, ball-and-chain* (for wife), *cake-eater, dumb Dora, dumbbell* (for stupid person), *nobody home,* and *you said it.* He also gave the world, "Yes, we have no bananas," though he did not write the song, and he seems to have originated *the cat's pajamas,* which was followed by a long series of similar superlatives. The sports writers, of course, are all assiduous makers of slang, and many of their inventions are taken into the general vocabulary. Thus, those who specialize in boxing have contributed, in recent years, *kayo, cauliflower-ear, prelim, shadow-boxing, slug-fest, title-holder, punch-drunk, brother-act, punk, to side-step* and *to go the limit* . . . and those who follow the golf tournaments have given currency to *birdie, fore, par, bunker, divot, fairway, to tee off, stance* and *onesome, twosome, threesome,* and so on—some of them received into the standard speech, but the majority lingering in the twilight of slang.

George Philip Krapp attempts to distinguish between slang and sound idiom by setting up the doctrine that the former is "more expressive than the situation demands." "It is," he says, "a kind of hyperesthesia in the use of language. *To laugh in your sleeve* is idiom because it arises out of a natural situation; it is a metaphor derived from the picture of one raising his sleeve to his face to hide a smile, a metaphor which arose naturally enough in early periods when sleeves were long and flowing; but *to talk through your hat* is slang, not only because it is new, but also because it is a grotesque exaggeration of the truth." The theory, unluckily, is combated by many plain facts. *To hand it to him, to get away with it,* and even *to hand him a lemon* are certainly not metaphors that transcend the practicable and probable, and yet all are undoubtedly slang. On the other hand, there is palpable exaggeration in such phrases as "he is not worth the powder it would take to kill him," in such adjectives as *breakbone* (fever), and in such compounds as *fire-eater,* and yet it would be absurd to dismiss them as slang. Between *blockhead* and *bonehead* there is little to choose, but the former is sound English, whereas the latter is American slang. So with many familiar similes, e.g., *like greased lightning, as scarce as hen's teeth;* they are grotesque hyperboles, but hardly slang.

The true distinction, in so far as any distinction exists at all, is that indicated by Whitney, Bradley, Sechrist and McKnight. Slang originates in the effort of ingenious individuals to make the language more pungent and picturesque—to increase the store of terse and striking words, to widen the boundaries of metaphor, and to provide a vocabulary for new shades of difference in meaning. As

Dr. Otto Jespersen has pointed out, this is also the aim of poets (as indeed, it is of prose writers), but they are restrained by consideration of taste and decorum, and also, not infrequently, by historical or logical considerations. The maker of slang is under no such limitations: he is free to confect his neologism by any process that can be grasped by his customers, and out of any materials available, whether native or foreign. He may adopt any of the traditional devices of metaphor. Making an attribute do duty for the whole gives him *stiff* for corpse, *flat-foot* for policeman, *smoke-eater* for fireman, *skirt* for woman, *lunger* for consumptive, and *yes-man* for sycophant. Hidden resemblances give him *morgue* for a newspaper's file of clippings, *bean* for head, and *sinker* for a doughnut. The substitution of far-fetched figures for literal description gives him *glad-rags* for fine clothing, *bonehead* for ignoramus, *booze-foundry* for saloon, and *cart-wheel* for dollar, and the contrary resort to a brutal literalness gives him *kill-joy, low-life* and *handout*. He makes abbreviations with a free hand—*beaut* for beauty, *gas* for gasoline, and so on. He makes bold avail of composition, as in *attaboy* and *whatdyecallem,* and of onomatopoeia, as in *biff, zowie, honky-tonk,* and *wow*. He enriches the ancient counters of speech with picturesque synonyms, as in *guy, gink, duck, bird,* and *bozo* for fellow. He transfers proper names to common usage, as in *ostermoor* for mattress, and then sometimes gives them remote figurative significances, as in *ostermoors* for whiskers. Above all, he enriches the vocabulary of action with many new verbs and verb-phrases, e.g., *to burp, to neck, to gang, to frame up, to hit the pipe, to give him the works,* and so on. If, by the fortunes that condition language-making, his neologism acquires a special and limited meaning, not served by any existing locution, it enters into sound idiom and is presently wholly legitimatized; if, on the contrary, it is adopted by the populace as a counterword and employed with such banal imitativeness that it soon loses any definite significance whatever, then it remains slang and is avoided by the finical. An example of the former process is afforded by *tommy-rot*. It first appeared as English school-boy slang, but its obvious utility soon brought it into good usage. In one of Jerome K. Jerome's books, *Paul Kelver,* there is the following dialogue:

"The wonderful songs that nobody ever sings, the wonderful

pictures that nobody ever paints, and all the rest of it. It's *tommy-rot!*"

"I wish you wouldn't use slang."

"Well, you know what I mean. What is the proper word? Give it to me."

"I suppose you mean *cant.*"

"No, I don't. *Cant* is something that you don't believe in yourself. It's *tommy-rot;* there isn't any other word."

Nor were there any other words for *hubbub, fireworks, foppish, fretful, sportive, dog-weary, to bump* and *to dwindle* in Shakespeare's time; he adopted and dignified them because they met genuine needs. Nor was there any other satisfactory word for *graft* when it came in, nor for *rowdy,* nor for *boom,* nor for *joyride,* nor for *slacker,* nor for *trust-buster.* Such words often retain a humorous quality; they are used satirically and hence appear but seldom in wholly serious discourse. But they have standing in the language nevertheless, and only a prig would hesitate to use them as George Saintsbury used *the best of the bunch* and *joke-smith.* So recently as 1929 the *Encyclopaedia Britannica* listed *bootlegger, speakeasy, dry, wet, crook, fake, fizzle, hike, hobo, poppycock, racketeer* and *O.K.* as American slang terms, but today most of them are in perfectly good usage. What would one call a racketeer if *racketeer* were actually forbidden? It would take a phrase of four or five words at least, and it would certainly not express the idea clearly.

On the other hand, many an apt and ingenious neologism, by falling too quickly into the gaping maw of the proletariat, is spoiled forthwith and forever. Once it becomes in Oliver Wendell Holmes's phrase, "a cheap generic term, a substitute for differentiated specific expressions," it quickly acquires such flatness that the fastidious flee it as a plague. The case of *strenuous* I have already mentioned. One recalls, too, many capital verb-phrases, thus ruined by unintelligent appreciation, e.g., *to freeze on to, to have the goods, to cut no ice, to fall for,* and *to get by;* and some excellent substantives e.g., *dope* and *dub,* and compounds, e.g., *to neck* and *to vamp.* These are all quite as sound in structure as the great majority of our most familiar words and phrases—*to cut no ice,* for example, is certainly as good as *to butter no parsnips*—but but their adoption by the ignorant and their endless use and

misuse in all sorts of situations have left them tattered and ob-
noxious, and soon or late they will probably go the way, as Brander
Matthews once said, of all the other "temporary phrases which
spring up, one scarcely knows how, and flourish unaccountably for
a few months, and then disappear forever, leaving no sign." Matthews was wrong in two particulars here. They do not arrive by
any mysterious parthenogenesis, but come from sources which, in
many cases, may be determined. And they last a good deal more
than a few months. *Shoo-fly* afflicted the American people for four
or five years, and *I don't think, aber nit, over the left, good night*
and *oh yeah* were scarcely less long-lived. There are, indeed, slang
terms that have survived for centuries, never dropping quite out of
use and yet never attaining to good usage. Among verbs, *to do* for
to cheat has been traced to 1789, *to frisk* for to search to 1781, *to
grease* for to bribe to 1577, and *to blow* for to boast to c. 1400.
Among nouns, *gas* for empty talk has been traced to 1847, *jug*
for prison to 1834, *lip* for insolence to 1821, *sap* for fool to 1815,
murphy for potato to 1811, *racket* to 1785, *bread-basket* for stomach
to 1753, *hush-money* to 1709, *hick* to 1690, *goldmine* for profitable
venture to 1664, *grub* for food to 1659, *rot-gut* to 1597 and *bones*
for dice to c. 1386. Among the adjectives, *lousy* in the sense of
inferior goes back to 1690; when it burst into American slang in
1910 or thereabout it was already more than two centuries old.
Booze has never got into standard English, but it was known to
slang in the first years of the fourteenth century. When *nuts* in
the sense revealed by "Chicago was *nuts* for the Giants" came
into popularity in the United States c. 1920, it was treated by most
newspaper commentators on current slang as a neologism, but in
truth it had been used in precisely the same sense by R. H.
Dana, Jr., in *Two Years Before the Mast,* 1840, and by Mark Twain
in *Following the Equator,* 1897. Sometimes an old slang word
suddenly acquires a new meaning. An example is offered by *to
chisel.* In the sense of to cheat, as in "He *chiseled* me out of $3,"
it goes back to the first years of the nineteenth century, but with
the advent of the N.R.A., in the late summer of 1933, it took on
the new meaning of to evade compliance with the law by con-
cealment or stealth. It has been credited to Franklin D. Roosevelt,
but I believe that its true father was General Hugh S. Johnson,
J. D.

With the possible exception of the French, the Americans now produce more slang than any other people, and put it to heavier use in their daily affairs. But they entered upon its concoction relatively late, and down to the second decade of the nineteenth century they were content to take their supply from England. American slang, says George Philip Krapp, "is the child of the new nationalism, the new spirit of joyous adventure that entered American life after the close of the War of 1812." There was, during the colonial and early republican periods, a great production of neologisms, . . . but very little of it was properly describable as slang. I find *to boost*, defined as to raise up, to lift up, to exalt, in the glossary appended to David Humphrey's *The Yankey in England*, 1815, but all the other slang terms listed, e.g., *duds* for clothes, *spunk* for courage and *uppish*, are in Francis Grose's *Classical Dictionary of the Vulgar Tongue*, published in London thirty years before. The Rev. John Witherspoon's denunciation of slang in *The Druid*, 1781, is a denunciation of English slang, though he is discussing the speech habits of Americans. But with the great movement into the West, following the War of 1812, the American vulgate came into its own, and soon the men of the ever-receding frontier were pouring out a copious stream of neologisms, many of them showing the audacious fancy of true slang. When these novelties penetrated to the East they produced a sort of linguistic shock, and the finicky were as much upset by the "tall talk" in which they were embodied as English pedants are today by the slang of Hollywood. That some of them were extremely extravagant is a fact: I need point only to *blustiferous, clam-jamphrie, conbobberation, helliferocious, mollagausauger, peedoodles, ripsniptiously, slang-whanger, sockdolager, to exflunctify, to flummuck, to giraffe, to hornswoggle, to obflisticate* and *to puckerstopple*. Most of these, of course, had their brief days and then disappeared, but there were others that got into the common vocabulary and still survive, e.g., *blizzard, to hornswoggle, sockdolager* and *rambunctious*, the last-named the final step in a process which began with *robustious* and ran through *rumbustious* and *rambustious* in England before Americans took a hand in it. With them came many verb-phrases, e.g., *to pick a crow with, to cut one's eye-teeth, to go the whole hog*. This "tall talk," despite the horror of the delicate, was a great success in the East, and its salient practitioners—for example, David Crockett—were popular heroes. Its example encouraged the production of like neologisms everywhere, and by 1840 the use of slang was very widespread. It is to those days before the Civil War that we owe many of the colorful American terms for strong drink, still current, e.g., *panther-sweat, nose-paint, red-eye, corn-juice, forty-rod, mountain-dew, coffin-varnish, bust-head, stagger-soup, tonsil-paint, squirrel-whiskey,* and so on, and for drunk, e.g., *boiled, canned, cockeyed, frazzled, fried, oiled, ossified, pifflicated, pie-eyed, plastered, snozzled, stewed, stuccoed, tanked, woozy.* "Perhaps the most striking difference between British and American slang," says Krapp, "is that the former is more largely merely a matter of the use of queer-sounding words, like *bally* and *swank,* whereas American slang suggests vivid images and pictures." This was hardly true in the heyday of "tall talk," but that it is true now is revealed by a comparison of current English and American college slang. The vocabulary of Oxford and Cambridge seems inordinately obvious and banal to an American undergraduate. At Oxford it is made up in large part of a series of childish perversions of common and proper nouns, effected by adding *-er* or inserting *gg.* Thus, breakfast becomes the *Queener, Jesus'* becomes *Jaggers,* and the Prince of Wales becomes the *Pragger-Wagger.* The rest of the vocabulary is equally feeble. To match the magnificent American *lounge-lizard* the best the Oxonians can achieve is a *bit of a lad,* and in place of the multitudinous American synonyms for *girl* there are only *bint* (Arabic for *woman*) and a few other such flabby terms. All college slang, of course, borrows heavily from the general slang vocabulary. For example, *chicken,* which designated a young girl on most American campuses until 1921 or thereabout was used by Steele in 1711, and, in the form of *no chicken,* by Swift in 1720. It had acquired a disparaging significance in the United States by 1788, as the following lines show:

> From visiting bagnios, those seats of despair,
> Where *chickens* will call you *my duck* and *my dear*
> In hopes that your purse may fall to their share,
> Deliver me!

GOOD AND BAD LANGUAGE *

Stephen Leacock

Quite apart from the technical aspect of the art of narration, there is the broader general question of good and bad language, of where speech ends and slang begins. To what extent must the language of literature and cultivated discourse accept and assimilate the innovations, the irregularities and the corruptions that perpetually appear in all languages as spoken by the mass of the people? To what extent are we to think of our language as a moving current, never the same except in its identity, and to what extent should we wish to check the flow of the current, so that stiller waters may run deeper! Obviously there is a limit in each direction. A current totally arrested means stagnation. Waters that run too fast end in the sand. Somewhere there may be a happy mean between the two.

Now this question arises for all languages. But it has a very peculiar importance for the English language since here the current flows in two parts, the American and the British; and many people are inclined to think that one tends to run too fast and the other tends to slacken. In other words we have here the problem of the American language and American slang. Every now and then controversy breaks out in regard to British English and American English—or it used to before the war stilled all babble—and it sometimes had a rather nasty edge to it. It carried in it one of the last faint survivals of the Stamp Act and the Boston Tea Party. Great quarrels die away to leave only generous memories; little quarrels live on. Hence the question of "slang" as between England and America (England, not Scotland; the Scots are not worrying) keeps its edge; all the more so, in that a lot of Americans think in their hearts, that the reason why the English don't use much slang is that they can't make it up, and a lot of English people think that the Americans use slang because they weren't

---

* Reprinted by permission of Dodd, Mead & Company from *How To Write* by Stephen Leacock. Copyright 1943 by Dodd, Mead & Company, Inc.

brought up properly—or, no, they don't think it, they know it. That's the provoking thing about the English (say the Americans); they don't think things, they know them. They did all their thinking years and years ago.

I can write on this controversy with the friendly neutrality of a Canadian. In Canada we have enough to do keeping up with two spoken languages without trying to invent slang, so we must go right ahead and use English for literature, Scotch for sermons and American for conversation.

Perhaps the highest point of controversy is reached in the discussion whether there is, whether there ought to be, whether it is a shame that there isn't, an "American" language. Some people feel very strongly on this point. They think that having your own language is a mark of independence like owning your own house, driving your own car and having your own shaving mug in the barber shop. Gangs of boys make themselves up a "language" and revel in its obscurity. The leading boys in this respect are the Irish, so anxious to have their own language that they are trying to learn Gaelic. If they are not careful, first thing they know they'll get to talk it and then they'll be sorry.

On the other hand, some people feel just the other way about it. A more interesting article appeared a little while ago in one of the leading British quarterlies, written by an American, and deprecating all idea of the creation of an American language as dangerous to our mutual dependence and kinship.

My own feeling about this, if I may put it in slang, is "I should worry." Or, in other words, there is not the faintest chance of there ever being an American language as apart from English. The daily intercommunication of telegraph, telephone, literature, and the press fuses all forms of "English" toward one and the broadcast and the talking pictures even fuse the toned voice. In the world of today languages cannot separate. That process belonged to epochs of distance and silence unknown now. Even then it was long. It took Latin a thousand years to turn into French.

The situation in the world today is this: There is a language called "English." It is too bad, if you like, that one country should seem to have stolen or to monopolize the claim to the name. But if the English stole the name of a language, the "Americans" stole the whole of two continents. Humble people, like the Canadians, and the Eskimos, have to live in "America" and speak "English," without fretting about it.

English is spoken by the people in England; is also spoken by the Scots, by the unredeemed Irish, the Australians—a lot of other people than Americans. Who speaks it best, no one knows; it's a matter of taste. Personally I think I like best the speech of a cultivated Scot, and perhaps least a certain high-grade English which calls a railroad a "wailwoad." I myself talk Ontario English; I don't admire it, but it's all I can do; anything is better than affectation.

Now by slang is meant the unceasing introduction into language of new phrases, and especially new nouns as names for things. There is no doubt that this peculiar fermentation of language has reached in America higher proportions than ever known anywhere else. For example—and my authority here is Mr. Eric Partridge, who cannot be wrong—a test was taken not long ago in a Wisconsin high school to see how many different words the boys and girls employed to express a low opinion of a person. Their list reads, mutt, bonehead, guy, carp, highbrow, tightwad, grafter, hayseed, hot-air artist, rube, tough-nut, chump and peanut. Perhaps they thought of more after they got home; these no doubt were only some of the things they called their teachers.

Many people, without being students of language, have observed the extraordinary number of ways in which American slang can indicate that a man has had too much drink. The chief authority on the subject (I refer to American slang and don't want to be ambiguous), H. L. Mencken, gives a partial list, brought up to 1923, and including *piffed, fiddled, spiflicated, tanked, snooted, stewed, ossified, slopped, jiggered, edged, loaded, het up, frazzled, jugged, soused, cornered,* and *jogged.*

Slang passes as it comes. It lives only when it deserves to live, when the word has something about it that does a real service. In the Wisconsin students' list above I can detect only two words that look permanent, *guy* and *highbrow. Guy* is a word with a history; it comes down to us from poor Guy Fawkes (Guido Faukes), tortured and executed for trying to blow up the English Parliament. His "Fifth of November" crime was kept alive in memory —still is—by toting around a tattered figure on a stick in a procession with the cry, "Oh, please to remember the fifth of November,

with gunpowder, treason and plot." So the word came to mean
a tattered-looking person and then just a queer-looking person, like
a professor. From that it began to mean just a person: *I was out
with another guy last night.*

The fact is we are always hard up for neutral words to mean
"just a person"; each new one gets spoiled and has to be replaced.
Be careful how you call a woman a "woman," and a "lady" is apt
to be worse; don't call a Frenchman an "individual," or an Englishman a "fellow." Hence the need for "guy," which will gradually
rise from ridicule to respectability, as already indicated. At some
future British coronation the Archbishop of Canterbury will say
to the Queen, "Will you take this guy to be your husband?" And
for all we know the Queen will answer, "Sez-you."

The other word, *highbrow,* will live for another reason. We
need it. It is a little different from *intellectual, learned, cultivated.*
It started like most slang as a brilliant image, or metaphor, taken
from the sweeping forehead, smooth as an egg, of a Shakespeare or
a Hall Caine. But, with perhaps a change of spelling, the thought
of *brow* will disappear and we shall use the term naturally and
effectively—*a highbrow audience,* the *opinion of highbrows,* etc.

The making of slang is, as I say, a sort of living process of language like the scum on wine. Without it there is no wine, no life,
no fermentation. Later on, the scum passes as dust and dregs and
leaves behind the rich fluid of the wine. A language that has ceased
to throw off slang has ceased to live. Thus came all our language.
Every syllable of it since the dawn of speech has been rolled over
and over in endless renewal. Our oldest words, our oldest names,
were once bright with the colors of the morning, striking some new
metaphor that brought into full relief the image of the thing seen.
Centuries ago some Roman called his fellow-Roman's head a
"pot" and put the word *testa* (tete) into the French language. His
genius for seeing resemblances was no greater than that of his
American successor who perceived that the human head was a
bean.

Now, the process of creating slang is not confined to America.
But I think the fermenting, slang-making process is livelier far in
America than in England. This would seem to be the consequence
of setting a language in a new country—with new lives, new scenes
to turn it to, and with the debris of other languages jostling
beside it. Under the wide canopy of heaven above the prairies a

preacher became a *sky-pilot.* In England he remained, among other things, an *incumbent,* still sitting there. A newcomer in the West was a *tenderfoot* or a *greenhorn,* a locomotive an *ironhorse,* and so on. Little snips of foreign idiom like the *something else again* of German, and *I should worry* of Yiddish, came snuggling into the language. *Yes, we have no bananas* carries with it the whole Mediterranean migration.

This process of change, like invention itself, became much more conscious in America than in England. What the English did for lazy convenience or by accident, the Americans did on purpose. Hence American slang contains a much greater percentage of cleverness than English. A lot of English slang words are just abbreviations. To call a professional at cricket a *pro,* or breakfast *brekker,* or political economy *pol. econ.,* saves times but that is all. To call a pair of trousers *bags* is a step up; there is a distinct intellectual glow of comparison. But it is only twilight as compared with such American effects as *lounge-lizard, rubber-neck, sugar-daddy, tangle-foot,* and *piece of calico.*

It is, moreover, a peculiar merit of American slang that a lot of it has the quality of vitality—vital force of renewed life. Take such words as a *hideout* and *frame-up,* or a *tie-up* (on a railway). To make these involves the process of *starting over again,* forming language from the beginning. Compare *sob-stuff, fade-out, send-off, side track,* and a host of others.

Everything, as the French say, has the defects of its merits. American slang forces the pace, and hence a lot of it *is* forced, pointless, of no literary or linguistic value. Especially tiresome is the supposed slang of the criminal class, as used in crime novels to heighten the reader's terror. Everyone recognizes such language, as *See here, pal, if the narks grab you for doing in that moll, the beak will send you up, see, and you'll burn.*

I don't know whether any people really use this stuff. I hope not. If they must be criminals, they might at least talk like gentlemen. But in any case English crime stories often run to the same kind of stuff; indeed I am not sure just where the words above belong.

But no one need be afraid that slang will really hurt our language, here or in England. It cannot. There is no dictatorship behind it. Words and phrases live only on their worth; they survive only on their merits. Nor does slang tend to separate America and England. As a matter of fact, the rising generation in England

reach out eagerly for American slang. If that means they're not rising but sinking, it's too bad. But anyway we'll sink together.

So much for the toleration of slang as bad language turning into
good, or dying from its very badness. What are we to say of bad
language in the other sense, the kind that really is bad? Are we to
put it in or leave it out? When we write a story our characters, if
they are what are called "red-blooded" men and women, are apt to
get profane; and even if they are thin-blooded they are apt to get
nasty, in fact the thinner, the nastier. The problem which all writers of fiction have to try to solve, and none have solved, yet, is how
to swear in print. Some writers of today think that they can solve
the problem by ignoring it—just go ahead and swear. We open the
pages of a typical novel and our eyes bounce off with a start at
the expression . . . *You miserable bastard!* . . .

This is not said to the reader. It is what the hero says to, or rather
throws at the villain, who has said something unbecoming in the
presence of a girl, something that a girl ought not to hear. The
hero is a splendid fellow. He has *guts*. The book says so. In fact
that's why the girl likes him. It says, "She threw her arms about his
neck and pressed her slim body close to him. 'You have guts,' she
murmured." You see, she herself is so awfully slim that naturally
—well, you get the idea. If not, you can read it all for yourself in
any new book, under such a title as *Angel Whispers*, or *Undertones*
or something like that, on the outside. On the inside it's full of
guts. The new books are like that.

But we are not talking about any particular book but about the
problem that is suggested—the question of how to deal with profanity in fiction—how can you swear in print?

We must, I fear, dismiss at once the old-fashioned Victorian expedient of telling the reader that one of the characters in the story
said something "with a terrible oath." That won't do now-a-days.
We want to hear it. What was it? This formula was the one used
in the pirate stories written for boys and girls.

For example:

"Har! har!" shouted the pirate with a foul oath. "They are in our
power."

"They certainly are," said the second pirate with an oath fouler
than the first.

"I'll say so," said the third pirate with an oath fouler still—a lot fouler.

The fourth pirate remained silent. He couldn't make it.

Now that won't do. We'll judge for ourselves how foul the oath is. If you can't say it, just whisper it. It's got to be pretty foul to get past us.

And I need hardly say, that it won't do to fall back on that old-fashioned trick that is used in novels "laid" in the Middle Ages —I mean the trick of making up a lot of fanciful stuff and calling it swearing.

Here's how it runs:

"Odd's piddlekins," cried Sir Gonderear, "by my halidome, thou art but a foul catiff. Let me not, or I'll have at you."

"Nay, by the belly of St. Mark," answered the Seneschal, "I fear thee not, false paynim . . . Have one on me!" (Or words to that effect.)

That was all right, as we shall see in the discussion of historical romances, from Sir Walter Scott. It won't do now. Such an epithet as *foul catiff* has been replaced by *you big stiff*, and a *paynim* is a *lobster*.

There used to be a special kind of swearing reserved by convention for the use of sailors in sea stories. "Shiver my timbers!" cried the bosun, "You son of a swob! Lift a finger, you lobscouse, and I'll knock the dead lights out of you." After which he spat a quid—a *quid pro quo*—into the lee scuppers.

Fenimore Cooper is a case in point. The public of his day was too strict in its ideas to allow a sailor even to shiver his timbers in print. A glance at any of Cooper's famous sea stories will reveal such a terrible profanity as d_____l, apparently hinting at *devil*, and d_____e, which may be interpreted with a thrill as "damme." Oddly enough, in Cooper's day the word "bloody" had not yet taken on in American its later offensive connotation, so that Cooper was at liberty to write, "D_____e," said the bosun, "what the d_____l does the bloody fellow mean?" But we may leave that to Fenimore Cooper. At present you couldn't navigate even a car ferry with a truck on it on that language.

You see, it was much easier to get away with such things a hundred years ago, at the beginning of modern fiction, than it is now. Take the case of Charles Dickens. He couldn't, of course, put real swearing into his books, and anyway he wouldn't have wanted to. So he set up a sort of jargon that he took straight out of the blood and thunder of the cheap London theater of which, as an impecunious youth, he was inordinately fond.

An example is seen in the language used by Bill Sykes, the murderer, in *Oliver Twist*. There is a scene, in which he is just going to do the murder—no, has just done it and is trying to escape. A child has got in the way and Sykes says to his associates, "Open the door of some place where I can lock this screeching hell babe. . . ." Why he didn't "bump the child off," I forget just now. The present point is the language he used. He would have had just as good a phrase for bumping it.

Compare the *hell's accursed,* and the *foul fiend,* and such mild phrases. With objurations of that sort you sometimes couldn't tell whether the characters were cursing or praying; in fact in origin the two are one.

That reminds me of the language I once heard used by a man showing a "picture panorama"—the kind of thing they used to have long ago before the real "pictures" replaced it. In these pictures, when the successive scenes were shown, there was a man who did the talking. "Here you see this," and "now you see that . . ." and so on, as the scene went by. The man I speak of was showing a scene representing a Swiss peasant, getting swallowed up in a morass, or nearly swallowed up, till an angel appeared to save him. I was quite unable, and I still am, to distinguish whether the Swiss peasant and the angel were praying or swearing. In fact I don't think the picture man had thought it out. He took a chance.

His talk ran:

> Here you see the Swiss Alps. In the foreground is one of those dangerous more-asses, where the treacherous surface, with all the aspect of firm ground, offers no real support. Here you see a Swiss peasant. Look! He is stepping out on the more-ass. The ground yields beneath his feet. He moves forward more rapidly to escape. He begins to sink. He tries in vain to withdraw his feet. He is slowly sinking to his doom. Look, he lifts his hands and cries aloud: "Oh, Heaven," he says, "get me out of this more-ass. Oh, God, this is damnedest more-ass. Christ! this is awful."

His prayer is heard. An angel appears, bending out from the clouds, her hand outstretched. "You poor soul," she says in a voice vibrating with pity. "You poor nut, you poor bastard . . . give me your hand, and come up." She takes him to her bosom, and he is saved.

So he would be, of course.

But to turn back again to advice to writers. Don't think you can get away with swearing by putting something very close to it, something nearly as good and much cheaper, by a shift of a letter or two. Some writers try, for instance, to use "ruddy" to stand for "bloody." This is used especially in the mouths of English army sergeants and such. It is supposed to give a barrackroom touch. But it is really just a left-over piece of Victorian evasion. Rudyard Kipling used this trick, not so stale in his hey-day as it is now. One recalls his Soudanese Negro Fuzzy-wuzzy, who was described as a "big, black, bounding beggar, who broke a British Square."

That's all right. Fuzzy-wuzzy was pretty close to that, but not just exactly that.

And here's another thing:

Don't try to get around the difficulty by turning the profanity into strokes (– – – – –), or making it into asterisks (***). That's just feeble.

Asterisks and dots and strokes are hopeless. You can't *swear* with those things. They won't read right . . . Read aloud, as they are, they would turn the pirate story into:

"Three asterisks!" shouted the Pirate.
"Four," shouted the next.
"I'll make it six," yelled a third, adding a stroke and a colon.

A person still young and inexperienced might think—surely there is no problem here. The true method would be to write down the very words that an actual person would actually use, to put the swearing in the book exactly as people swear it. But that, of course, would never do. Leaving out all question of whether the law allows it, art forbids it. It wouldn't sound right. Try it. Put down a set of four profane, obscene words—not samples, but the whole set used in what is called a string of profanity. It would sound awful for one paragraph, flat and stale after two, and beyond that utterly nauseating—in fact just like swearing. And you know how that sounds.

The only advice that can be given to the writer is, don't go further than others do. In fact, keep just a little behind them. If they say "guts," you say "bowels of compassion."

~ C ~

suggestions for discussion

1. The subject of coherence was introduced in Chapter Two and is brought up again in this chapter. In the earlier lesson, the emphasis was put on coherence within the paragraph; here it is on coherence between and among paragraphs. In this latter sense, coherence is the mortar that cements the building blocks that are the paragraphs into a sensible, effective arrangement.

Now, with reference to the first eight or ten paragraphs of Bergen Evans' article, see how frequently you find Evans repeating in one paragraph some of the important words and ideas used in the preceding one. For example, the second paragraph, which is very short, repeats *language, slang, standard,* and the idea of the absorption of slang words by the standard language—all of which appear in the first paragraph.

2. Select a paragraph that appears toward the middle of any of the three selections above. Now, see how frequently you find the author repeating words and ideas (including pronouns to refer to words and ideas already identified) that occurred two, three, or four paragraphs earlier.

Clearly such a practice of extended repetition is of great value in keeping the reader's mind centered on what is important. It is a device that you should practice using.

3. None of the authors represented in this chapter makes use of a paragraph in which he says in so many words, "In the pages that follow, I shall discuss such-and-such a matter. In doing so, I shall first treat so-and-so and then proceed to this-and-that."

Select a passage of four to six paragraphs in whichever selection you wish; write a paragraph introducing the passage. Remember that your purpose is to add to the coherence of the passage.

4. In Stephen Leacock's essay, "So much for the toleration of slang as bad language turning into good, or dying from its very badness" is about as good an example as can be found in our three selections of the transitional paragraph. Above it the author has been discusing slang as a process of growth in English; below it he discusses the use of "bad words"—profane and obscene ones—that occur in the speech of many persons and that the writer must sometimes repeat, represent, or suggest—or else look bad in dodging them.

See if you can identify other examples, perhaps less striking, of the transitional paragraph in any one or more of the selections that you have read in this chapter.

5. Identify a point in one of the selections where a transitional paragraph *could* have been used but wasn't. Now, write an appropriate transitional paragraph for the passage that you have identified.

~ D ~

suggestions for writing

1. Of the three selections in this chapter, those by Evans and Mencken are extended definitions of slang. Evans went about his task of definition by considering the several aspects of slang—the enormous amount of it, historical instances of slang that has entered the standard language, the secret purpose of some of it, etc.— each in its turn. Mencken works chiefly by citing dictionaries and scholars and by examining critically their assertions about slang.

Select one or two of the characteristics of slang that are recognized by both writers and, in your own words, write a short piece in which you combine their methods. Thus, your paper, when finished, should identify a prominent characteristic, or two characteristics, of slang; it should illustrate; and it should draw from Mencken those authoritative works that have recognized the same feature(s) of slang; it should also contain an element of your own criticism— or evaluation—of the aptness of the observations expressed in your sources.

2. Consider all three of the selections on slang as you look up in your dictionary the long lists of entries under *kick, hard,* and *blue.* Using what you have learned of the nature of slang and your own judgment—with, of course, any special instructions given by your teacher—write a paper of six to ten paragraphs in which you discuss the difficulty of deciding what is slang and what is not. (Notice that at one time *blue* for "sea," as in "The ship sailed on the blue" must have been slang or something very much like it.) You will find that the lists that you are to look up contain many entries that illustrate the thin border between slang and the standard language.)

3. At least one of the desk dictionaries commonly owned by college students calls *three-bagger* (a triple or three-base hit in baseball) slang but does not place any restrictive or status label on *four-bagger* (a home run in baseball); another calls both slang; another calls neither slang; a fourth lists *two-bagger* and *three-bagger,* but not *four-bagger,* as baseball terms but without calling them slang or colloquial. Drawing on what you know of slang, write a paper in which you advocate the practice of one of four dictionaries or of whatever dictionary you own.

4. What is your opinion on how a writer should represent profane and obscene language? Express your view in a short essay. (You may wish to treat profane language as one thing and obscenity as another.)

In any papers you write in these and following exercises, be sure to practice what you have learned about coherence among paragraphs.

~ E ~

additional readings

Roberts, Paul, *Understanding English* (New York: Harper & Row, Publishers, 1958), Ch. 24, "Slang and Its Relatives."

Myers, L. M., *Guide to American English*, 3rd ed. (Englewood Cliffs, N.J.: Prentice-Hall, Inc., 1962), Ch. 2, "Areas of Usage."

Hinton, Norman D., "The Language of Jazz Musicians," *Publications of the American Dialect Society*, No. 30 (1958), 38-48. Partially reprinted in Charlton Laird and Robert M. Gorrell, *English as Language: Backgrounds, Development, Usage* (New York: Harcourt, Brace & World, Inc., 1961), 259-61.

Chapter Eight

~ A ~

the effective beginning

The term used to describe the rhetorical element to be discussed in this chapter is "introduction." But whatever the terminology, we are concerned now with the most effective way to begin a piece of writing. An effective beginning should have built into it some quality that is attractive enough to make the reader want to continue reading what you have written. It may be true that what you have written is so important and vital that the contents are, in fact, attraction enough to the reader. However, if this is so, you have the greater urgency in giving it an introduction that may appeal to your reader, for the better your writing and the more cogent your thinking, the less you should be content with seeing them ignored. Drawing attention to them is the chief purpose of your introduction.

Besides serving as a kind of lure, an introduction is a statement of the subject matter of your paper. What has just been said may very well be a statement of the obvious, but it is not uncommon to find examples of the writer's forgetting to tell the reader just what he is getting into. Sometimes the omission of a statement about a subject may be purposeful, but surprise openings in practical exposition are usually incongruous.

How much of the subject must be written about? How long must the introduction be? These are unanswerable questions. But the beginning should be so attractive that it will keep the reader from dropping what you have written and going on to other matters, and it should present enough of your subject and purpose to allow him to gather a minimum of information from the very beginning of the first paragraph.

~ B ~

the english language in school

IGNORANCE BUILDS A LANGUAGE *

John S. Kenyon

A chemist whose training had been limited to the dusty retorts and the alcohol lamp in a village high-school laboratory of the 1890's would get short shrift if he applied for a position in a great industrial plant; nor would a quack bonesetter get a look-in at a position in a modern clinic. Yet in our American system of training in the use of the mother tongue, which Sir Henry Newbolt in his distinguished Report on British Education has declared to be the one essential foundation of national education, we are employing by the hundreds, in this country today, teachers of English whose scientific training in the language is fairly comparable to that of the aforesaid chemist or quack doctor. A distinguished English Inspector of Schools, Mr. George Sampson, has stated that "A teacher of speech untrained in phonetics is as useless as a doctor untrained in anatomy," and every teacher of English is a teacher of speech. It would be safe to estimate that less than one per cent of the American teachers of English have had any training in phonetics worth mentioning—that is to say, in the indispensable elements of their subject.

* Reprinted from *The American Scholar,* Volume 7, Number 4, Autumn, 1938. Copyright © 1938 by the United Chapters of Phi Beta Kappa. By permission of the publishers.

And not only in the present teaching and use of the English language, but in the development of our language, ignorance has been at least as important a factor as knowledge. I am not thinking of the inert ignorance of the uneducated about their language—that indeed has had a profound and on the whole a progressive effect on language, manifesting itself in an almost miraculously intricate and regular operation of known laws of linguistic behavior. I am thinking rather of the linguistic ignorance of the cultivated, ignorance of a growing body of knowledge; of that aggressive ignorance which adopts the technique of knowledge and is powerfully influencing the language we use.

It is not surprising, in the present state of English teaching in American schools and colleges, that among the educated there should be a profound and widespread ignorance of the nature and normal operation of the linguistic processes, past and present, that govern the English we speak and write. Fortunately this does not prevent the literate from enjoying the use of good English; it is when this ignorance dons the armor of the critic that the fact becomes important. Swift's proposal "for Correcting, Improving, and Ascertaining the English language" and for "fixing our language for ever" furnishes a good instance. It would be hard to exaggerate the lack of comprehension here exhibited of the nature and processes of the growth of English from the earliest times. For though some of Swift's predecessors and followers recognized the fact that no living language can be fixed and secured from change, none of them had any adequate idea of the regularity and method of its constant growth or of the function of this unobserved growth in the formation of cultivated idiom.

Swift was followed by a group of grammarians and lexicographers earnestly engaged in rescuing the English language from imminent ruin—Lowth, Dr. Johnson, Campbell, Blair, Priestly, Lindley Murray, Walker, and others. Some of the basic assumptions that governed the thinking of these men were:

(1) Grammar was a system of logic, most perfectly exhibited in Latin. Until recently *grammar* had meant exclusively Latin grammar, a sense preserved in *grammar school* and in our grammatical terminology.

(2) English had little grammar of its own and had to be subjected, therefore, to a perfect external grammatical system. This is reflected in Johnson's remark, "English has been subjected so little

and so lately to grammar." Out of this assumption grew the usual definition of grammar: "The art of speaking and writing the English language with propriety" (Murray). There is a great gulf fixed between this concept of grammar and the scientific concept casually stated by the late American scholar Edward S. Sheldon: "Grammar is a description of the facts of language."

(3) From the conception of grammar as an external logical system applicable to a language followed the notion that all forms of a language are "correct" or "incorrect"—that there is, in the universe somewhere, an inherently correct way of saying or writing everything. This simplified the difficult task of adjusting usage to theories of correctness: if great writers violated "grammar" they were simply wrong. Therefore there was no hesitation in correcting the "mistakes" of Shakespeare, Milton, Addison, Swift, and the rest.

(4) Since in the eighteenth century there was no science of linguistics, no body of knowledge of the principles of the growth and structure of English, ideas about the laws of pronunciation (especially in its relations to the written language) were of the vaguest. In his dictionary of 1791 John Walker dealt, more fully than any one up to his time, with pronunciation. He based his treatment on the letters of the alphabet, a practice followed in dictionaries to this day. He shared the views of his predecessors that the letters were the "elements" of English; that they had "powers" of sound, as if they were seed from which words sprouted. Of the word *quay* he says, "Sometimes seen written *key;* for if we cannot bring the pronunciation to the spelling, it is looked upon as some improvement to bring the spelling to the pronunciation: a most pernicious practice in language." There was little conception of English as a living language, to which spelling was a mere incident in its long history.

Most of these conceptions are still more or less current and in the main control the views of the educated on "correct" grammar and pronunciation. It is true that the scientific attitude toward English has made remarkable strides in America in the last ten years. There are encouraging signs that the scientific point of view is penetrating to the great body of teachers of English in schools and colleges. But the general body of the literate is not likely to keep pace with the scientific advance in their language. As a result of this perennial ignorance our English is constantly, and will continue to be, shaped to a considerable extent by the ignorant efforts of the cultivated to improve it.

Since it is solely usage that not only accepts or rejects but first creates grammatical forms, syntactical constructions, meanings of words, and pronunciations (though this is ignored in practice by thousands who have theoretically accepted it since Horace stated it), the scientific observer of language meets no fact more frequently than that many usages and pronunciations now unquestioned had their origin in ignorant blunders—i.e., in violations of usages valid at the time. For instance before the fourteenth century *you* was only a plural objective pronoun. By a misunderstanding of certain ambiguous constructions (as *if you like* "if it please you") *you* came to be accepted as a nominative (as *you are strangers*). By another shift *you* also came to be used for one person. Usage, and usage alone, has now made *you* just as "grammatically" singular and nominative as it was plural and objective. This was not accomplished without protest. Professor Fries quotes a beautiful sample from George Fox (1660) objecting to singular *you:* "O Vulgar Professors and Teachers, that speaks Plural when they should Singular . . . Come you Priests and Professors, have you not learnt your Accidence?" Here Fox condemns one construction while using another equally open to objection. He not only uses *speaks* as plural but shows no hesitation in using *you* as nominative, though he could have argued just as soundly that it was only objective as he did that it was only plural. His criticism is typical of much of today's. He attacked what suited his purpose and ignored the other accepted usages equally open to attack.

A whole series of blunders in verb form has given us the forms *baked, carved, crept, stepped, bound, bit, spoke, have sat, have shone, have stood,* and some 100 others, mistakes once parallel to *knowed, drinked, have rode, have rang, have ate, have fell,* etc. Some of them were recognized as blunders; but inexorable usage took advantage of the general linguistic ignorance of the cultivated, so that we now declare *have sat* "grammatical" and should oppose any attempt to restore the regular form *have seaten* as vigorously as we now deny place to Shakespeare's *have spoke,* Gray's "Elegy Wrote in a Country Churchyard" or the historically correct *have went.*

In contrast to adopting mistakes, we also refuse admittance to usages that accord with the laws of English, in our ignorance overlooking parallel usages that we accept without question. This is well illustrated in the field of semantics. Acting on the baseless assumption that a word can have but one "proper" meaning, the critic stands like Canute to keep back the tide of shifts and new adaptations of meaning which mark a living language in the midst of busy life that uses words for its own purposes and not to please the purist. Moreover the "proper" meaning to which the critic would restrict us is itself usually a shift from former "proper" meanings. A recent letter to a literary journal asserts "Know all men by these presents that this word, *alibi*, should never be used for the word *excuse*. This word, *alibi*, has a very specific, limited, and legalistic denotation that does not permit its being used as a synonym for *excuse* in any connection whatsoever." Whether the extended figurative meaning of *alibi* is yet general is here incidental. The statement is of interest as showing that the writer's mind, like that of hundreds of the educated, has no place in its scheme for such shifts of meaning. Have no other legal terms become figurative and generalized? Who now hesitates to use *entail* in a generalized sense?

The irony of this attitude is shown in Swift's phrase itself—"ascertaining and fixing." To the younger generation some attention to context is required to insure the "right" meaning of *fix*, and it is doubtful whether the majority of the educated would at first glance know Swift's meaning of *ascertain*; they might wonder, in the proposal for "correcting, improving, and ascertaining," why the *ascertaining* should come last.

A precious list of examples of this Canutish attempt to prevent words from adapting their meanings to new conditions may be seen in R. G. White's *Words and their Uses,* a once admired and—alas! —still influential book. See particularly his objections to *animal* (in the sense "lower animal"), *catch* (a train), *dirt* ("earth"—as in Shakespeare, Milton, Bunyan), *execute, ice-water, real estate, rooster.* Two samples are typical: *"Consider,"* he says, "is perverted from its true meaning by most of those who use it." Among the "most" were standard writers of the past 400 years; but actual cultivated usage stands no chance in the presence of a "true meaning." Again, he made the usual objection to the conversational *have got* for *have* on grounds of "true meaning" (for no well-informed person denies its currency among the cultivated), refusing acceptance to an established idiom while ignorantly accepting parallel meanings open to the same objection—for every speaker who uses *shall, may, can, dare, must, ought,* is employing the same shift of meaning in the preterit-present verb that has taken place in *have got* for *have;* and *ought* has done the thing twice over under the noses of the purists. "But that was long ago" they say; "we mustn't let it happen again." This kind of criticism of meaning is still popular with the educated. "Oh, you are Professor Syntax, are you? Well, now, tell me: what about this misuse of the word *healthy?* A climate is *healthful,* isn't it?" Desiccated instances of such theoretical distinctions of meaning not supported by general use are scattered throughout the body of American teachers as part of their stock in trade, and their influence on usage is considerable. It would be a healthy exercise for all such critics to ponder the prefatory article on Signification in the great *Oxford Dictionary*—and better still to study the scores of different meanings therein exhibited from the living language of common words like *get, go, see.*

In pronunciation—the basis of all living language—our English teaching leaves us ignorant of such elementary facts as the nature and formation of the sounds we use, the simplest laws and most constantly operative facts of sound-change, the relation of spelling-forms to the living language, and the historical development and prevalence of standard types of speech with their interrelations. Errors arising from this ignorance have been adopted, and usage—to which error is as good grist as truth—has fixed them in accepted English. We are horrified at *drownd* for *drown, gownd* for *gown, acrost* for *across* and *onced* for *once;* but we have accepted the *d* in *astound, sound,* and *thunder,* and the *t* in *against* and *midst,* which originated in the same "mistakes."

If Tennyson had known anything about historical sound-change he might not have insisted on pronouncing *knowledge* like *know,* adopting a theory of earlier generations. Walker (1791) partly knew the principle involved and remarked,

> Some speakers, who had the regularity of their language at heart, . . . with heroic fortitude have opposed the multitude by pronouncing the first syllable of this word as it is heard in the verb to *know.* The pulpit and the bar have for some years given a sanction to this pronunciation; but the senate and the stage hold out inflexibly against it; and the nation at large seems insensible of the improvement.

Preoccupation with writing and print has made it hard for the average educated person to think habitually of the English language as pursuing its intricate development and adaptation to the needs of life independently, in the main, of letters and spelling. He does not distinguish without an effort between the traditional utterance of his language and its variable, inconsistent, and irrational spelling-forms. So, while usage has in the main accepted the traditional oral development, spelling-pronunciation has played a larger and larger part in the formation of standard speech; and usage accepts this spelling-pronunciation as freely as the traditional.

Tacit assumption of the authoritative nature of spelling leads the pots of spelling to black the kettles of tradition. When a large group of words like *honor, humble, horrible, hospital,* etc. came from Old French into English they had had no *h*-sound for centuries. But since they were often spelt with *h* (in imitation of Latin), the literate, taking the usual view that the spelling-form prevailing in their time was the word itself, began to sound the *h*. Hence one by one most of these words have acquired the *h* sound, and the historical pronunciations *'umble, 'orrible, 'ospital* etc. are material for caricature. Only *hour, honest, honor, heir* have escaped this pious reform. Of course those in which the *h* ceased to be spelt, as *able, arbor,* have acquired no *h* sound. Our habit of putting the cart before the horse is seen in the *clerk-clark* controversy. We blame the English for giving the traditional *ar* sound to *Derby, clerk, Berkshire* etc. while we ignorantly accept the same *ar* sound normally developed from the same source (the *e* sound as in *very*) in numerous words like *carve, far, smart, star* etc. So spelling-bound are we that we are content to sound *ar* if it is spelt with *a;* but so sacred is the now irrational spelling *Derby, clerk* etc. that instead of also adopting the correct spelling *ar* in the few remaining words we enshrine the bad spelling and condemn the historically correct pronunciation. As Dr. Fuhrken says, we are willing to mispronounce words just to show that we know their miserable spelling. The spellbinders have their shibboleths, such as *often.* The letter *t* in its spelling, silent long since by regular sound-change, has been canonized and the schoolteacher reverences it accordingly; but she continues to omit the *t* sound in *soften, listen, fasten, bristle, castle,* and many others; and likewise (horrible!) in *last night, next door, mustn't,* and others, though she is unaware of it and might deny it.

Spelling-pronunciation as a corrective is fragmentary and inconsistent. Its practitioners pounce on the scattered victims that fall within their linguistic range, leaving the unobserved words of the same class unregenerate. Thus usage has accepted the *o* sound in *combat* but keeps the original *u* sound in *come, love, honey, some, front* etc. It has adopted the *th* sound in *theater, throne, Arthur, Elizabeth, Katherine, Martha, Nathan, Theodore,* in which *th* formerly spelt the *t* sound; but it keeps the original *t* sound in *Thomas, Thompson, Esther, Thames,* and all the nicknames *Art, Betty, Kate, Marty, Nate, Ted. Anthony* seems fated to a *th* sound in spite of dictionaries and of *Mark Antony* and *Tony. Anthonio* in *The Merchant of Venice* has preserved the *t* sound by a changed spelling.

Few spelling-pronouncers have any idea how upsetting a consistent application of their principle to the living language would be. They might hesitate to apply it to *heard-beard, treat-great-threat, done-tone-gone, early-nearly, eight-height, goes-does-shoes,—* the list is endless. But after usage has unquestionably sanctioned a spelling-pronunciation contrary to former good use, it must then be accepted as correct. Ignorant as many such changes were in their inception, usage has in fact adopted many of them. This impressive company, bastard offspring of literacy and linguistic ignorance, mingle on equal terms with the legitimate children of phonetic law and say "Don't despise us; you will beget others like us who will be received into good society as we have been." This is a safe prediction under an educational system in which uninformed legislators compel prospective teachers of English to spend their time of preparation bandying "quartiles" and "percentiles" in place of getting aware of the facts of the language they are to teach; when neither the teachers nor most other educated persons know even the names of the scholars who have slowly established these facts; when a leading news magazine does not mention the sudden death and irreparable loss of the greatest historical grammarian of the English language.

The most influential linguistic ignorance is ignorance of usage itself. To many of the educated who accept the authority of usage in theory the statement "It is not in good use" means, practically, "I disapprove it." It is not easy to ascertain the actual usage of large bodies of the educated on specific points. There is a temptation to substitute the ignorant claims of quack treatises on "Correct English," "Write it Right" etc. for the actual practice of the cultivated. A Mopsa-like faith in print inhibits the one needful question, "What linguistic acquirements give this writer a claim to speak?" Still, there is by now so large an accumulated body of expert observation on past and current English usage that on most points good usage is ascertainable. The work of Sweet, Storm, Jespersen, Wright, Wyld, Poutsma, Luick, McKnight, Baugh, and many more, and especially that vast storehouse of first-hand information on usage, the *Oxford Dictionary,* are now available in first-class libraries. Above all, if his eyes are open for them, the educated reader can observe disputed points for himself in the best writing. He cannot read far in British novels without discovering that in cultivated speech there is no hesitation in saying "Who did you meet there?" or "Everybody got what they wanted."

A clear instance of the disparity between theoretical and actual good usage is the use of a final preposition. The objection to it never was warranted by standard practice. As Curme has shown, Dryden gave currency to the heresy on the above-mentioned false assumption that Latin practice is valid for English. Only a few tried to follow Dryden. The great monuments of English since before the time of Chaucer have freely used this ancient and effective construction, which accords with other progressive features of English idiom. Objection to it is stock in trade of second-rate teachers and of manuals of usage; it keeps bobbing up among the semi-literate. An occasional good writer ruins his sentences by avoiding it on theory instead of following his sense of style. Thus I find in *The Forsyte Saga* "Of what she was thinking," "Turning to see at what she was looking"—instead of the normal "What she was thinking of" and "What she was looking at." Especially in the carefully doctored English of radio announcers one hears "A good place in which to live," "An object for which to work," in contrast to the simple dignity of the biblical "bought the potter's field, to bury strangers in," Hamlet's "fly to others that we know not of," Burke's "the sphere she just began to move in," Washington's "the command I am honored with," or Lowell's "soil good to be born on, good to live on, good to die for and to be buried in." Every real master of English style knows that the final preposition is not only anciently established but is compact, simple, natural, and effective. Ignorance has not succeeded in eradicating it and is not likely to do so. In Milton's phrase, "What a fine conformity would it starch us all into!"

But in another instance a baseless theory, founded on the same fallacy of a Latin model, has gained complete acceptance in English—avoidance of a double negative. Not a single good reason except the tyranny of usage can be given for not using two or more negatives to strengthen negation. It is wholly in accord with linguistic principle, being in the best of use in many other languages, as formerly in English, and is extremely effective, as in Chaucer's famous four-negative sentence. It is still in full vigor in folk speech, where its great value keeps it alive; and it frequently occurs in disguise in cultivated use. The case is typical of my thesis: the objection regularly offered by the critic is the false one—that two negatives necessarily make an affirmative; not the real one—that usage has rejected it, decisively, though ignorantly.

Thus, unawareness of what actual cultivated usage is goes along with failure to recognize its decisive function in every case. The occupation of the teacher and the scholar of English becomes more and more the dissemination of the facts of the language in past and present living usage. The need of information on the part of both teacher and public dwarfs all the panaceas perennially offered for improving our English. A fine group of young American, English, Scandinavian, and Dutch scholars are attacking the task with vigor and breadth of mind, and with marked success; but toward a general acquaintance with the facts indispensable for intelligent decisions hardly a beginning has been made.

The Social Significance of Differences in Language Practice and the Obligation of Schools *

Charles C. Fries

"English" maintains its place as the most frequently *required subject* of our school and college curriculums because of the unanimous support given it both by the general public and by education authorities. This support rests upon the general belief that the mastery of *good English* is not only the most important asset of the ambitious, but also an obligation of every good citizen. There is, however, in many quarters, a very hazy idea of the specific ele-

---

* *American English Grammar* (English Monograph No. 10, National Council of Teachers of English; New York: Appleton-Century-Crofts, Inc., 1940), Ch. I. Reprinted with the permission of The National Council of Teachers of English and Charles C. Fries.

ments which make *good English*. A great deal of vigorous controversy ignores all the larger problems of effective communication and centers attention upon the criteria to be applied in judging the acceptability of particular words and language forms. All of this controversy is direct evidence that there do exist many differences in the language practice of English speaking people; for no controversy could arise and no choice be offered unless differing language forms presented themselves in the actual practice of English speech. It is the purpose of this chapter to set forth the general character of these differences and to analyze their significance in relation to the obligations resting upon our schools. The chapter as a whole will therefore present the principles underlying this whole investigation and the point of view which has determined its material and method.

Underlying many of the controversies concerning words and language forms is a very common attitude which I shall call here the "conventional point of view." Frequently stated explicitly, sometimes only implied, it appears in most handbooks and manuals of correct English, in grammars and rhetorics, in educational tests and measures, and in many editorials of the press. This conventional point of view assumes not only that there is a correctness in English language as absolute as that in elementary mathematics but also that the measures of this correctness are very definite rules. The following quotations are typical:

"A college professor rises to defend 'ain't' and 'It is me' as good English. The reed upon which he leans is majority usage. . . . 'Ain't,' as a legitimate contraction of 'am not,' would not require defense or apology if it were not for widespread misuse. Unfortunately the same cannot be said of 'it is me.' This solecism could not be given the odor of good English by a plurality as great as Warren G. Harding rolled up in 1920. . . . A vast amount of wretched English is heard in this country. The remedy does not lie in the repeal of the rules of grammar; but rather in a stricter and more intelligent enforcement of those rules in our schools. . . . This protest against traditional usage and the rules of grammar is merely another manifestation of the unfortunate trend of the times to lawlessness in every direction. . . . Quite as important as keeping undesirables out of the vocabulary is the maintaining of respect for the rules of grammar, which govern the formation of words into phrases and sentences. . . . Students should be taught that correct speaking is evidence of culture; and that in order to speak correctly they must master the rules that govern the use of the language." [1]

---

[1] [From an editorial in *The Detroit Free Press,* December 9, 1928.]

"Grammar consists of a series of rules and definitions. . . . Since . . . ninety-five per cent of all children and teachers come from homes or communities where incorrect English is used, nearly everyone has before him the long, hard task of overcoming habits set up early in life before he studied language and grammar in school. . . . Such people are exposed to the ridicule of those who notice the error, and the only way in which they can cure themselves is by eternal vigilance and the study of grammar." [2]

---

[2] [W. W. Charters, *Teaching the Common Branches,* rev. ed. (New York: The Macmillan Company, 1924), pp. 96, 98, 115.]

"This is a test to see how well you know correct English usage and how well you can select the *rule or principle in accordance with which a usage is correct.* In the left hand column a list of sentences is given. In each sentence there are two forms in parentheses, one correct, and the other incorrect. In the right hand column a list of rules or principles is given, some one of which applies to each sentence. . . .

Sentences	*Principles*
( ) 1. (Whom) (Who) did you meet?	a. The indirect object is in the objective case.
( ) 2. He told John and (I) (me) an interesting story.	b. The subject of the verb is in the nominative case.
	c. The object of a verb is in the objective case.

. . . Read the first sentence in Section I; then mark out the incorrect form. Read the rules in Section I, until you find one that applies to this first sentence. Place the letter of this rule in the square preceding the first sentence. . . ." [3]

"One purpose of this report is to describe and illustrate a method of constructing a grammar curriculum upon the basis of the errors of school children . . . it is apparent that the first step is to *ascer-*

---

[3] [T. J. Kirby, "Grammar Test," University of Iowa Standard Tests and Scales, Iowa City, Iowa.]

tain the rules which are broken and to determine their relative importance." [4]

The point of view expressed in these quotations, assuming as it does that certain definite rules are the necessary standards by which to measure language correctness, also repudiates *general usage* as a valid guide to acceptability, even the usage of the so-called "educated." The following quotation represents dozens of similar statements:

> "The truth is, however, that authority of general usage, or even of the usage of great writers, is not absolute in language. There is a misuse of words which can be justified by no authority, however great, and *by no usage however general.*" [5]

From this, the "conventional point of view," the problem of the differences in our language practice is a very simple one. Only two kinds of forms or usages exist—correct forms and mistakes. In general, the mistakes are thought to be corrupt forms of illegitimate meanings derived by carelessness from the correct one. In some cases a grudging acquiescence accepts some forms which are contrary to the rules when these forms are sanctioned by an overwhelming usage, but here the view remains that these forms, although established by usage, are still *incorrect* and must always be incorrect. To this point of view these incorrect forms sanctioned by usage are the "idioms" of the language. In all the matters of differing language practices, therefore, those who hold this point of view regard the obligation of the schools as perfectly clear and comparatively simple —the schools must root out the *mistakes* or *errors* and cultivate the language uses that are *correct according to the rules.*

Opposed to this "conventional point of view" is that held by the outstanding scholars in English language during the last hundred years. I shall call it here "the scientific point of view." Typical expressions of it abound.

> "In considering the use of grammar as a corrective of what are called 'ungrammatical' expressions, it must be borne in mind that

---

4 ["Minimal Essentials in Language and Grammar," *Sixteenth Yearbook of the National Society for the Study of Education* (Bloomington, Ind.: Public School Publishing Co., 1917), pp. 86-87.]

5 [R. G. White, *Words and Their Uses,* rev. ed. (Boston: Houghton Mifflin Company, 1899), p. 14.]

the rules of grammar have no value except as statements of facts: whatever is in general use in a language is for that very reason grammatically correct." [6]

"The grammar of a language is not a list of rules imposed upon its speakers by scholastic authorities, but is a scientific record of the actual phenomena of that language, written and spoken. If any community habitually uses certain forms of speech, these forms are part of the grammar of the speech of that community." [7]

"It has been my endeavor in this work to represent English Grammar not as a set of stiff dogmatic precepts, according to which some things are correct and others absolutely wrong, but as something living and developing under continual fluctuations and undulations, something that is founded on the past and prepares the way for the future, something that is not always consistent or perfect, but progressing and perfectible—in one word, human." [8]

"A Grammar book does not attempt to teach people how they ought to speak, but on the contrary, unless it is a very bad or a very old work, it merely states how, as a matter of fact, certain people do speak at the time at which it is written." [9]

In these typical expressions of "the scientific point of view" there is, first of all, a definitely stated opposition to the fundamental principle of the "conventional attitude." All of them insist that it is unsound to take the rules of grammar as the necessary norms of correct English and to set out to make all usage conform to those rules. In these expressions of the scientific view there is, also, a clear affirmation of the fundamental principle of the attitude that usage or practice is the basis of all the *correctness* there can be in language. From this, the scientific point of view, the problem presented by the differences in our language is by no means a simple one. Instead of having to deal with a mass of diverse forms which can be easily separated into the two groups of *mistakes* and *correct language* according to perfectly definite measures, the language scholar finds himself confronted by a complex range of differing

---

6 [Henry Sweet, *New English Grammar* (Oxford: Clarendon Press, 1891), I, 5.]
7 [Graltan and Currey, *One Living Language* (London: Thomas Nelson & Sons, 1925), p. 25.]
8 [Otto Jespersen, *A Modern English Grammar* (Heidelberg, 1909), I, Preface.]
9 [H. C. Wyld, *Elementary Lessons in English Grammar* (Oxford: Clarendon Press, 1925), p. 12.]

practices which must be sorted into an indefinite number of groups according to a set of somewhat indistinct criteria called "general usage." Those who hold this scientific point of view insist, therefore, that the first step in fulfilling the obligation of the schools in the matter of dealing with the English language is to record, realistically and as completely as possible, the facts of this usage.

ENGLISH AS SHE'S NOT TAUGHT *

Jacques Barzun

At an educational conference held in Vancouver last summer, leaders of the Canadian school system generally agreed that from half to three quarters of their students in the first year of college were incompetent in grammar, syntax, and analysis of thought. What was notable in the discussion was that nearly every participant used the English language with uncommon force and precision. Any looseness or jargon heard there came from the three American guests, of whom I was one. Most of our hosts—Canadian teachers, principals, supervisors, and university instructors—had obviously gone through the mill of a classical education; the chairman made a mild pun involving Latin and was rewarded with an immediate laugh. Yet they declared themselves unable to pass on their linguistic accomplishment to the present school generation, and they wanted to know why.

In the United States the same complaint and inquiry has been endemic, commonplace, for quite a while. You come across it in the papers. You hear parents, school people, editors and publishers, lawyers and ministers, men of science and of business, lamenting the fact that their charges or their offspring or their employees can neither spell nor write "decent English." The deplorers blame the modern progressive school or the comics or TV; they feel that in school and outside, something which they call discipline is lacking, and they vaguely connect this lack with a supposed decline in morality, an upsurge of "crisis." Like everything else, bad Eng-

---

* *Atlantic Monthly*, CXCII, No. 6 (December, 1953), 25-29.

lish is attributed to our bad times, and the past (which came to an end with the speaker's graduation from college) is credited with one more virtue, that of literary elegance.

The facts seem to me quite different, the causes much more tangled, and the explanation of our linguistic state at once more complex and less vague. For many years now I have been concerned with the art of writing and kept busy at the invidious task of improving other people's utterance, and I cannot see that performance has deteriorated. The level is low but it has not fallen. As a reader of history I am steadily reminded that the writing of any language has always been a hit-and-miss affair. Here is Amos Barrett, our chief source on the battles of Concord and Lexington: "It wont long before their was other minit Compneys . . . We marched Down about a mild or a mild half and we see them acomming . . ." and so on. An illiterate New England farmer? Not so, since he could write; he had been taught and in some way represents "the past." The question he poses is, how do people write who are not professionals or accomplished amateurs? The answer is: badly, at all times.

Writing is at the very least a knack, like drawing or being facile on the piano. Because everybody can speak and form letters, we mistakenly suppose that good, plain, simple writing is within everybody's power. Would we say this of good, straightforward, accurate drawing? Would we say it of melodic sense and correct, fluent harmonizing at the keyboard? Surely not. We say these are "gifts." Well, so is writing, even the writing of a bread-and-butter note or a simple public notice; and this last suggests that something has happened within the last hundred years to change the relation of the written word to daily life.

Whether it is the records we have to keep in every business and profession or the ceaseless communicating at a distance which modern transport and industry require, the world's work is now unmanageable, unthinkable, without *literature.* Just see how many steps you can take without being confronted with something written or with the necessity of writing something yourself. Having been away for a couple of weeks during the summer, I find a bill from the window washer, who luckily came on a day when the cleaning woman was in the apartment. He has therefore scribbled below the date: "The windows have been cleaned Wed. 12:30 p.m. Your maid was their to veryfey the statement"—perfectly clear and adequate.

One can even appreciate the change of tenses as his mind went from the job just finished to the future when I would be reading this message from the past. Call this bad writing if you like, it remains perfectly harmless. The danger to the language, if any, does not come from such trifles. It comes rather from the college-bred millions who regularly write and who in the course of their daily work circulate the prevailing mixture of jargon, cant, vogue words, and loose syntax that passes for prose. And the greater part of this verbiage is published, circulated, presumably read. A committee won't sit if its drivelings are not destined for print. Even an interoffice memo goes out in sixteen copies and the schoolchildren's compositions appear verbatim in a mimeographed magazine. Multiply these cultural facts by the huge number of activities which (it would seem) exist only to bombard us with paper, and you have found the source of the belief in a "decline" in writing ability—no decline at all, simply the infinite duplication of dufferism. This it is which leads us into false comparisons and gloomy thoughts.

NB
" dufferism "

THE BEST REASON FOR STUDYING GRAMMAR AND THE SECOND-BEST REASON FOR STUDYING GRAMMAR *

Paul Roberts

The best reason for studying grammar is that grammar is interesting. Most readers will find this statement shocking and absurd. But that is because in their early school days they did not take grammar straight but had it mixed with a number of bitter ingredients. Writers of many elementary grammar books would also, presumably, consider the statement heretical; for in the prefaces to such books we find repeated the remark that grammar, though profitable (it enables us to write powerful and accurate English) is unfortunately not pleasurable. This might be called the medicine approach to grammar: we know it has a frightful taste, but you

* Pp. 1-4, *Understanding Grammar* by Paul Roberts. Copyright 1954 by Harper & Brothers. Reprinted with the permission of Harper & Row, Publishers.

must take it to get well. Pedagogically, this has two faults: first, it sets the student against the subject; second, it is untrue.

Anyone teaching a subject as a means rather than as an end may expect trouble, especially if the students are immature. Most youngsters are rather less intent on improving themselves than on enjoying themselves. This is disheartening, but we may as well face it. Even college students are reluctant to submit to a stiff discipline in grammar in order to strengthen and brighten their prose styles. Many of them don't give a hang about their prose styles, and many others consider their prose styles regrettable but hopeless. Consequently, grammar presented as a means, not an end, has no appeal to them. Students are rather like Communists; ends interest them, not means.

Happily, it is not very difficult to present grammar as an interesting and desirable end in itself. We all of us wish to know about things; this is merely a consequence of being human. Sometimes we wish to know about impersonal things, like insects or airplanes or atoms. But more often we want to know about things connected with ourselves, and since nothing is more closely connected with ourselves than the language we speak, we want to know about grammar. It is true that in most people this particular curiosity has been throttled by the time high-school days are over, but we all begin with it. It is no harder to interest the student in the way he says things than in, say, Shakespeare, or the Crimean War, or the dank mysteries of zoology. Further, it is not a grammatical system. Many elementary teachers have noticed that children like—of all things—diagraming, useless though this activity may be. The only advantage that puzzles and cryptograms have over grammatical problems is that puzzles and cryptograms are not so likely to improve us. For it happens that grammar does have practical value, apart from its intrinsic interest.

We can best understand what grammar can do for us by understanding what grammar is. Grammar is a body of generalizations about how people say things. In order to make generalizations, we must first agree on the meaning of terms for the things we wish to talk about. That is grammatical definition.

The first task of the grammarian is to group the words that occur in sentences so that he can talk about them. When he discovers which words naturally go together in groups, he gives the groups names, for convenience of discussion. For example, if he examines the sentences "The apple was ripe," "The car was old," "The moon was low," he notes *apple, moon,* and *car* are similar words. In other English sentences he finds other words which in form and behavior are similar to *apple, moon,* and *car,* and presently it is clear that *apple, moon,* and *car* are part of a large group of words. The grammarian then tries to define the group—that is, to state in general terms what it is that the members of the group have in common. The next step is to give the group a name—in this case, the name *noun.* Then, instead of saying, "Words like *apple, moon,* and *car* behave such and so," he can say more simply, "Nouns behave such and so."

This paves the way for discussion of language problems. It makes ~~sic~~ possible the teaching of language. Suppose the problem is whether to use *is* or *are, was* or *were* after nouns like *apple, apples, car, cars.* Instead of explaining each detail, each individual sentence as it occurs, the teacher uses a generalization: "In English, plural subjects are commonly followed by plural verbs." If we know what the terms mean, and if we understand that a generalization is just a general—ization and not a divine commandment, we have a useful guide to a problem of language.

It should not be supposed, however, that learning generalizations about the detail of a language is the same thing as learning a language. We are not competent in a language until we can use its materials automatically in response to situations, without stopping to ponder the pertinent generalization. The generalization serves merely as a guide during the learning period, checking and correcting us while the details are becoming fixed.

Generally speaking, the student's need of grammatical information is in inverse proportion to his competence in the language. For example, a foreign student beginning the study of English can make use of such a generalization as "In statements the normal word order is subject-verb-object: 'Ed milked the cow.'" The native speaker has less use for the generalization, since it would not occur to him to vary the pattern to "Ed the cow milked" or "Milked Ed the cow." Native speakers, however, can utilize very simple generalizations when they are trying to change from one dialect to another. For example, the person who habitually says "Him and me milked the cows" learns the generalization, "In standard English, pronouns used as subjects are in the nominative case." Grammatical generalizations are useful also to those seeking skill in writing, for they give a clearer idea of the resources of the language.

Does it follow then that he who uses the language expertly needs no knowledge of grammar? Yes, it does. For ability to use a language does not presuppose ability to describe it. Millions of people who use English very competently cannot describe it at all. In America most children do not study grammar earlier than the seventh grade, when for the first time they encounter such terms as *subject, verb, singular, present, passive*. But long before this they have learned how to make subjects and verbs agree, how to form the past tense, how to make singular nouns plural, even how to use dependent clauses and to execute complicated maneuvers with participles and infinitives. The grammar class, when they reach it, does not teach them how to speak but rather how to describe their speech and name the parts thereof. Nor is the child's further progress in language entirely dependent on his learning a technique of description. Some people have skipped the grammar class entirely and gone on to become not only competent but even expert users of the language.

In practice, however, most people do not escape instruction in language. Even professional writers seek the advice and criticism of formal or informal teachers. And instruction in language presupposes knowledge of grammar, since grammar is the means by which teacher and student talk about language.

~ C ~

suggestions for discussion

1. The four selections reproduced in this chapter have good but not spectacular introductions. And the student will be well advised to put the lesson implied by this practice to use in his own writing: The good introduction is suitable in tone and content to the rest of the theme.

In composing an introduction, a writer has an almost unlimited number of ways to proceed. (It should be needless to say that no one way should always be used.) With a bit of oversimplification, some common gambits employed by good writers as introductory devices are (1) an announcement of one's purpose, and perhaps the method of treatment; (2) an introductory question; (3) a preliminary quotation; (4) an anecdote; and (5) a short narrative or story used to orient one's own work to the history of the subject. An introductory device that consists of an assertion of what may be true enough but is not the conventional view of the subject is another effective way to begin. This unexpected assertion is represented by Roberts' sentence, "The best reason for studying grammar is that grammar is interesting." A variation of this opening is the assertion of a truth that is so clearly recognized that no one will argue against it.

Now, try to provide one sentence classification of the introductions of the first three selections in this chapter. Remember that the introduction is likely to take a full paragraph or more. (Of course, in a book-length study, it may occupy one full chapter or more.)

2. Among the common introductory devices listed in the second paragraph of question 1 are the opening question and the quotation. These devices must pass the severest tests of relevance if they are to be effective. Nothing falls flatter than the opening question that does not command a response suitable to the writer's purpose; questions that would alienate the reader must be avoided, and quotations should be selected to fit both the spirit and the subject of the work.

Using the question as an opening device, write your own introduction to one of the selections reprinted in this chapter.

3. Write an introduction to one of the selections above in which you employ a quotation from one of the others.

4. Which of the four selections in this chapter has the longest introduction? Which has the shortest? Does the length of an introduction have any special virtue? Would length be a secondary concern?

~ D ~

suggestions for writing

1. Write a short paper on your own views of the obligation of the schools in the teaching of English.

2. Write a review-article of Kenyon's essay, "Ignorance Builds a Language." In your article give a short resume of the content of Kenyon's essay and then give your own reasons for accepting or rejecting his position.

3. Write a paper of six to ten paragraphs on the subject "Good English and Bad." Draw from your own ideas and from selections reprinted in this book, regardless of whether they appear in Chapter Eight or not.

4. Write two alternate introductions using different introductory devices to one of the pieces you have written for questions 1-3 above.

~ E ~

additional readings

Perrin, Porter G., *Writer's Guide and Index to English,* 3rd ed. (Chicago: Scott, Foresman & Company, 1959), Ch. 1, "The Varieties of English."

Baugh, Albert C., *History of the English Language,* 2nd ed. (New York: Appleton-Century-Crofts, 1957), Ch. 9, "The Appeal to Authority, 1650-1800."

Roberts, Paul, *Understanding English* (New York: Harper & Row, Publishers, 1958), Ch. 10, "Grammarian's Funeral."

Chapter Nine

~ A ~

the effective ending

One of the most difficult of the rhetorical elements to master is the conclusion or ending. Many pieces of writing lose the effectiveness gained by an excellent presentation of ideas simply because the writer concluded in a hazy, anticlimactic manner. Most poor conclusions are the result of little or no planning; in fact some pieces of writing have no real conclusion at all. In the latter case, when the reader arrives at the end of the material, he immediately assumes that something will follow. How frustrated he becomes when he is unable to continue is easily imaginable. He, in fact, has the same reactions as the unfortunate young man who lived in a dormitory room below that of a student who kept late hours. Upon going to bed our young man always prepared himself for the loud noises made by his inconsiderate neighbor. And since he was prepared, he always went back to sleep with little or no damage to his nervous system. One night, however, the latecomer pulled one shoe off and dropped it to the floor: This of course, was the signal for the long-suffering resident below to begin making his preparations for going back to sleep. Unfortunately, for some inexplicable reason, the second shoe never fell. And all night long our sufferer waited for the shoe to fall so that he could turn in for an undisturbed sleep.

Each piece of writing demands a different ending. Some endings

review what has been said. Others state the last idea in a series or
the last step in a process. Needless to say the ending should be
organic, growing from the needs of the individual piece of writing.
Ultimately some way must be found to drop the other shoe.

~ B ~

the future of english

LANGUAGE AND SOCIETY *

Simeon Potter

The greater languages tend to extend their domains at the expense of the smaller ones and yet in many parts of the world we see
determined efforts to preserve and fortify minority-tongues. After
all, language is a symbol of high spiritual worth. When there is any
kind of interference with the free speaking of a given language or
dialect, or an endeavour to enforce its use, much more than the
linguistic factor is at stake. Language then ceases to be a mere
means of communication and becomes an emblem or token, tied up
with the whole complex problem of personal liberty. In principle,
therefore, it is clear that state interference either for or against a
particular language is politically unsound except in so far as it becomes necessary for the conduct of government itself. Prohibitions
and commands alike arouse resentment. A policy of complete linguistic toleration is both just and expedient. Only when a minority-
language is used as a means to stir up subversive violence is state
action justified. By the inexorable constitution of society, speakers
of minority-languages are liable to certain social and economic disadvantages. Three courses are then open to them: (a) they may, left
to themselves, remain as they are and continue to suffer disadvan-

---

* *Language in the Modern World* (Harmondsworth: Penguin Books Ltd, 1960),
pp. 184-87.

tages; (b) they may, if ambitious, become bilingual; or (c) they may, perhaps in a later generation, discard their inherited speech altogether in favour of the majority-language. Examples of (a) are the Bretons in France, the Catalans in Spain, and, to some extent, the Irish in parts of the Gaeltacht along the west coast of Eire; examples of (b) are seen in the French *habitants* in Quebec, the speakers of Rumansch in northeast Italy and Switzerland, and, very largely, the Welsh in Wales; whereas examples of (c) are now furnished by the Scottish Highlanders who are gradually forgetting their Gaelic altogether and following the path already taken by the speakers of Cornish in the nineteenth century and of Manx in the twentieth.

If complete tolerance is the only sane policy for civilized governments to adopt towards minority-tongues, it is no less applicable to great languages also. Their future is quite unpredictable. Will one world language eventually emerge with the gradual spread of one accepted culture? In some measure a world language has already emerged with the rapid advance of science and with the creation of the United Nations Educational Scientific and Cultural Organization, which we call UNESCO, but which H. G. Wells would doubtless have christened *World Brain*. Side by side with the development of this new scientific vocabulary, we see considerable progress being made, especially in the cities of Russia and China, in the diffusion of those artificial languages like Esperanto and Interlingua. . . .

UNESCO is one of the Specialized Agencies of the Economic and Social Council of the United Nations, and so too is that much older organization now known as the Universal Postal Union, inaugurated by the Treaty of Berne in 1874, long before it was incorporated into UNO in 1948. The highest compliment we pay to UPU is that we often forget its very existence. It has functioned so efficiently all these years that we just take it for granted that a letter posted in London will be delivered to its proper destination in Vladivostok or Tierra del Fuego. In recent years UPU has taken a further step forward in world communication by issuing in Roman script a complete list of the post offices in all the five continents. This must surely be regarded as a signal triumph in view of the fact that, apart from numerous lesser ones, there are four other major scripts still in use in the world, namely, Cyrillic, Arabic, Devanagari, and Chinese. Even the Soviet Union and the Chinese People's Republic have been persuaded to accept the Union's stabilized transliterations of the names of their post offices into Roman script. If this process could be extended to other names in Russia and China as well as in the rest of Asia and Africa, one formidable difficulty would be overcome. National governments should now be encouraged to compile gazetteers of all place-names in use within their borders with received pronunciations recorded phonetically as in the pioneer publications of the British and Columbia Broadcasting Corporations. In tasks so important for world peace, many existing institutions should join, such as the Committee of Onomastic Sciences, the International Library Commission, and the International Standards Organization. Inevitably the Universal Postal Union will work in close association with UNESCO itself and also with the International Telecommunications Union. Collaboration between these three United Nations Specialized Agencies will surely make substantial contributions towards the advancement of world trade and communication in the coming years.

Meantime, universal literacy, nothing less, becomes year by year a pressing necessity. The pace quickens in the race on our planet between education and catastrophe. The problem of illiteracy is not solved by compulsory schooling alone, if, as in Britain, many men's reading is limited to the gutter press, or, as in America, many people assume a "mucker pose" and shun as affectation anything that suggests conscious refinement or ennoblement of life. Literacy is not a state, but a process: it cannot be finally guaranteed in any society. It involves hard toil in teaching the young and it demands the subsequent enlistment of every conceivable means of enlightening grown-ups—sound radio, television, cinema, theatre, press, museum, art gallery, public library, university extension, and adult education. It is useless to teach the alphabet and the three R's to young people and then turn them back into a society that remains stubbornly uncultured and unlettered. It is essential to fortify them continually against the insidious depravity of soul-destroying slogans; to train them to be wary of all absolutes and oversimplified either-or choices; to show them how to distinguish word from thing, and how to discriminate intelligently between facts and inferences and between inferences and value-judgements; to teach them to see how language really works in action; and to help them to recognize and respect life's fundamental loyalties. In other words, it is essential to create and secure for present-day society a "climate of literacy" in which alone national democracy is able to function and world government can be achieved.

THE FUTURE OF ENGLISH *

Albert Marckwardt

The analysis of the development of American English . . . has attempted to show the relationship of this development to the most salient features in the cultural life and history of the American people. It would be equally interesting for someone to make a complementary study of the particular facets of British English, and indeed of the English spoken in the various dominions of the Empire, indicating the relationships between language and culture which exist there as well.

But when all is said and done, English, despite the vast numbers who speak it and its widespread dissemination over the globe, is still but a single language, and to paraphrase an earlier commentator, the differences between its widest extremes, though extensive in certain features of the language, are still remarkably few. As a language it is highly unified; more so than many tongues spoken by a far smaller number of people.

This raises the question of the probable future of English. We have already noted that 230 million speakers of English as a first language are spread over four continents. We have noted too that this represents more than a fortyfold, almost a fiftyfold, increase over the number of speakers who used the language in 1600. At that time it was fifth among the languages of the Western world, surpassed in numbers by speakers of French, German, Spanish, and Italian. In 1750 it was still fifth, Russian having replaced Italian as a fourth. A century later English had gone ahead of the others, the sudden addition of twenty-three million speakers of the language in the United States apparently sufficing to put it into first place.

With this as a background, it might be argued that if the fiftyfold multiplication of the last four centuries were to be cut to merely a fivefold increase over the next four, we might expect one billion speakers of English by 2350—nearly one-half of the present world population. Or the recent rate of increase of from fifteen to twenty million per decade would give us very nearly the same result. The probability of such an increment may be questioned on the ground that the nineteenth-cenutry aggrandizement of English was largely dependent upon the opening up of the North American continent to settlers who eventually adopted the language. With the twentieth century more than half over, it does not seem likely that any single English-speaking country will repeat the feat of the United States in the nineteenth century. Yet Australia, South Africa, and Canada will unquestionably show pronounced gains, and a total of 300 million speakers of English as a first language some time in the twenty-first century is by no means inconceivable. It could reach 350 million. At any rate no other European language, not even Russian, is currently in a position to compete with it.

It is, however, in its development as a second language that the real opportunities for the future development of English seem to lie. It is probably fair to say that after some tinkering with international languages, we can only conclude that no one of them has yet been sufficiently successful to justify much confidence in its future. Consequently, if we are to look forward to any single language which might serve as an international auxiliary—and the increase in rapidity and extent of travel and communications somehow leads us to expect this—such a language will undoubtedly be one of those in use at the present time. The English language would seem to be the best candidate for a number of reasons.

In the first place it is the native language of *two* of the most powerful and influential nations of the world. This is not true of French, German, Russian, Spanish, or Chinese. Moreover, it is used today both in speech and in writing to an extent unsurpassed by any other. It has been estimated that three-fifths of the world's radio stations broadcast in English and that three-fourths of the world's mail is written in the language.

There are in particular certain features of English which make for its convenience as an international auxiliary. Its vocabulary is composed of vast numbers of words both of Teutonic and of Latin origin, making large portions of its word stock readily comprehensible to millions of speakers of other languages. The words are short; the language is free from a complicated inflectional system, giving at least the illusion of ease of mastery. At the same time we must not fail to observe that our wretched spelling system, which so successfully obscures any consistent relationship between the spoken and written forms of the language, will undoubtedly act as a deterrent to some degree, but probably not enough to counterbalance the other factors which have been cited.

It is extremely difficult to estimate the number of speakers of English as a second language: some authorities place the number at fifty million, others at 125 million. Whatever the facts may be, there can be no doubt that it is on the increase. It is replacing French as a second language in the schools of Latin America and in some of the European countries. It has always been important as an auxiliary language in Holland and the Scandinavian countries. Until very recently Russia placed considerable emphasis upon the teaching of English in her schools. Various types of pidgin English serve as a trade language in the Far East. If, within the next century, a more highly interdependent world will have to depend upon bilingualism to conduct its affairs, a doubling of the numbers who now speak English as a second language is not inconceivable. At the end of that time we may assume that probably 500 million people will be speaking some form of English, either as a first or a second language.

This leads to a further question—what kind of English will these half a billion speakers use? What will the language be like? In attempting to answer this, we must remember that English has never been anything like a uniform language. No academy has ever attempted to rule upon its vocabulary and grammar. In America, at least, this lack of uniformity has been due in part to a constant increase in the number of speakers. If the increase should continue at anything like its present rate, it is not likely that a greater uniformity will be established, despite the leveling influence of improved means of communication. This may not be a bad thing; undoubtedly the English language owes much of its vigor to the variety existing within it.

We have seen that a language may be considered from the point of view of its words, its sounds, its inflectional endings, and its patterns of word order. We know also that for the last several centuries the vocabulary of English has been very large, that some words have been borrowed from languages in almost every part of the world. Certain languages, principally Latin, French, and the Scandinavian tongues, have contributed heavily to our present lexicon. Moreover, the dictionaries of the English language at various periods of its history seem to reflect a consistent present lexicon. Moreover, the dictionaries of the English language as it was used approximately 1000 years ago, contain about 37,000 words. A fairly complete dictionary of Middle English—that is, of the language of 500 years ago—would have between 50,000 and 70,000 entries. It is likely that a dictionary of Early Modern English, the period of Shakespeare and his contemporaries, would contain at least 140,000 words, and it is a well-known fact that unabridged dictionaries of present-day English have approximately half a million entries.

Even if we consider the probability that the early records of our language are so fragmentary that the numbers just cited for Old and Middle English fall far short of what the language actually contained, yet the apparent quadrupling of our stock of words during the last three and a half centuries is significant evidence of a strong tendency toward vocabulary increase. There is no reason to suppose that this will not continue.

We have noticed, in addition, that the recent extensions of our vocabulary have come not so much through word borrowing as from the manipulation of elements which are already in the language. Such processes as compounding, the addition of derivative prefixes and suffixes, and change in grammatical function account for considerably more than half of our new words today. Without question we shall continue to borrow some words from foreign languages in the future. We did so during both world wars, and as the language spreads over areas of the Far East, for example, it is reasonable to look forward to new words coming from Malay, as well as from Russian, possibly even from Swahili and Bantu, but the principal growth in the English vocabulary will undoubtedly come as the result of the processes which have just been mentioned —up to what point is hard to guess. A doubling of the vocabulary in the next two centuries is not difficult to conceive in the light of what has happened since 1600.

If the area over which English is spoken and the number of speakers of English increase, as we expect them to, it is highly probable that a considerable number of words will be used in one regional form of English but not in another. It is likely, too, that the increasing complexities of modern life and modern technology will demand a larger vocabulary of the individual, as has been evidenced by the replacement of the horse by the automobile, of the town crier by the newspaper, of the candle by electric lighting. But there has always been a large gap between the vocabulary of the individual and the total word count of the language, and this will very likely increase as time goes on.

We may ask next, "How will the English of the future sound?" To most of us the language of Chaucer sounds somewhat more like the present-day speech of one of the Low Countries than like Modern English, and the early pages of this volume demonstrate clearly enough that Shakespeare's lines, uttered as we think he and his contemporaries pronounced them, ring somewhat strangely in our ears. Will the speech of our descendants 300 years hence sound equally strange? Or has the English language attained a phonetic stability? There is really no reason to believe that it has. Present differences in the way in which English is pronounced throughout the world may, and in fact do reflect certain differences in the rate at which sound changes have operated in the past.

We shall probably make more progress in attempting to answer this question if we consider it in the light of the various kinds of sounds: consonants, long and short vowels. On the whole our consonants have changed relatively little since the period from the twelfth to the fourteenth centuries, when such pairs as *s* and *z, f* and *v* became meaningfully distinct instead of mere variants of the same sound. Prior to that time such contrasts as those of *feel* and *veal* or *ice* and *eyes* could not have occurred in English. It was just about the same time that the *ng* as in *sing* and *long* emerged as a sound in its own right. Since that time English has acquired but one new consonant, the *zh* sound of *vision* or *measure*. Other changes have been confined either to individual words or at most to particular phonetic situations: the development of the *sh* sound in *sugar* and of *j* in *soldier*. There may be more changes of this nature ahead of us, but any basic alteration of the whole consonant system would be surprising.

At the other extreme, the popularly called "long" vowels have always changed considerably, particularly within the last 500 years. At the beginning of the Christian era, the stressed vowel of the word *home* was pronounced with the sound of *ī*, as it still is in the cognate German word *Heim*. By the time of King Alfred the vowel in this word had acquired the sound of *ah*, which then developed to *aw* at approximately 1200. The word attained its present *o*-like quality probably by 1500, as did most others with the same stressed vowel sound. Nor is this a rare or exceptional instance. In the 200 years separating the period of Chaucer from that of Shakespeare, virtually every long vowel in English underwent some sort of change, not only in its own quality but very often in respect to its relationship to other vowel sounds in the language. It is only since the time of Shakespeare, or slightly before, that words such as *read* and *reed, caught* and *brought, pain* and *pane* have come to be pronounced with the same vowel sound, and conversely words such as *coat* and *cot* or *made* and *mad,* then having the same quality of sound, have become differentiated.

Despite the extent and variety of this change, much of it does fit into a pattern. What seems to be involved here is a gradual raising of the tongue and jaw position for making the sounds in question until they reach a point where they cannot be raised any more, after which they develop into diphthongs. Thus the word which Chaucer and his contemporaries pronounced as *moos* is now given the diphthongal pronunciation *mouse.* Conversely, most diphthongs in the earlier periods of the language are now simple vowels—*law* was pronounced earlier with an *ow* sound; today, despite its spelling, it has but a single vowel. Developments as striking as these may easily continue. In fact we may have the beginnings of something like it in the *eh-oo* one encounters in the British pronunciation of words like *know* and *home.*

In comparison, the so-called "short" vowels have changed very little in the course of the last 1000 years. Words like *bed, this, ox,* and *full* have been pronounced with the same vowels for the last ten centuries and even more. It would seem reasonable, then, to conclude that they will undergo no major changes in the immediate future.

Another kind of pronunciation change is confined particularly to foreign words taken into the language: a shift of stress or accent toward the front. This is occurring today with such words as *ciga-rette, Detroit, inquiry,* and *robust,* all of which are heard from time to time with the stress on the first syllable. This happened centuries ago to words like *liquor, pleasant,* and *nation,* originally pro-nounced with principal stress on the final syllable. From one point of view, the disappearance of secondary stress in the British pronun-ciation of words like *secretary* and *circumstance* could be considered as a part of the same general development. Without question this tendency will continue to operate, although it is impossible to know which particular words will be affected.

The comparative freedom of English from inflectional or grammatical endings—at least as compared with Latin or German—has often been considered one of its strongest claims as a potential international language. What has happened is that through the years certain other devices have come to take the place of inflections. First, though, let us look at those inflectional suffixes which are indispensable to the structure and operation of English today. The two most important of these are the -s plural of nouns and the -ed which forms the past tense and past participle of the vast majority of English verbs.

The first of these, originally only one of eight or nine ways of indicating the plural, has expanded to a point where today there are relatively few native nouns which form their plural in any way other than the addition of -s. A small number of foreign words, such as *antenna, nucleus,* and *phenomenon,* at times retain the plural inflection of their language of origin. It is possible that the -s plural will be extended to some of these, particularly when they pass, as *antenna* has already done, from the learned into everyday language.

In much the same manner the regular -ed verb inflection has encroached upon all others during the last ten centuries. Verbs newly admitted into the language have adopted this inflection. Such old verbs as *help* and *climb* have lost their irregular past forms *holp* and *clomb,* which have been replaced in the standard language by *helped* and *climbed.* Even now the very uncertainty which many speakers and writers feel with respect to *strive* and *wake* indicates that a change is under way. The 360 verbs in Old English which indicated changes in tense through alterations of their principal vowel (e.g. *sing, sang, sung*) have been reduced to a mere sixty. The language as a whole now has only about 125 irregular verbs of any kind. It seems safe to predict that this number will become smaller as time goes on.

A few other inflections are now in the process of being replaced by constructions involving what are often called function words. For example, the inflected genitive, or possessive, often alternates with a construction employing the preposition *of: the horse's head, the head of the horse.* Throughout the last several centuries the sphere of *of* has been steadily increasing at the expense of the inflectional ending. We can no longer say *water's glass* for *glass of water,* or *ours one* for *one of ours.* We may well ask whether in time it will seem equally awkward to say *year's vacation, world's fair,* or *St. Joseph's Hospital.* Likewise, the comparative and superlative adjective endings *-er* and *-est* have slowly given way to constructions with *more* and *most.* We are no longer able to employ such formations as *interestinger* and *honestest.* Could this taboo ultimately extend to *prettier* and *hottest?* Finally, it would not seem unreasonable to expect that the few situations where the inflected subjunctive of the verb still remains intact will eventually give way to formations with such auxiliaries as *may, might,* and *should.*

There are also situations in English where the few remaining forms specifically indicative of case, e.g. *me, who, him,* conflict with the normal word-order patterns of the language. In general, an object form such as *me* will follow the verb, whereas a subject form such as *who* will precede it. This tendency toward the fixation of word order accounts for such apparent solecisms as *It is me, Who are you looking for?* Even more important is the general principle behind such developments. When the choice of a form based upon word order conflicts with the choice of a form based upon an inflectional paradigm or pattern, word order generally turns out to be the determining factor. No matter how we feel about these particular constructions, they are undoubtedly here to stay, but because of the scarcity of case-distinctive forms, it is not likely that many more changes of this type will occur.

Word order is, however, one aspect of the larger problem of syntax. In general, largely to compensate for the loss of inflectional endings, English word order has become more rigid. Shakespeare had more freedom than we have now. Will our great-grandchildren have less?

For example, when the modifying elements of place, manner, and time are all included within a single sentence, we are able to say:

> *He wrote the exercise carefully at home this afternoon.*
> *This afternoon he wrote the exercise carefully at home.*
> *He carefully wrote the exercise at home this afternoon.*

Certainly the following constructions seem somewhat more awkward and would occur less frequently:

He wrote the exercise at home carefully this afternoon.
He wrote the exercise carefully this afternoon at home.

We would be even less likely to say:

He wrote the exercise at home this afternoon carefully.
He wrote the exercise this afternoon at home carefully.

Moreover, although we may begin the sentence with the time element, we may place neither the modifier of place nor of manner in initial position. Consequently we cannot say:

Carefully he wrote the exercise this afternoon at home.
At home he wrote the exercise this afternoon carefully.

It is not unreasonable to expect a further fixation and limitation of such patterns as time goes on.

Another kind of syntactical development concerns the shift in the function of inflection and auxiliary verbs. In the language of King Alfred, even in that of Chaucer, the auxiliary *can* literally and specifically meant "to know" or "to know how." At that time the verb *may* was employed to indicate ability, where as the inflected subjunctive denotes possibility. At present, *can* indicates ability, *may* indicates possibility and upon occasion permission, and the inflected subjunctive has all but disappeared. In fact, *can* now often usurps the function of possibility and permission: *It could rain. Can I go?* Is the next step the disappearance of *may* and the replacement of *can* by some other construction?

Our present use of the verb *got* raises a series of similar questions. *Have got,* indicating possession, at times replaces *have* which in turn displaced an earlier *owe, ought.* *Have got to,* meaning necessity or obligation is likewise taking the place of *ought* and *must.* Will these latter auxiliaries disappear altogether, as certain others, notably *thearf,* "to need" and *dow,* "to avail, befit" have done in the past? It is already evident that *going to* is encroaching upon the domain of *shall* and *will* to indicate future time.

Speculations of this nature might go on indefinitely, but at least some of the possible lines of development the English language may follow in the future have been suggested. To sum up: as possible developments in the English language of the next few centuries, we may expect that it will be spoken by more people, that it will include more words, that the pronunciations of its stressed vowels may change, that the noun plural and regular past tense inflections will be strengthened and that certain other inflections will gradually disappear, that there will be a continued fixation of word-order patterns, and a shift in some verb auxiliaries.

In considering the future of English one inevitably comes up against the question which has been one of the concerns of the present work, the differences between the language as spoken in England and in America. Will these become greater as time goes on, or will they tend to disappear?

This question can best be answered in terms of the particular facets of American culture . . . reflected in the English language as it is spoken here. We have seen that American English reflects, among other things, the melting pot aspect of American culture chiefly through its verbal borrowings. By preserving some of the words, meanings, and features of the pronunciation of sixteenth- and seventeenth-century English, it mirrors the cultural lag so often reflected in a colony separated from the mother country by some distance. The sinewy vigor of the frontiersman, his ingenuity born of necessity, and his disregard of convention find their counterpart in the bold creation of new compounds and derivatives, the free employment of functional changes, and the bizarre blended forms; even his lusty humor is matched by his playfully hyperbolical tall talk. On the other hand, the glorification of the commonplace and an accompanying tendency toward euphemism betokens the squeamishness of a somewhat culturally insecure middle-class and a mid-nineteenth-century deference to feminine taste. To the extent that these culture traits are likely to persist and be strengthened, it may be presumed that the language will continue to reflect them. When or as they become less prominent their influence will diminish.

The verbal borrowings from immigrant nations have clearly become less numerous. Many of our early loan words are now obsolete, and the languages spoken by the bulk of our late nineteenth- and early twentieth-century immigrant peoples have left little trace upon English. With immigration during the last three decades reduced to a mere trickle, any further influx of borrowings beyond an occasional adoption here and there seems unlikely. The retention of features of sixteenth- and seventeenth-century English is not likely to be influenced greatly over the years. There are few, if any, indications that our drugstore will become a chemist's shop, or that the r coloring of our vowels will grow less prominent. Though the gap between American and British English in this respect is not likely to close, there are certainly no indications that it will widen. We shall undoubtedly continue to develop new compound and derivative formations; word blending and functional change will continue as active processes, but it must be remembered that these are confined to certain quite definitely circumscribed areas of the vocabulary. Many of our most ludicrous euphemisms have already disappeared from current use, and on the question of cultural insecurity we shall have something to say a little later. All in all, there would seem to be little reason for anticipating a further divergence between British and American English.

There is also the question of the extent to which British English is being influenced by Americanisms, a question which can best be answered accurately and scientifically by one who speaks British English. There is no question that the availability of American books, newspapers, and films has served to acquaint millions of Englishmen with American features of the language which, however, they do not normally employ. Recognition or passing acquaintance does not necessarily mean adoption, and while it is possible here and there to point to English acceptance and use of an American term, there is no more reason for expecting that American cooking and food terminology, political jargon, or the lexicon of the automobile is going to be taken over bodily than there is to suppose that the English are going to cook like Americans or to alter their political organizations and practices.

One must remember, however, that no matter how striking the differences between British and American English may be, the similarities far outweigh them, for it is in grammatical structure and syntax—essentially the operational mcahinery of the language —that the difference is negligible. It is neither exaggeration nor idle chauvinism to say that the English language, with an exceptional past behind it, appears to be on the threshold of a still greater future. Moreover, this future is to a considerable extent in the hands of those who regularly speak and write the language. What can they do to insure and even to further the development which lies ahead?

This basic question may best be answered by considering the dangers which may conceivably beset a language in the particular situation in which English finds itself today. There would seem to be two such perils, diametrically opposed to each other. On the one hand there are some who have seen, even in certain of the developments which have been mentioned earlier in this chapter—for example, the disappearance of the inflected subjunctive, the establishment of *who* in pre-verbal position, the use of *have got* to indicate possession—indications of a too great liberty, if not license. The unchecked development of tendencies such as these, it is argued, could lead to developments so divergent that the English language would lose its unity, and consequently its utility as a medium of communication. Opposed to this is the view that highly restrictive rules and conservative attitudes springing from a fear of solecism and leading to a denial of what is actual usage will exert such a confining influence upon the language that its flexibility will be lost and its ultimate potentialities remain unrealized.

Although there may be some danger from the first of these, the present social and cultural situation, in the United States especially, would seem to indicate that the greater of the two perils is the second. A number of factors enter into this situation. We have seen that from the beginning until late in the nineteenth century there was always a frontier, an area where unlettered pioneers toiled to secure cultural advantages for their children—including the mastery of standard English. Moreover, the children of foreign-speaking immigrants felt the sting of social disapproval if their language betrayed their origin. The spread of higher education to social groups who in Europe would have remained comfortably within the confines of a regional or class dialect, also brought with it an emphasis upon correctness of speech and writing.

In learning a language, whether it be a different form of our native tongue or a totally foreign idiom, we operate inductively. We learn specific facts and usages first. When we have absorbed enough of these, we begin to synthesize—we form patterns, general behavior traits, upon which we then rely when a new situation faces us. The more uncertain we are of ourselves, culturally or in any other way, the more insistent we are upon guidance in specific facts and instances, and the more reluctant we are to rely upon an instinctive grasp of these general patterns. As far as raising the level of English is concerned, American textbooks and teaching practices have too seldom taken the students beyond the level of instruction in specific matters. As a consequence, most people in the United States carry about with them a strange assortment of linguistic taboos. The feeling against *ain't,* even as a first person interrogative, is very widespread. Some react against *like* for *as.* For many the pronunciation *ice cream* with primary stress on the first syllable is taboo; for others the taboo against *John and me* so powerful that it prompts them to use *John and I* even when it is structurally objective and *me* would normally be demanded.

It may be reasonably argued that these taboos, which are after all the results of a primarily negative approach to language, or to expression, have performed their function and outlived their usefulness. They should be replaced with something positive. We are at a point where the doctrine of original sin, linguistically speaking, must be replaced by a faith in intuition, by dependence upon the established, unconsciously known patterns of the language. Such an instinct can be developed only by giving attention to the broader aspects of structure and the evolving tendencies of the language.

The history of English during the last two centuries demonstrates that highly restrictive and unrealistic rules of grammar do not have a lasting effect upon the language as a whole. The more incredible portions of the body of rules developed by Nathaniel Ward, Dr. Johnson, Lindley Murray, and their followers have generally disappeared. In the present situation, however, the attitude behind the creation of a mass of non-pertinent and unscientific linguistic legislation can still do positive harm. It can create and preserve taboos, which ought never to have been created, against certain expressions and constructions. It can develop anxiety neuroses in many of the people who employ the language. Both of these are undesirable conditions for the future development of the English language. We cannot expect a medium of communication to develop in advance of the courage and resourcefulness of the people who employ it.

It is our responsibility to realize whither the language is tending, and the duty of our schools and teachers to promulgate healthy linguistic attitudes. If this is done, we may be certain that some individuals can and will attain greatness in the use of the language, which in turn will make of it a more flexible and sensitive medium for the rest of us. In this sense, a new era lies before all the English-speaking peoples.

WORLD ENGLISH? *

Stuart Robertson
Frederick Cassidy

If the English language in the past century or so has entered a
new phase of growth to suit it to the rapidly developing democratic-
industrial society of today, a phase in which it necessarily breaks
free of the eighteenth century's static ideals, and gradually becomes
adapted to the needs of a more dynamic age, we must realize that
it does not throw over all tradition or historical continuity—indeed,
with language that would be suicidal. The chief patterns of the
language, in its modern stage, remain firm: what proves good in
past usage, and what proves good of new acquisition, continues.
Just as the stylists of the Restoration laid aside the Latinized bro-
cade, splendid as it was, of Sir Thomas Browne, and put on the
plain English broadcloth of Defoe and Dryden, so the writer of
today weaves a new fabric of his own, experimenting in many types.
The prose of today (if any generalization can be made about so
various a thing) is less formal, more rapid and practical; it travels
light, throwing off the weight of convention, decoration, or structural complexity. At its worst this makes it seem harried, mean,
flaccid, or flat; but at its best it can be pungent, sinewy, clear, and
wrought, but achieving an art of its own, reaching a larger number
of minds, and supporting a larger number of artisans than has
been possible in former ages. Mass-production, in its early stages,
scorns art—but once established, it returns to art. This explains
why it can be said with some measure of truth that more people
are using the language better today than ever before. It is also true,
no doubt, that there is a larger audience for cheap, inartistic, stupid,
and vulgar uses of language than ever before. The Elizabethan
broadsides and chapbooks have their innumerable, and equally
ephemeral, modern counterparts. If language is mechanized, like

---

* *The Development of Modern English* (Englewood Cliffs, N.J.: Prentice-Hall,
1954), pp. 408-17.

everything else it is dehumanized and dies; but the forces of renewal are perpetually at work, and whatever is really vital survives. The English language is changing and will change still, but it is in no serious danger of decay.

Meantime, as we have remarked before, one of the most important considerations for the future of the language is that English, in the past three centuries, has spread all over the world. Its use as an international language is constantly increasing. That some general medium of expression is really to be desired we have the experience of history to testify. In the Middle Ages, Latin occupied this position, and in modern times French has approximated it, especially as the language of international diplomatic relations. Is English, possibly, in line for the succession? Before examining the claims of English as a world auxiliary language, however, we must first consider whether a natural language or an artificial one—such as Esperanto—holds out the best hope of effective use and general acceptance. [Esperanto is an artificial language first devised, by L. L. Zamenhof, in 1887.]

The ideal of an artificial speech, scientifically constructed so as to combine the merits of some of the leading naturally developed languages and at the same time embody none of their defects, is by no means a new thing. Some of the projected artificial languages do not, it is true, fulfill the first of these conditions; that is, they are based not on one or more existing languages, but are purely *a priori* schemes. None of these, however, is seriously advocated at present; it is quite generally recognized that a universal language must be founded on one or more of the vernaculars of the world. To go into the many variations of the project—such as Volapuk, Ido, "Latino sine flexione," Movial—would take us too far afield. A few words must nevertheless be said about Esperanto, the claimant favored by the majority of the advocates of a universal language.

Esperanto has Latin, the most nearly international and neutral of elements, as the chief basis of its vocabulary; its grammar is exceedingly simple and its spelling is phonetic. That it has won a real, though necessarily limited, measure of successful adoption, is indicated by the support given it after the first World War by the League of Nations, the International Telegraphic Union (1925), and the Union Internationale de Radiophonie (1927). The second World War, of course, set the movement back considerably, and the United Nations has been less hospitable to Esperanto than was the League: it has five official languages—English and French as "working languages" and in addition Chinese, Russian, and Spanish. The Esperantists have resumed activity, however, as witness their thirty-fifth annual conference, which met in Paris in 1950, with 2500 delegates from 34 countries. Nevertheless, they can lay claim to only one and a half million people who use Esperanto daily, which is less than the number who speak even a minor natural language, and is utterly dwarfed by the daily users of any major one. No more than five thousand daily users are claimed for the United States—yet a dozen natural foreign languages are spoken by more people than that in the United States. Thus even the most successful of the artificial languages, after more than sixty years of existence, has achieved very little actual acceptance, and not even the acceptance of all who favor an artificial auxiliary language.

Furthermore, the arguments that have been urged against Esperanto in the past are still valid. The uniformity claimed for it all over the world is partly vitiated by its different pronunciation in various countries. And while its grammatical system is simple by European standards, it is still very difficult for speakers of non-European languages. A recent Esperantist publication makes much of the international misunderstandings that have resulted through mistranslation from one natural language to another (French, English, Russian). The implication is that the use of Esperanto would remove all such difficulties. But of course this is quite without foundation, since the various languages would themselves have to be translated into Esperanto words, and the possibilities for misunderstanding would be just as great.

If, then, the project of an artificially constructed universal language has so far met with only a very limited measure of success, what claims may be advanced for English as an international language? It seems more and more certain that if any living speech attains this position, it will be English. In our own day, English has come to rival French in the field of diplomacy, and since the second World War, has virtually replaced French as the "second" language—the language most useful for the traveler—all over Europe. In other parts of the world, its prestige and usefulness are still more commanding. Though India gained independence in 1950 and might have been expected to set up one of its native languages as a national standard, the rivalry existing among them, combined with the fact that English was already known everywhere among educated people, has led to the retention of English. As someone has said, the Indians, in coming together to throw off the British yoke, found it necessary to communicate with each other in the language of the British.

Beach-la-Mar or Sandalwood-English, spoken and understood all over the Western Pacific, and Pidgin-English, known in China and to some extent in Japan and in California, are the most conspicuous examples of corrupt forms of English that have been evolved from the contact with exotic tongues and spread over large areas. It is said, incidentally, that the American share in these trade languages is becoming larger than the British. But it is not, of course, merely in such corrupt jargons that Modern English has gained a world-wide ascendancy; in its more standard British and American forms, it is, especially since the first World War, more and more dominating the civilized, and a large part of the uncivilized, world.

This leadership among the languages of the world has been achieved well within the Modern English period. In the Renaissance, and probably as late as the period of the Restoration, the speakers of English were fewer than the speakers of at least four other European languages—German, French, Spanish, and Italian. Even in the eighteenth century, English was still, for a time, outdistanced in numbers of speakers by four other European languages, since, if Italian had been left behind, a new rival, Russian, had asserted itself. In the nineteenth century, however, English came rapidly to the front, largely as a result of the swift increase in the population of the United States and of the British colonies. Probably by the middle of the century it had outdistanced its competitors. Estimates, in millions of speakers, made at several times since then, are as follows:

	English	*German*	*Russian*	*French*	*Spanish*
1868	60	52	45	45	40
1890	111	75 +	75	51 +	42 +
1900	116 (123)	75 (85)	70 (85)	45 (52)	44 (58)
1912	150	90	106	47	52
1921	170	87½	120½	45	65
1936	191	85	90	—	100
1952	225	—	180	—	110

The figures, necessarily only approximations, have at least the merit of coming from a number of different sources and representing various points of view. Their testimony to the recent and rapid increase in the number of those speaking English is perhaps for this very reason the more impressive. It is evident, of course, that they do not tell the whole story as to the languages of the world; but China's 450 millions speak dialects that are mutually unintelligible and that, besides, scarcely spread beyond her borders; and a similar situation holds for those who speak cognate varieties of Indic—the Indo-European languages of India—perhaps 325 millions. Clearly, any rivalry for the position of a world language must come from the tongues of Europe; and the figures that have been quoted are a striking evidence of the way in which English has outdistanced its European competitors. In numbers of native speakers, English is rivalled only by North Chinese; in numbers of native *and foreign* speakers, it is quite unrivalled by any language in the world. The fact that English has gained the ascendancy is not to be disputed. There may be difference of opinion, however, as to *why* it has done so.

The reason for the spread of English is probably quite unconnected with the language as such, or with any intrinsic virtues over other languages which it may be thought to have: England's rise as a world power, beginning in the days of Elizabeth, is accompanied, step by step, by the ascendancy of English as a world language. The political union of England and Scotland under James I in 1603, followed by the formation of the United Kingdom of Great Britain and Ireland, helped to make it certain that English would be used, and in a form substantially the same, throughout the islands and in the newly founded Colonies. In the New World, the fall of New Amsterdam in 1664 and that of Quebec in 1759 assured the triumph of English over two important rivals, Dutch and French; and the expansion of the United States brought it about that Spanish, the only remaining competitor of English on the North American continent, was reduced to a decidedly subordinate position. In the latter half of the eighteenth century and throughout the nineteenth century, the English language was established in every corner of the earth through conquest, colonization, and the commercial ascendancy of the English-speaking peoples. It may even be conjectured, as Krapp suggests, that the tenacity with which the British and the Americans hold to their own language and their own ways has been a real factor in spreading the English language; for if the English-speaking people would not learn a foreign language, it is evident that foreigners, to trade with them, had to learn English. The contrast has been observed, for example, in the far greater readiness of the Germans, as compared both with the English and with the Americans, to learn the Spanish language and adapt themselves to Latin ways, when engaged in commerce with South America. Doubtless, the more complacent Anglo-Saxon attitude is bad for trade, when better linguists, like the Germans, are competitors; but, just as evidently, it has proved in the past to be an appreciable factor in the world-wide use of English.

Having, by the mid-nineteenth century, won first place among the languages of the world, English has been favored by more recent developments so that its primacy is less and less questioned. Inventions that make communication between nations easier have inevitably lent themselves to the spread of English. So we may regard the telephone, the telegraph, the radio, the movies, and no doubt, once its range is increased, television. Here too, it may be said, it is often the American brand of English that is spread abroad, frequently to the chagrin of the British. The second World War, particularly, took great numbers of Americans into places where they had never been before; and airplane travel takes tourists, businessmen, and many others in increasing numbers almost everywhere. The fact that since the close of the war only Americans have been in the economic position to travel much beyond their national borders has made English even more the language that goes abroad.

But what of the intrinsic merits of English? Is it on the whole well- or ill-fitted for the role of auxiliary world speech? Has it not spread, in part, because it is a better language than its competitors? This is a dangerous question! In the first place, linguists nowadays are agreed that there is no real evidence to prove any one language better than any other *as a language*. That is, though languages compared will certainly be found to differ in structure and resource, the "advantages" of one sort in any language will generally be offset by its "disadvantages" of another sort. The structure of "primitive" languages is no less complex, and no different in potentiality, than that of "cultivated" languages. To make value-judgments about them, therefore, is not a matter for the linguist. But the greatest danger in such questions comes from the fact that our emotions are so deeply and secretly involved with our native language that it is almost impossible to be objective. The best medicine, in such a case, is to read Edward Sapir's excellent tenth chapter of *Language,* "Language, Race, and Culture."

Once alert to the dangers of subjectivity, however, we may note with some interest what has been said about the values of English by competent observers. One foreign scholar who has studied English and other languages intensively, and who can more dispassionately assess merits and shortcomings, Otto Jespersen, has written, "The English language is a methodical, energetic, businesslike, and sober language"; and again (with particular reference to its increasing use as a world language), "It must be a source of gratification to mankind that the tongue, spoken by two of the greatest powers of the world is so noble, so rich, so pliant, so expressive and so interesting. . . ." In still another place, he states his view of English as compared with other languages in these terms: ". . . it seems to me positively and expressly *masculine,* it is the language of a grown-up man and has very little childish or feminine about it."

The foregoing terms represent, with entire adequacy, the usual favorable view of Modern English. It is most frequently praised for its businesslike simplicity—in sound-system, in grammar, and in at least the more frequently used core of its vocabulary. This simplicity, it is commonly thought, makes it easy for a foreigner to learn, and hence makes it particularly adaptable for use as a world tongue. To modify this judgment, however, we have such an admission as the following, from the pen of an enthusiastic defender of this very quality of simplicity: "The foreigner essaying it, indeed, finds his chief difficulty, not in mastering its forms, but in grasping its lack of forms." More subtly, and from a different angle, the apparent simplicity of English has been declared to be a delusion and a snare:

> The fact that a beginner in English has not many paradigms to learn gives him a feeling of absence of difficulty, but he soon learns to his cost that this is only a feeling. . . . The simplicity of English in its formal aspect is . . . really a pseudo-simplicity or a masked complexity. . . . He [the foreigner] may well feel that the apparent simplicity of English is purchased at the price of a bewildering obscurity.

Granting that there is some truth in these strictures and that the superficial impression of simplicity that English gives is somewhat ambiguous, one may still feel that its forms, its words, and its sounds compare favorably, in the ease with which at least approximate mastery of them can be attained, with those of other languages. Its vocabulary has the enormous advantage of being compounded almost equally of Germanic and Romanic elements, so that a good part of it is already familiar to the speakers of many other European languages. Its morphology is so inconsiderable that the language has been called "the grammarless tongue"—which is, of course, inaccurate, since what it lacks in morphological complexity is fully counterbalanced by syntactical complexity; yet the phrase does emphasize its simplicity in one respect. In inflections and word order, as we have seen, the modern speech has greatly simplified and regularized the practices of Old English. (On the other hand, it has acquired a complex array of phrase-groupings, using function-words, which are no less difficult than the inflections of Old English.)

The greatest stumbling-block in the way of the foreigner who would acquire English is, as will be granted on all sides, the spelling—"that pseudo-historical and anti-educational abomination." On the subject of English as a world speech it is perhaps worth recalling that long ago the great German linguist Jacob Grimm congratulated other Europeans that the English had not yet discovered that only one thing prevented the universality of English from being completely apparent: its "whimsical, antiquated orthography." Today, with the English language perceptibly nearer the indicated goal, the same handicap remains. If it could be removed, or at least reduced, that might bring English still nearer to acceptability as a world language. Even with this handicap, English can perhaps qualify on its merits—insofar as these can be judged. But it is worth remarking that the point will be decided in the future, however it goes, not on linguistic grounds, but on grounds of the continued rise in world influence—or the fall—of those whose language is now English.

~ C ~

suggestions for discussion

1. In the headnote to this chapter, two ways of concluding a piece of writing are cited: the review of what has been said and the presentation of the last idea in a logical succession of ideas.

But as the number of good ways to begin a paper is large and indefinite, so too is the number of ways to end one. Other ways include the common devices: (1) a return to at least the sense—and frequently the words—of a quotation or a question used in the introduction; (2) a statement of a fact or an emotion that was implicit in the body of the paper; (3) "the other side of the coin"—a note of hope if the paper began on one of despair, or of calm resolution if the opening was one of grief or uncertainty; and (4) a return to an anecdote or historical narrative used in the introduction.

Try, now, to give short descriptions of the endings of the three selections that you have read in this chapter.

2. As is true of the introduction, the conclusion has no set length. The final paragraphs of the three selections in this chapter range from about seventy-five words to over 250 words.

For one or more of the selections, replace the ending with a short —two-or-three-line conclusion of your own writing; for a different selection, prepare a conclusion of about a hundred words.

3. To your way of thinking, is there generally a connection between the length of the ending and the likelihood that it will summarize the body of the paper? Is there a connection between the length of the ending and your ability to remember how a piece of writing is concluded? Test your responses against the endings of the selections in this chapter.

4. Again refer to the selections in this chapter and observe whether any of them has a conclusion that contains echoes from its introduction.

~ D ~

suggestions for writing

1. In "World English?" from *The Development of Modern English* by Robertson and Cassidy, the following statement appears: "The reason for the spread of English is probably quite unconnected with the language as such, or with any intrinsic virtues over other languages which it may be thought to have. . . ."
Write a paper of six to ten paragraphs on the general subject of non-linguistic reasons for the prominence of English among the languages of the world. You will find information or, at least, helpful hints, in all the selections in this chapter.

2. The authors represented in this chapter avoid making an error sometimes made by writers comparing English with other languages; that is, declaring or implying that because we use so little inflection (change of word form to reflect grammatical usage, such as, the change of *man* to *men* or *boy* to *boys* to denote the change from singular to plural number, or of *run* to *ran* and *jump* to *jumped* to reflect the change from present to past tense) our language is one of great simplicity.

Now, after rereading Marckwardt on word order and Robertson and Cassidy on the simplicity of English, look into your dictionary and study the entries *get, take,* and *run,* with their various meanings and with their many groupings into such expressions as *run after, run a temperature,* and the like. When you have prepared yourself for the task, write a paper of six to ten paragraphs with the aim of examining the "simplicity"—or the "complexity"—of English. (You may, of course, use any other material that you feel relevant or that your teacher may assign.)

3. In the selection from Simeon Potter's book, *Language in the Modern World,* you will find a social-political view of language and its use. Write a short paper on the idea contained in Potter's sen-

tence "Literacy is not a state, but a process." You might try your hand at opening and closing your paper with appropriate quotations from Potter.

~ E ~

additional readings

Bryant, Margaret M., *Modern English and Its Heritage,* 2nd ed. (New York: The Macmillan Company, 1962), Ch. 5, "Modern English."

Baugh, Albert C., *A History of the English Language,* 2nd ed. (New York: Appleton-Century-Crofts, 1957), Ch. 1, "English Present and Future."

Quirk, Randolph, *The Use of English* (New York: St. Martin's Press, Inc., 1962), Ch. 1, "Who Uses English?"; Ch. 2, "On Users and Uses."

Chapter Ten

~ A ~

organizing the whole composition

After a discussion of the beginning and the ending of your composition, the next logical step is to concentrate on the development of the middle of your writing effort. To use a cliché, every piece of writing must have a beginning, a middle, and an end if it is to be complete.

Obviously, the middle or body of the paper, containing its essence or content, must be well-organized to be effective. Clear presentation of the content is achieved by some plan of attack or by an outline. A practical way to go about outlining your material is the following: First, state in a single sentence the central idea of your paper. (There are many names for this central idea, such as topic idea, controlling idea, theme, and thesis.) Then collect and jot down all the ideas that seem to be pertinent to this central idea and correlate them into groups, with a controlling idea or topic for each group. Check, at this point, to see if the controlling ideas of the groups are logical subdivisions of the central idea, discard any that are not. Finally, put the groups in order.

This sequence is outlined in the following schemes. For a short paper a paragraph outline is the most convenient:

Central idea (a single sentence statement)
  I. Topic sentence for the first paragraph
 II. Topic sentence for the second paragraph
III. Topic sentence for the third paragraph

For more comprehensive and longer papers topic and sentence outlines are more practical. The topic outline resembles the following plan:

Central idea (a single sentence statement)
  I. A phrase identifying the controlling idea of the first major part of the paper
     A. A phrase to denote a point subordinate to I.
        1. Phrase to denote a point subordinate to A.
        2. Another phrase to indicate a point that is equal to 1 in importance.
     B. A phrase to denote a point equal in importance to A.
 II. A phrase identifying the controlling idea of the second major part
     A. A phrase to denote a point subordinate to II.
     B. A phrase to denote a point equal in importance to A.
        1. Phrase to denote a point subordinate to B.
        2. Another phrase to indicate a point that is equal to 1 in importance.

The sentence outline differs from the topic outline only in that each topic is developed in a complete sentence.

In any case, the use of an outline will serve two purposes: as a test for unity, and as a guide in helping you write your theme quickly and easily. In reading the following essays, observe particularly the organizational structure, from which you should be able mentally to reconstruct the outlines.

~ B ~

the language of literature

AN INSTRUMENT OF COMMUNICATION *

John Wain

It would be interesting to know whether there is anyone left who still accepts the traditional distinction between "mind" and "body." (If there is, what does he do about "soul"?) It is, generally speaking, accepted by everyone today that the older conception of intelligence is obsolete. If a boy was articulate, handled words and ideas, "took to his book," he was intelligent. True, there was always *mens sana in corpore sano* to give the athlete his formal justification. But, on the whole, it is a real advance to have got rid of that rather oppressive classification—to realize that intelligence is of different kinds, that one man may have it in his hands, another in his eyes, another in the exceptional speed and accuracy with which his muscles respond to the instructions of his brain. Where is the "intelligence" of Mr. Stirling Moss? Yet it would be a bold man who would maintain that such feats as his are performed independently of "the mind." In fact, as anyone can see, the best athletes and sportsmen differ from the second-best not by being stronger but by having more mind, more intelligence. And along with this realization goes the realization that certain kinds of "intelligence" are not to be encouraged too wholeheartedly. A man who handles abstract ideas fluently, and the more fluently because he never feels them as anything more than abstract ideas, can do only a limited amount of good and may, in many circumstances, do harm. There is nothing "modern" about this point of view; the doctrine that what human beings need is humanity, fullness of being, completeness of devel-

---

* *The Times Literary Supplement,* August 15, 1958, p. xxii.

opment, has been voiced in every age and has been orthodox in some.

This is not an article about education, and in any case I would never pick a quarrel with a theory of education which laid the emphasis on a basic training in literary and scientific knowledge. In fact I should rather like to go back to a world in which the classroom was expected to provide knowledge, and the rest of the boy's education was given to him by his father and uncles, and animals, and other children. In that world, it was reasonable to single out a bookish boy and call him "intelligent." Now that we expect education to do so much more, to be responsible for every side of the development of the young human creature, it is not. To take to his book shows one kind of ability in a boy; to take to his camera, his spanner, his logarithmic table, to be able to nurse a sick bird back to life—all these show other kinds. And there seems to be no readily demonstrable hierarchy of value. Because, of course, none of them has any value unless the boy is growing up as a human being.

These preliminaries should indicate, by implication, most of what I shall have to say about the future of "the book." Of one thing we may be sure: the book, as a physical object, will be with us; we shall not go back to the papyrus or forward (if it is "forward") to the reading-machines of *Brave New World*. The codex or hinged book is one of the great inventions of man; it is comparable with the wheel, the domestication of fire, musical instruments, and so forth. That old nightmare of the literary man, a house of the future in which there will be no such thing as a bookshelf, is no nearer than it ever was, and gets no nearer as time moves on.

We live in a strange and shifting world in which it is no longer true that certain forms and appearances have an inherent status. Yet the notion dies hard. There are still people who think or at any rate consistently act as if they thought, that the most banal drawing-room comedy performed by living players is superior to a film—any film—because it involves "theatre," which is eternally higher than cinema. There are likewise people who cling to the idea that to read a book is *ipso facto* a worthier activity than to watch television, listen to sound radio or talk to your neighbour over the garden fence. And, absurd as these ideas are, it would be unwise to deride them too fiercely. It is human and natural, and may at times even be useful, that a certain respect should cling to the idea of an acted play or a printed book. They are, and have been throughout history, important symbols of man's effort to build rather than tear down. Nevertheless, we must not allow them to obscure our serious thinking; for the plain fact is that there is no inherent superiority in the traditionally revered implements. It is a sound instinct to respect a man more for being a poet than for writing, say, television features. Yet the "poet" may be a purveyor of drunken, incoherent *Ersatz*, and the television writer might be genuinely imaginative. I personally detest detective stories; but I see no reason why a well-written detective story might not be more worth reading, in any sense I can give to that expression, than a ponderously point-missing essay on Shakespeare's tragedies. *Might;* there is much virtue in that *might;* but we must not slam the door.

For this reason I am never very happy about statistics which aim to show how literature is surviving in the face of competition. So many thousand people bought or borrowed so many thousand books. But what books did they borrow? The process of skimming off all volumes with titles like *Valve-Tappet Adjusting for Beginners* and *Let's Play Rugger* would involve very complicated statistics indeed; yet these would be the only kind we could work from.

It is, indeed, arguable that to get the most unbookish person to handle a book from time to time is a success in itself. A family whose members are continually turning to books for light entertainment and practical instruction will at least have a bookshelf, and there is the possibility that "real" books might alight, thistle-down-fashion, on it. I am sympathetic to this argument, but I think it will have to be abandoned. The reader who turns to a book *faute de mieux* can never be relied on to fight in our ditch when it comes to a battle. After all, if you want to know how to adjust tappets, reading a book is rather a cumbrous way of learning. Neither the diagram nor the written word is as good as demonstration, and television has made the demonstration possible. And if it is light entertainment you want, after a hard day's work, who would not rather *see* the kiss-kiss, bang-bang fantasy enacted before his eyes? No, the conclusion must be, I think, that only those readers are worth having, and worth trying to count in statistics, who feel a need for the printed word which cannot be supplied by anything else.

This means that we shall have to stop being hypnotized by mere numbers. And, after all, that should not be difficult. No one is hypnotized by numbers in his personal life. Anyone would rather have a few warm and reliable friends than a crowd of faint ones. Any speaker would rather address a small and interested audience than a large bored one. And from the point of view of practical usefulness, one pair of stout shoes is better than ten that leak. In a word, "the book" can afford to shed its passengers and continue with crew alone. The thriller-writer, the maker of books for a rainy evening or a long dead Sunday, will largely drop out. There will still be a market for his talents, but it will be a different market. He will take his audience with him, and the genuine book-readers will be left in an uncluttered field.

What will the typical member of this reduced, bedrock public for the printed book be like? First, and most important, he will be someone to whom the *sound* of words is a pleasure. Those to whom a language is merely utilitarian, a means of conveying narrative and fact, will welcome more direct means of communication. The reader of books will be the lover of language; he will want his narratives, his descriptions, his philosophies in permanent written form so that he can turn back repeatedly, through the years, to a passage that appeals to him as felicitous or moving. In fact the nearest parallel to the serious book is not the utilitarian or "light" book but the gramophone record. To the genuine reader, to possess a book and read it only once would be as unthinkable as to play a gramophone record only once. It may not be worth playing more than once, but in that case he will probably get rid of it.

The direction in which my argument is moving will now be plain. There are people in whose experience language is a sensuous and emotional reality, a pleasure for its own sake. To others, it is simply a means of communication. This distinction cuts across all divisions of social status or education. The love of language is found among speakers who do not handle it "correctly," and many of its most devoted worshippers are quite lacking in relish for "ideas" and could certainly not be called intellectual. On the other hand, many people who live intensely through the mind handle words as if they were slabs of processed cheese. In fact the position is even more complicated. As with all forms of worship, some of the loudest protesters seem not to have the root of the matter in them. Many of the writers who regard themselves, and induce others to regard them, as "stylists," fine writers, masters of cadence and echo, turn

out on examination to handle language inertly: their very preoccupation with "style" reveals a coldly external attitude to what
should be a living thing.

To come back to our main thread. The printed page stores language; film, radio, television and theatre direct a stream of it
through our heads. (In all these cases, naturally, the script can be
printed; but that is slightly to one side of our argument.) It follows
that the book is the instrument of those to whom language is
capable of being a focus for emotions, images and ideas. There are
many such people; they are the people to whom poetry and oratory
are addressed, who delight in turns of phrase, puns, proverbs, anything in which the run and feel of words is an important part of
the meaning. When Samuel Butler remarked that "The Ancient
Mariner" would probably not have attracted any attention if it
had been called "The Old Sailor," he was indicating the essential
division; because there are, obviously, people to whom the two
titles are as one, who are simply dead to words as others are dead
to colours or sounds.

Naturally one does not wish to exaggerate. A person who is entirely dead to the concrete and tangible pleasure of using language
is a rarity, and so is one who gulps words like a dram-drinker. Perhaps the distinction, in this as in so many other matters, is between
those who carry it beyond puberty and those who lose it there.
Virtually all children, during the years when they are learning to
speak, take delight in words: they enjoy the catch-phrases of
comedians; in their compulsory reading, they are most easily attracted by the "Aroint-thee-witch-the-rump-fed-ronyon-cries" kind
of line. In adolescence, many people fall in love with a poet or a
succession of poets. But this love, I think, is always a complicated
matter, owing at least as much to the poet's "meaning" as his language. (It is significant that Shelley and Swinburne should be
favourites but not Wordsworth; Housman but not Gray.) George
Orwell, for example, was evidently confusing two things when he
remarked in an account of his development (*Why I Write*):

> "When I was about sixteen I suddenly discovered the joy of mere
> words, i.e., the sounds and associations of words. The lines from
> *Paradise Lost—*
>
> > So hee with difficulty and labour hard
> > Moved on: with difficulty and labour hee,

which do not now seem to me so very wonderful, sent shivers down my backbone; and the spelling 'hee' for 'he' was an added pleasure."

What he had "suddenly discovered," it seems clear, was his own moral universe; no doubt there was a dawning technical interest in writing, which made Milton's idiosyncratic spelling seem delightful; but the young Orwell whose backbone decided to shiver at these two lines out of a long poem, and a poem remarkable for the grandeur of its harmonies, was obviously setting forward already on the strenuous path he had marked out for himself.

In such a world, the author is in the position of Harry the Fifth before Agincourt, giving all cowards leave to depart. He has no wish to address a captive audience. Those whose most intense experiences are visual, or tactile, or abstractedly intellectual, can be of no essential help to him, nor he to them. For, of course, it is not merely a question of pleasure. Language communicates most effectively to those who love it, just as food more easily nourishes a man who is hungry. And, as Mr. Orson Welles was asking recently, "If man cannot communicate, can he be expected to control his destiny?"

How Should One Read a Book? *

Virginia Woolf

In the first place, I want to emphasize the note of interrogation at the end of my title. Even if I could answer the question for myself, the answer would apply only to me and not to you. The only advice, indeed, that one person can give another about reading is to take no advice, to follow your own instincts, to use your own reason, to come to your own conclusions. If this is agreed between us, then I feel at liberty to put forward a few ideas and suggestions because you will not allow them to fetter that independence which is the most important quality that a reader can possess. After all, what laws can be laid down about books? The battle of Waterloo was certainly fought on a certain day; but is *Hamlet* a better play than *Lear*? Nobody can say. Each must decide that question for himself. To admit authorities however heavily furred and gowned, into our libraries and let them tell us how to read, what to read, what value to place upon what we read, is to destroy the spirit of freedom which is the breath of those sanctuaries. Everywhere else we may be bound by laws and conventions—there we have none.

But to enjoy freedom, if the platitude is pardonable, we have of course to control ourselves. We must not squander our powers, helplessly and ignorantly, squirting half the house in order to water a single rose-bush; we must train them, exactly and powerfully, here on the very spot. This, it may be, is one of the first difficulties that faces us in a library. What is "the very spot"? There may well seem to be nothing but a conglomeration and huddle of confusion. Poems and novels, histories and memoirs, dictionaries and blue books; books written in all languages by men and women of all tempers, races, and ages jostle each other on the shelf. And outside the donkey brays, the women gossip at the pump, the colts gallop across the fields. Where are we to begin? How are we to bring order into this multitudinous chaos and so get the deepest and widest pleasure from what we read?

It is simple enough to say that since books have classes—fiction, biography, poetry—we should separate them and take from each what it is right that each should give us. Yet few people ask from books what books can give us. Most commonly we come to books with blurred and divided minds, asking of fiction that it shall be true, of poetry that it shall be false, of biography that it shall be flattering, of history that it shall enforce our own prejudices. If we could banish all such preconceptions when we read, that would be an admirable beginning. Do not dictate to your author; try to become him. Be his fellow-worker and accomplice. If you hang back, and reserve and criticise at first, you are preventing yourself from getting the fullest possible value from what you read. But if you open your mind as widely as possible, then signs and hints of almost imperceptible fineness, from the twist and turn of the first sentences, will bring you into the presence of a human being unlike any other. Steep yourself in this, acquaint yourself with this, and soon you will find that your author is giving you, or attempting to give you, something far more definite. The thirty-two chapters of a novel—if we consider how to read a novel first—are an attempt to make something as formed and controlled as a building: but words are more impalpable than bricks; reading is a longer and more complicated process than seeing. Perhaps the quickest way to understand the elements of what a novelist is doing is not to read, but to write; to make your own experiment with the dangers and difficulties of words. Recall, then, some event that has left a distinct impression on you—how at the corner of the street, perhaps you passed two people talking. A tree shook; an electric light danced; the tone of the talk was comic, but also tragic; a whole vision, an entire conception, seemed contained in that moment.

But when you attempt to reconstruct it in words, you will find that it breaks into a thousand conflicting impressions. Some must be subdued; others emphasized; in the process you will lose, probably, all grasp upon the emotion itself. Then turn from your blurred and littered pages to the opening pages of some great novelist—Defoe, Jane Austen, Hardy. Now you will be better able to appreciate their mastery. It is not merely that we are in the presence of a different person—Defoe, Jane Austen, or Thomas Hardy—but that we are living in a different world. Here, in *Robinson Crusoe,* we are trudging a plain high road; one thing happens after another; the fact and the order of the fact is enough. But if the open air and adventure mean everything to Defoe they mean nothing to Jane Austen. Hers is the drawing-room and people talking, and by the many mirrors of their talk revealing their characters. And if, when we have accustomed ourselves to the drawing-room and its reflections, we turn to Hardy, we are once more spun round. The moors are round us and the stars are above our heads. The other side of the mind is now exposed—the dark side that comes uppermost in solitude, not the light side that shows in company. Our relations are not towards people, but toward Nature and destiny. Yet different as these worlds are, each is consistent with itself. The marker of each is careful to observe the laws of his own perspective, and however great a strain they may put upon us they will never confuse us, as lesser writers so frequently do, by introducing two different kinds of reality into the same book. Thus to go from one great novelist to another—from Jane Austen to Hardy, from Peacock to Trollope, from Scott to Meredith—is to be wrenched and uprooted; to be thrown this way and then that. To read a novel is a difficult and complex art. You must be capable not only of great fineness of perception, but of great boldness of imagination if you are going to make use of all that the novelist—the great artist—gives you.

But a glance at the heterogeneous company on the shelf will show you that writers are very seldom "great artists"; far more often a book makes no claim to be a work of art at all. These biographies and autobiographies, for example, lives of great men, of men long dead and forgotten, that stand cheek by jowl with the novels and poems, are we to refuse to read them because they are not "art"? Or shall we read them, but read them in a different way, with a different aim? Shall we read them in the first place to satisfy that curiosity which possesses us sometimes when in the evening we linger in front of a house where the lights are lit and the blinds are not yet drawn, and each floor of the house shows us a different section of human life in being? Then we are consumed with curiosity about the lives of these people—the servants gossiping, the gentlemen dining, the girl dressing for a party, the old woman at the window with her knitting. Who are they, what are they, what are their names, their occupations, their thoughts and adventures?

Biographies and memoirs answer such questions, light up innumerable such houses; they show us people going about their daily affairs, toiling, failing, succeeding, eating, hating, loving, until they die. And sometimes as we watch, the house fades and the iron railings vanish and we are out at sea; we are hunting, sailing, fighting; we are among savages and soldiers; we are taking part in great campaigns. Or if we like to stay here in England, in London, still the scene changes; the street narrows; the house becomes small, cramped, diamond-paned, and malodorous. We see a poet, Donne, driven from such a house because the walls were so thin that when the children cried their voices cut through them. We can follow him, through the paths that lie in the pages of books, to Twickenham; to Lady Bedford's Park, a famous meeting-ground for nobles and poets; and then turn our steps to Wilton, the great house under the downs, and hear Sidney read the *Arcadia* to his sister; and ramble among the very marshes and see the very herons that figure in that famous romance; and then again travel north with that other Lady Pembroke, Anne Clifford, to her wild moors, or plunge into the city and control our merriment at the sight of Gabriel

Harvey in his black velvet suit arguing about poetry with Spenser. Nothing is more fascinating than to grope and stumble in the alternate darkness and splendour of Elizabethan London. But there is no staying there. The Temples and the Swifts, the Harleys and the St. Johns beckon us on; hour upon hour can be spent disentangling their quarrels and deciphering their characters; and when we tire of them we can stroll on, past a lady in black wearing diamonds, to Samuel Johnson and Goldsmith and Garrick; or cross the channel, if we like, and meet Voltaire and Diderot, Madame du Deffand; and so back to England and Twickenham—how certain places repeat themselves and certain names!—where Lady Bedford had her Park once and Pope lived later, to Walpole's home at Strawberry Hill. But Walpole introduces us to such a swarm of new acquaintances, there are so many houses to visit and bells to ring that we may well hesitate for a moment, on the Miss Berry's doorstep, for example, when behold up comes Thackeray; he is the friend of the woman whom Walpole loved; so that merely by going from friend to friend, from garden to garden, from house to house, we have passed from one end of English literature to another and wake to find ourselves here again in the present, if we can so differentiate this moment from all that have gone before. This, then, is one of the ways in which we can read these lives and letters; we can make them light up the many windows of the past; we can watch the famous dead in their familiar habits and fancy sometimes that we are very close and can surprise their secrets, and sometimes we may pull out a play or a poem that they have written and see whether it reads differently in the presence of the author. But this again rouses other questions. How far, we must ask ourselves, is a book influenced by its writer's life—how far is it safe to let the man interpret the writer? How far shall we resist or give way to the sympathies and antipathies that the man himself rouses in us—so sensitive are words, so receptive of the characters of the author? These are questions that press upon us when we read lives and letters, and we must answer them for ourselves, for nothing can be more fatal than to be guided by the preferences of others in a matter so personal.

But also we can read such books with another aim, not to throw light on literature, not to become familiar with famous people, but to refresh and exercise our own creative powers. Is there not an open window on the right hand of the bookcase? How delightful to stop reading and look out! How stimulating the scene is, in its unconsciousness, its irrelevance, its perpetual movement—the colts galloping round the field, the woman filling her pail at the well, the donkey throwing back his head and emitting his long, acrid moan. The greater part of any library is nothing but the record of such fleeting moments in the lives of men, women, and donkeys. Every literature, as it grows old, has its rubbish-heap, its record of vanished moments and forgotten lives told in faltering and feeble accents that have perished. But if you give yourself up to the delight of rubbish-reading you will be surprised, indeed you will be overcome, by the relics of human life that have been cast out to moulder. It may be one letter—but what a vision it gives! It may be a few sentences—but what vistas they suggest! Sometimes a whole story will come together with such beautiful humour and pathos and completeness that it seems as if a great novelist had been at work, yet it is only an old actor, Tate Wilkinson, remembering the strange story of Captain Jones; it is only a young subaltern serving under Arthur Wellesley and falling in love with a pretty girl at Lisbon; it is only Maria Allen letting fall her sewing in the empty drawing-room and sighing how she wishes she had taken Dr. Burney's good advice and had never eloped with her Rishy. None of this has any value; it is negligible in the extreme; yet how absorbing it is now and again to go through the rubbish-heaps and find rings and scissors and broken noses buried in the huge past and try to piece them together while the colt gallops round the field, the woman fills her pail at the well, and the donkey brays.

But we tire of rubbish-reading in the long run. We tire of searching for what is needed to complete the half-truth which is all that the Wilkinsons, the Bunburys and the Maria Allens are able to offer us. They had not the artist's power of mastering and eliminating; they could not tell the whole truth even about their own lives; they have disfigured the story that might have been so shapely. Facts are all that they can offer us, and facts are a very inferior form of fiction. Thus the desire grows upon us to have done with half-statements and approximations; to cease from searching out the minute shades of human character, to enjoy the greater abstractness, the purer truth of fiction. Thus we create the mood, intense and generalised, unaware of detail, but stressed by some regular, recurrent beat, whose natural expression is poetry; and that is the time to read poetry when we are almost able to write it.

> Western wind, when wilt thou blow?
> The small rain down can rain.
> Christ, if my love were in my arms,
> And I in my bed again!

The impact of poetry is so hard and direct that for the moment there is no other sensation except that of the poem itself. What profound depths we visit then—how sudden and complete is our immersion! There is nothing here to catch hold of; nothing to stay us in our flight. The illusion of fiction is gradual; its effects are prepared; but who when they read these four lines stops to ask who wrote them, or conjures up the thought of Donne's house or Sidney's secretary; or enmeshes them in the intricacy of the past and the succession of generations? The poet is always our contemporary. Our being for the moment is centred and constricted, as in any violent shock of personal emotion. Afterwards, it is true, the sensation begins to spread in wider rings through our minds; remoter senses are reached; these begin to sound and to comment and we are aware of echoes and reflections. The intensity of poetry covers an immense range of emotion. We have only to compare the force and directness of

> I shall fall like a tree, and find my grave,
>   Only remembering that I grieve,

with the wavering modulation of

> Minutes are numbered by the fall of sands,
> As by an hour glass; the span of time
> Doth waste us to our graves, and we look on it;
> An age of pleasure, revelled out, comes home
> At last, and ends in sorrow; but the life,
> Weary of riot, numbers every sand,
> Wailing in signs, until the last drop down,
> So to conclude calamity in rest,

or place the meditative calm of

> whether we be young or old,
> Our destiny, our being's heart and home,
> Is with infinitude, and only there;

> With hope it is, hope that can never die,
> Effort, and expectation, and desire,
> And something evermore about to be,

beside the complete and inexhaustible loveliness of

> The moving Moon went up the sky,
> And nowhere did abide:
> Softly she was going up,
> And a star or two beside—

or the splendid fantasy of

> And the woodland haunter
> Shall not cease to saunter
>   When, far down some glade,
> Of the great world's burning,
> One soft flame upturning
> Seems, to his discerning,
> Crocus in the shade,

to bethink us of the varied art of the poet; his power to make us at once actors and spectators; his power to run his hand into character as if it were a glove, and be Falstaff or Lear; his power to condense, to widen, to state, once and for ever.

"We have only to compare"—with those words that cat is out of the bag, and the true complexity of reading is admitted. The first process, to receive impressions with the utmost understanding, is only half the process of reading; it must be completed, if we are to get the whole pleasure from a book, by another. We must pass judgment upon these multitudinous impressions; we must make of these fleeting shapes one that is hard and lasting. But not directly. Wait for the dust of reading to settle; for the conflict and the questioning to die down; walk, talk, pull the dead petals from a rose, or fall asleep. Then suddenly without our willing it, for it is thus that Nature undertakes these transitions, the book will return, but differently. It will float to the top of the mind as a whole. And the book as a whole is different from the book received currently in separate phrases. Details now fit themselves into their places. We see the shape from start to finish; it is a barn, a pig-sty, or a cathedral. Now then we can compare book with book as we compare building with building. But this act of comparison means that our attitude has changed; we are no longer the friends of the writer, but his judges; and just as we cannot be too sympathetic as friends, so as judges we cannot be too severe. Are they not criminals, books that have wasted our time and sympathy; are they not the most insidious enemies of society, corrupters, defilers, the writers of false books, faked books, books that fill the air with decay and disease? Let us then be severe in our judgments; let us compare each book with the greatest of its kind. There they hang in the mind the shapes of the books we have read solidified by the judgments we have passed on them—*Robinson Crusoe, Emma, The Return of the Native*. Compare the novels with these—even the latest and least of novels has a right to be judged with the best. And so with poetry—when the intoxication of rhythm has died down and the splendour of words has faded, a visionary shape will return to us and this must be compared with *Lear,* with *Phedre,* with *The Prelude;* or if not with these, with whatever is the best or seems to us to be the best in its own kind. And we may be sure that the newness of new poetry and fiction is its most superficial quality and that we have only to alter slightly, not to recast, the standards by which we have judged the old.

It would be foolish, then, to pretend that the second part of reading, to judge, to compare, is as simple as the first—to open the mind wide to the fast flocking of innumerable impressions. To continue reading without the book before you, to hold one shadow-shape against another, to have read widely enough and with enough understanding to make such comparisons alive and illuminating—that is difficult. It is still more difficult to press further and to say, "Not only is the book of this sort, but it is of this value; here it fails; here it succeeds; this is bad; that is good." To carry out this part of a reader's duty needs such imagination, insight, and learning that it is hard to conceive any one mind sufficiently endowed; impossible for the most self-confident to find more than the seeds of such powers in himself. Would it not be wiser, then, to remit this part of reading and to allow the critics, the gowned and furred authorities of the library, to decide the question of the book's absolute value for us? Yet how impossible! We may stress the value of sympathy; we may try to sink our own identity as we read. But we know that we cannot sympathise wholly or immerse ourselves wholly; there is always a demon in us who whispers, "I hate, I love," and we cannot silence him. Indeed, it is precisely because we hate and we love that our relation with the poets and novelists is so intimate that we find the presence of another person intolerable. And even if the results are abhorrent and our judgments are wrong, still our taste, the nerve of sensation that sends shocks through us, is our chief illuminant; we learn through feeling; we cannot suppress our own idiosyncrasy without impoverishing it. But as time goes on perhaps we can train our taste; perhaps we can make it submit to some control. When it has fed greedily and lavishly upon books of all sorts —poetry, fiction, history, biography—and has stopped reading and looked for long spaces upon the variety, the incongruity of the living word, we shall find that it is changing a little; it is not so greedy, it is more reflective. It will tell us that there is a quality common to certain books. Listen, it will say, what shall we call this? And it will read us perhaps *Lear* and then perhaps the *Agamemnon* in order to bring out that common quality. Thus, with our taste to guide us, we shall venture beyond the particular book in search of qualities that group books together; we shall give them names and thus frame a rule that brings order into our perceptions. We shall gain a further and a rarer pleasure from that discrimination. But as a rule only lives when it is perpetually broken by contact with the books themselves—nothing is easier and more stultifying than to make rules which exist out of touch with facts, in a vacuum—now at last, in order to steady ourselves in this difficult attempt, it may be well to turn to the very rare writers who are able to enlighten us upon literature as an art. Coleridge and Dryden and Johnson, in their considered criticism, the poets and novelists themselves in their unconsidered sayings, are often surprisingly relevant; they light up and solidify the vague ideas that have been tumbling in the misty depths of our minds. But they are only able to help us if we come to them laden with questions and suggestions won honestly in the course of our own reading. They can do nothing for us if we herd ourselves under their authority and lie down like sheep in the shade of a hedge. We can only understand their ruling when it comes in conflict with our own and vanquishes it.

If this is so, if to read a book as it should be read calls for the rarest qualities of imagination, insight, and judgment, you may perhaps conclude that literature is a very complex art and that it is unlikely that we shall be able, even after a lifetime of reading, to make any valuable contribution to its criticism. We must remain readers; we shall not put on the further glory that belongs to those rare beings who are also critics. But still we have our responsibilities as readers and even our importance. The standards we raise and the judgment we pass steal into the air and become part of the atmosphere which writers breathe as they work. An influence is created which tells upon them even if it never finds its way into print. And that influence, if it were well instructed, vigorous and individual and sincere, might be of great value now when criticism is necessarily in abeyance; when books pass in review like the procession of animals in a shooting gallery, and the critic has only one second in which to load and aim and shoot and may well be pardoned if he mistakes rabbits for tigers, eagles for barndoor fowls, or misses altogether and wastes his shot upon some peaceful cow grazing in a further field. If behind the erratic gunfire of the press the author felt that there was another kind of criticism, the opinion of people reading for the love of reading, slowly and unprofessionally, and judging with great sympathy and yet with great severity, might this not improve the quality of his work? And if by our means books were to become stronger, richer, and more varied, that would be an end worth reaching.

Yet who reads to bring about an end, however desirable? Are there not some pursuits that we practise because they are good in themselves, and some pleasures that are final? And is not this among them? I have sometimes dreamt, at least, that when the Day of Judgment dawns and the great conquerors and lawyers and statesmen come to receive their rewards—their crowns, their laurels, their names carved indelibly upon imperishable marble—the Almighty will turn to Peter and will say, not without a certain envy when He sees us coming with our books under our arms, "Look, these need no reward. We have nothing to give them here. They have loved reading."

Literature of Knowledge and Literature of Power *

Thomas DeQuincey

What is it that we mean by *literature?* Popularly, and amongst the thoughtless, it is held to include everything that is printed in a book. Little logic is required to disturb *that* definition. The most

---

* "Alexander Pope," *The North British Review,* 1848.

thoughtless person is easily made aware that in the idea of *literature* one essential element is some relation to a general and common interest of man—so that what applies only to a local, or professional, or merely personal interest, even though presenting itself in the shape of a book, will not belong to literature. So far the definition is easily narrowed; and it is as easily expanded. For not only is much that takes a station in books not literature, but inversely, much that really *is* literature never reaches a station in books. The weekly sermons of Christendom, that vast pulpit literature which acts so extensively upon the popular mind—to warn, to uphold, to renew, to comfort, to alarm—does not attain the sanctuary of libraries in the ten-thousandth part of its extent. The drama again—as, for instance, the finest part of Shakespeare's plays in England, and all leading Athenian plays in the noontide of the Attic stage—operated as a literature on the public mind, and were (according to the strictest letter of that term) *published* through the audiences that witnessed their representation some time before they were published as things to be read; and they were published in this scenical mode of publication with much more effect than they could have had as books during ages of costly copying or of costly printing.

Books, therefore, do not suggest an idea coextensive and interchangeable with the idea of literature; since much literature, scenic, forensic, or didactic (as from lecturers and public orators) may never come into books, and much that does come into books may connect itself with no literary interest. But a far more important correction, applicable to the common vague idea of literature, is to be sought not so much in a better definition of literature as in a sharper distinction of the two functions which it fulfills. In that great social organ which, collectively, we call literature, there may be distinguished two separate offices, that may blend and often do so, but capable, severally, of a severe insulation, and naturally fitted for reciprocal repulsion. There is, first, the literature of *knowledge,* and secondly, the literature of *power.* The function of the first is to *teach;* the function of the second is to *move;* the first is a rudder, the second an oar or a sail. The first speaks to the mere discursive understanding; the second speaks ultimately, it may travel towards an object seated in what Lord Bacon calls "dry light"; but proximately it does and must operate—else it ceases to be a literature of power—on and through that *humid* light which clothes itself in the mists and glittering iris of human passions, desires, and genial emo-

tions. Men have so little reflected on the higher functions of literature as to find it a paradox if one should describe it as a mean or
subordinate purpose of books to give information. But this is a
paradox only in the sense which makes it honourable to be para-
doxical. Whenever we talk in ordinary language of seeking information or gaining knowledge, we understand the words as connected
with something of absolute novelty. But it is the grandeur of all
truth which can occupy a very high place in human interests that
it is never absolutely novel to the meanest of minds; it exists
eternally by way of germ or latent principle in the lowest as in the
highest, needing to be developed, but never to be planted. To be
capable of transplantation is the immediate criterion of a truth that
ranges on a lower scale. Besides which, there is a rarer thing than
truth—namely *power,* or deep sympathy with truth. What is the
effect, for instance, upon society of children? By the pity, by the
tenderness, and by the peculiar modes of admiration which connect
themselves with the helplessness, with the innocence, and with the
simplicity of children, not only are the primal affections strengthened and continually renewed, but the qualities which are dearest
in the sight of heaven—the frailty, for instance, which appeals to
forbearance, the innocence which symbolizes the heavenly, and the
simplicity which is most alien from the worldly—are kept up in
perpetual remembrance, and their ideals are continually refreshed.
A purpose of the same nature is answered by the higher literature,
viz. the literature of power. What do you learn from *Paradise Lost?*
Nothing at all. What do you learn from a cookery-book? Something
new, something that you did not know before, in every paragraph.
But would you therefore put the wretched cookery-book on a higher
level of estimation than the divine poem? What you owe to Milton
is not any knowledge, of which a million separate items are still but
a million of advancing steps on the same earthly level; what you
owe is *power*—that is, exercise and expansion to your own latent
capacity of sympathy with the infinite, where every pulse and each
separate influx is a step upwards, a step ascending as upon a Jacob's
ladder from earth to mysterious altitudes above the earth. All the
steps of knowledge, from first to last, carry you further on the same
plane, but could never raise you one foot above your ancient level
of earth; whereas the very first step in power is a flight—is an ascending movement into another element where earth is forgotten.

Were it not that human sensibilities are ventilated and continually called out into exercise by the great phenomena of infancy, or of real life as it moves through chance and change, or of literature as it recombines these elements in the mimicries of poetry, romance, etc., it is certain that, like any animal power or muscular energy falling into disuse, all such sensibilities would gradually droop and dwindle. It is in relation to these great *moral* capacities of man that the literature of power, as contradistinguished from that of knowledge, lives and has its field of action. It is concerned with what is highest in man; for the Scriptures themselves never condescended to deal by suggestion or cooperation with the mere discursive understanding; when speaking of man in his intellectual capacity, the Scriptures speak not of the understanding, but of "the understanding heart," making the heart, i.e., the great *intuitive* (or non-discursive) organ, to be the interchangeable formula for man in his highest state of capacity for the infinite. Tragedy, romance, fairy tale, or epopee, all alike restore to man's mind the ideals of justice, of hope, of truth, of mercy, of retribution, which else (left to the support of daily life in its realities) would languish for want of sufficient illustration.

What is meant, for instance, by *poetic justice?* It does not mean a justice that differs by its object from the ordinary justice of human jurisprudence, for then it must be confessedly a very bad kind of justice; but it means a justice that differs from common forensic justice by the degree in which it attains its object—a justice that is more omnipotent over its own ends, as dealing, not with the refractory elements of earthly life, but with the elements of its own creation, and with materials flexible to its own purest preconceptions. It is certain that, were it not for the literature of power, these ideals would often remain amongst us as mere arid notional forms; whereas, by the creative forces of man put forth in literature, they gain a vernal life of restoration, and germinate into vital activities. The commonest novel, by moving in alliance with human fears and hopes, with human instincts of wrong and right, sustains and quickens those affections. Calling them into action, it rescues them from torpor. And hence the preeminency over all authors that merely *teach,* of the meanest that *moves,* or that teaches, if at all, indirectly by moving. The very highest work that has ever existed in the literature of knowledge is but a provisional work—a book upon trial and sufferance, and *quamdiu bene se gesserit.* Let its teaching be even partially revised, let it be but expanded—nay, even let its teaching be but placed in a better order—and instantly it is superseded. Whereas the feeblest works in the literature of power, surviving at all, survive as finished and unalterable amongst men. For instance, the *Principia* of Sir Isaac Newton was a book militant on earth from the first. In all stages of its progress it would have to fight for its existence: first, as regards absolute truth; secondly, when that combat was over, as regards its form or mode of presenting the truth. And as soon as a Laplace, or anybody else, builds higher upon the foundations laid by this book, effectually he throws it out of the sunshine into decay and darkness; by weapons won from this book he superannuates and destroys this book, so that soon the name of Newton remains as a mere *nominis umbra,* but his book, as a living power, has transmigrated into other forms. Now, on the contrary, the *Iliad,* and *Prometheus* of Æschylus, the *Othello* or *King Lear,* the *Hamlet* or *Macbeth,* and the *Paradise Lost,* are not militant, but triumphant for ever, as long as the languages exist in which they speak or can be taught to speak. They never *can* transmigrate into new incarnations. To reproduce these in new forms, or variations, even if in some things they should be improved, would be to plagiarize. A good steam-engine is properly superseded by a better. But one lovely pastoral valley is not superseded by another, nor a statue of Praxiteles by a statue of Michael Angelo. These are separated not by imparity, but by disparity. They are not thought of as unequal under the same standard, but as different in *kind,* and, if otherwise equal, as equal under a different standard. Human works of immortal beauty and works of nature in one respect stand on the same footing: they never absolutely repeat each other, never approach so near as not to differ, and they differ not as better and worse, or simply by more and less—they differ by undecipherable and incommunicable differences, that cannot be caught by mimicries, that cannot be reflected in the mirror of copies, that cannot become ponderable in the scales of vulgar comparison. . . . At this hour, five hundred years since their creation, the tales of Chaucer, never equalled on this earth for their tenderness and for life of picturesqueness, are read familiarly by many in the charming language of their natal day, and by others in the modernizations of Dryden, of Pope, and Wordsworth. At this hour, one thousand eight hundred years since their creation, the pagan tales of Ovid, never equalled on this earth for the gaiety of their movement and the capricious graces of their narrative, are read by all Christendom.

This man's people and their monuments are dust, but *he* is alive; he has survived them, as he told us that he had it in his commission to do, by a thousand years, "and shall a thousand more."

All the literature of knowledge builds only ground-nests, that are swept away by floods, or confounded by the plough; but the literature of power builds nests in aerial altitudes of temples sacred from violation, or of forests inaccessible to fraud. This is a great prerogative of the *power* literature, and it is a greater which lies in the mode of its influence. The *knowledge* literature, like the fashion of this world, passeth away. An encyclopaedia is its abstract; and, in this respect, it may be taken for its speaking symbol—that before one generation has passed an encyclopaedia is superannuated; for it speaks through the dead memory and unimpassioned understanding, which have not the repose of higher faculties, but are continually enlarging and varying their phylacteries. But all literature properly so called—literature [par excellence]—for the very reason that it is so much more durable than the literature of knowledge, is (and by the very same proportion it is) more intense and electrically searching in its impressions. The directions in which the tragedy of this planet has trained our human feelings to play, and the combinations into which the poetry of this planet has thrown our human passions of love and hatred, of admiration and contempt, exercise a power for bad or good over human life that cannot be contemplated, when stretching through many generations, without a sentiment allied to awe. And of this let every one be assured—that he owes to the impassioned books which he has read many a thousand more of emotions than he can consciously trace back to them. Dim by their origination, these emotions yet arise in him, and mould him through life, like forgotten incidents of his childhood. . . .

~ C ~

suggestions for discussion

1. Here let us take careful notice of the organization of John Wain's essay, "An Instrument of Communication," that is reproduced above.

On the most superficial level, we may say that the introduction consists of the first two paragraphs, that the third paragraph is a transitional one, and that the conclusion comes in the last paragraph; the body of the paper begins with the fourth paragraph and continues through the one that appears next to last.

On a subtler level of analysis, we observe that the first paragraph and the second put a clear emphasis on the idea that in a human being it is fullness or completeness of development that counts. In fact, both paragraphs end with explicit statements to that effect. The final paragraph presents a comparison of the author of books with King Henry V before the battle at Agincourt (in Shakespeare's *King Henry the Fifth*). One who is familiar with the speech made by the young King Henry will know that the writer of our essay is but returning to the theme that he presented in the introduction. For the King bids those to depart who would not fight against an enemy who outnumbers them by five to one. Then, only "we few, we happy few, we band of brothers" will remain; the incomplete now will have gone their little ways. And, in the essayist's view, the author and the true readers—those who hunger for and who feed their spirits on language, who truly would *communicate*—will be also a band of brothers.

If the beginning and ending of the essay are indeed as we have described them, the remaining test of it as an essay is its middle. Is the body of the paper consistent with what the introduction leads you to expect of it? Does the body of the paper lead logically to the conclusion? (Notice that you are not asked to agree—or to disagree —with the essayist; you are asked only to try to reach a generalization or a judgment on the way the parts of the essay fit together.)

2. In the manner demonstrated in question 1, identify the body of the second essay reprinted in this lesson; recall that you will first recognize the limits of the introduction and conclusion.

3. The second essay is considerably longer than the first. Is it more complex in its structure or less? One good way to compare the two selections in this respect is to write a one-paragraph digest or summary of each of them.

4. The third essay, a celebrated one in which its author drew a basic distinction between two kinds of literature, is by a writer who is often held to have had a discursive, i.e., rambling, style. Employing the kinds of analysis used in questions 1 and 2 and, if you wish, the writing of a digest as in 3, judge the essay as a composition with a beginning, middle, and end; reach a critical judgment of the coherence of the parts.

5. Incidentally, all three selections in this chapter were written by English authors. The third one was written over a hundred years ago and is no longer typical of British usage. In the first two, however, which are of recent composition, notice such spellings as *criticise* (where the American preference is for *criticize*), the use of the word *spanner* (for *wrench*), and the fictional book title *Let's Play Rugger*. You may wish to look for other small signs of British— as opposed to American—usage. (The differences between the two are not especially numerous or serious in writing; they are more noticeable, of course, in speech.)

~ D ~

suggestions for writing

1. Recall what you have learned earlier about the terms *abstract, concrete,* and levels of *abstraction*. Consider, now, Wain's statement toward the end of his first paragraph: "A man who handles abstract ideas fluently, and the more fluently because he never feels them as anything more than abstract ideas, can do only a limited amount of good and may, in many circumstances, do harm." Do you agree

with this assertion? Does it relate to those persons who led—success-fully—political rebellions but who, once the "chains of tyranny" were cast off and "liberty" gained, lacked the ability to design a political scheme that would enable themselves and their com-patriots to preserve their freedom and to avoid anarchy on the one hand, and a reversion to tyranny on the other? How is one to regard a Hitler and his dream of Aryan supremacy? Can you think of other examples of persons whose wholehearted acceptance of an abstraction, without due regard for its effects following resolution into specific measures, has led them and perhaps others to harm?

Write a paper of six to ten paragraphs in which you examine these questions. (Caution: In writing on a rather highly abstract subject or in dealing with abstractions, you must avoid lapsing into a sequence of general statements without support in fact, in ex-amples, or in reasoned thinking. In your paper, therefore, use enough concrete material to show that you are really thinking about your subject.)

2. "But we tire of rubbish-reading in the long run," said the author of the second essay in this chapter. Is her conception of rub-bish the same as yours? Try to state in so many words what literary rubbish is. (Notice that pornography, impiety, and outright false-hood seem not to be involved at all.) Write an essay of six to ten paragraphs contrasting what you regard as rubbish and what you accept as real literature.

3. All three essays in this chapter could be read as works pointing toward the difference between the literature of *knowledge* and the literature of *power*. Write a paper of eight to twelve paragraphs in which you try to express a composite view of the subject. (Be care-ful not to misrepresent any of your authors. Remember that De-Quincey, the writer of the third essay, was the only one of them who actually used the terms that you are to write about.)

4. In addition to the two categories of literature recognized by DeQuincey—referred to in question 3—should other classes be estab-lished? The cookbook or the instruction manual that one gets with a new power mower are obviously well enough called the literature of knowledge, and the book of Job and *King Lear* are examples of the literature of power; but what about mystery stories, science fiction, or cowboy stories? In an essay of six to ten paragraphs, try your own hand at classifying literature.

~ E ~

additional readings

Donald P. Costello, "The Language of the Catcher in the Rye," *American Speech,* 34 (1959), 176-181. Reprinted in Elizabeth M. Kerr and Ralph M. Aderman, *Aspects of American English* (New York: Harcourt, Brace & World, Inc., 1963), pp. 167-77.

Charles F. Hockett, *A Course in Modern Linguistics* (New York: The Macmillan Company, 1958), Ch. 63, "Literature."